WHAT NEXT YOU BASTARD

WHAT NEXT YOU BASTARD
An Autobiography

Ken Hall
with
Monika McFerran

© Ken Hall and Monika McFerran 2001

This book is copyright. Apart from any fair dealing for the purposes of study, research, criticism, review, or as otherwise permitted under the Copyright Act, no part may be reproduced by any process without written permission. Inquiries should be made to the publisher.

First published in 2001

Typeset by
Midland Typesetters Pty Ltd
Maryborough, Victoria 3465

Printed and bound by
Southwood Press Pty Ltd
76–82 Chapel St, Marrickville, NSW 2204

For the publisher
Hale & Iremonger Pty Ltd
PO Box 205, Alexandria, NSW 2015
www.haleiremonger.com

National Library of Australia
Cataloguing-in-Publication entry:

Hall, Ken, 1940- .
What next you bastard: an autobiography.

ISBN 0 86806 705 9.

1. Hall, Ken, 1940- . 2. Illiterate persons - Australia - Biography. 3. Sick children - Australia - Biography. I. McFerran, Monika. II. Title.

305.90633092

Contents

1.	No way, not me!	7
2.	Pins and needles	18
3.	The last holiday	27
4.	Give the boy a broom	30
5.	Horses don't care	44
6.	Palomino	53
7.	Heading west	63
8.	Jackaroo	78
9.	Kyuna	94
10.	Droving	108
11.	Art of the game	121
12.	Big Red	133
13.	The mob	144
14.	Kilterry	155
15.	The sander	166
16.	Nasho	177
17.	Tug-o'-war	186
18.	An angel on her way to heaven	195
19.	Janice	206
20.	Hervey Bay	217
21.	Narrow escapes	225
22.	The island	237
23.	On the beach	252
24.	Spell Australia for me	270
Epilogue		284
Acknowledgments		286

1. *No way, not me!*

My childhood was very short. It ended soon after my twelfth birthday in early 1952, when I arrived flat on my back at the Royal Brisbane Hospital.

Being sick was nothing new to me – I had been in and out of hospitals ever since I was born – only this time they didn't take me to the children's wing. Rules were rules. When you turned twelve you were an adult, and that meant the men's ward for me.

What hit me first was the terrible silence. I was used to the sounds of children laughing and crying and calling for their mothers to come and make it all better. Even a room full of sick children has a feeling of life and hope and future, and that funny mixture of happiness and sadness when friends get well enough to go home.

Ward 1A had none of that. It had bare walls and faded screens and a sour unfriendly smell. The only sounds I heard were the sick old men groaning and coughing, tossing and turning, afraid to sleep in case they never woke up again. Those who left the place didn't walk out. They were wrapped in a bedsheet and wheeled away on a tin trolley.

Ward 1A was the terminal ward, but I didn't know that at the time.

When I first arrived I was tired and hungry and angry as hell for being taken out of the children's ward that I knew so well, so I did my best to ignore my wardmates. They weren't too happy about my being there either. Some of them complained about having a boy beside them, whining that they just couldn't cope with that. Looking back, I realise it must have made them uncomfortable having to share their pain and misery with a youngster like me. And maybe the idea that one day soon they would have to watch me being wheeled away under a sheet was just too hard to take. But as a young boy I didn't understand this. I just felt lonely and unwanted.

Early the next morning I was still on strike, so I pretended not to notice the tests they made on me, and even managed to ignore the nurse who gave me my bed-bath. But when she turned me onto my side and I found myself being stared at by Mr Bell in the next bed, it was suddenly too much. I glared at him, hoping to make him feel as uncomfortable as he was making me. He was very good at this game. Our eyes locked together and I was damned if I was going to blink before he did. It was only when the nurse had finished towelling me dry and went to start on him that I discovered his secret. He had died during the night.

Death. I just couldn't grasp it. I had always thought it was something that only happened to very old or very bad people. Mr Bell hadn't looked all that old, so I told myself he must have done some pretty rotten things in his life.

Mr Wallace from two beds down was trembling with fear. 'You're not moving me into that bed,' he screamed at the nurse. 'I don't want to die!'

I was born without tonsils or adenoids, which meant that my body couldn't fight the infections I kept getting. Every germ that came along, I caught. But that wasn't the whole story, because somewhere along the line I also picked up a weak heart. It was nothing for me to spray blood from my nostrils like a human sprinkler, or to keel over at the drop of a hat, all without warning.

None of this made me very popular at school, not that I spent much time there. Short periods in the classroom were usually interrupted by long periods at home, where my dog Darkie and I spent our days sprawled on a mattress in the dining room, listening to Biggles, Smokey Dawson and Hopalong on the radio till the others came home.

The worst part about being sick so often was all the medicine I had to take – bitter white chalky tablets by the handful, day after day. Getting them down was quite a job. Keeping them down was even harder. Mum had tried everything, even crushing them up and hiding them in my food. She could have saved herself the trouble. Even Darkie knew better than to fall for that old trick.

Missing out on so much school didn't really bother me, but I hated the shame and humiliation each time I returned. Catching up on the work was impossible. They would be doing things I had never seen before. Spelling – that was always out of my range, with even the simplest words causing me problems. And times tables? Never heard of them.

No way, not me!

A few times the teachers wanted to put me back a couple of grades because I was so far behind, but Mum raged at them, pointing out that it would mean being in the same grade as my little brother. Whether she was concerned about Mark's feelings or mine I'm still not sure, and in the end it doesn't really matter. One thing you should know about Mrs Myrtle Hall – when it came to her kids, she got her own way every time.

In every grade the seat right in front of the teacher's desk was reserved for the 'bottom of the class'. That seat was always mine. But even when I was right there under their noses the teachers were usually too busy to help me. Maybe they thought it was a waste of time bringing me up to date, with all my comings and goings.

One of the teachers, Miss Turnbull with the big bosom and the grey bun – now she was a nasty one. She had all the boys scared to death of her, threatening us with a kiss if we misbehaved. A kiss from those lips! I still shudder whenever I think of them: dry and flaky, except for the very corners of her mouth where saliva glistened.

At the end of that year she asked everyone who had never been kissed by her to stand up. At first I thought it might be some kind of trick, but I had worked my butt off to make sure I would never be punished by that old witch! So when a couple of the other boys stood up, so did I.

'Ken Hall! What are you standing up for?'

'You've never kissed me, Miss.'

'You are a liar, boy!' Miss Turnbull shouted. 'I don't believe you. Sit down at once!' Then she turned to the other three boys, top students, all of them. 'Let's give these boys a hand for their good behaviour and excellent achievement all year.' To this day I'll never forgive her.

There were plenty of others over the years, but the last teacher I had was definitely the worst.

'Mr Hall,' he'd said, on my first day back after many months away, 'please stand up and face the class.' Thirty curious faces gazed up at me. 'This, class, is our new Dummy. Most of you already know him. We have a job to do, and that is to make sure that by the end of this year his name won't be Dummy any more. With your help, we will build him up so that this class can be proud of him.'

He could have saved himself the speech. At the end of that first week Mr Scott ordered me to join in the school football match.

When I reminded him that I wasn't allowed to do sport of any kind he just laughed it off. 'Nonsense, boy,' he said, 'there's nothing wrong with you that a bit of good old-fashioned exercise won't fix.'

I didn't have too much experience with team games. And for Christmas I had always been given colouring books or tin soldiers instead of the football I'd hoped for. So I messed up pretty badly, sending the ball straight into the arms of the opposing side.

Mr Scott was disgusted, punishing me with ten sit-ups. 'Bloody weak creature,' he sneered. 'Do five more!'

That was my last day at school. Next morning I was here in the hospital.

Being sick so much of the time was no fun for me, but my parents felt the strain too. Well, my father, Stan, must have, anyway. He was a 'ladies' man' – whatever that meant. He was tall and slick with neatly combed hair, groomed like one of the racehorses he liked to bet on. Dad changed his shirts three times a day, his trousers twice, and gave Mum hell if they were less than perfectly pressed. After leaving the Air Force, Dad went back to being a shop assistant in the local store. He also spent a good amount of time down at the local pub, and got his kicks from knocking his four sons around with the ironing cord. His idea of a joke was to sneak his cigarette under the table at meal times and find an unsuspecting knee or two to burn.

I was seven when he walked out. Mum found the winning Golden Casket ticket in her purse, Dad went out to claim first prize and never came back.

Did he ever love us? I don't know. He must have loved Mum though, despite the way he used to lay into her when he'd had a few too many, because at some later stage he did ask her to join him – on condition that she place us all in a foster home first. She refused and that was the end of it.

A nurse came by with a screen and placed it around my bed, blocking my view of the other patients. The ward sister and some doctor I had never seen before entered this tent and stood by my side. He was a very old doctor. He looked like he belonged in one of the beds. Fixing his eyes on the ceiling, he pressed a cold stethoscope against my chest and listened carefully.

'Breathe in and out for me, son,' he said kindly.

No way, not me!

When he had finished, he stood back and looked at me long and hard, as if he wasn't quite sure what to say. He bent over and ran his bony old hand gently over my head, then straightened up, sighed softly and left.

Within minutes I was surrounded by staff. It was like a beehive around me. They pushed my bed into the middle of the ward, right beside the sister's table. A screen was set up around me and all the struggling and fighting in the world didn't get me out of having something I had come to hate with a passion – an enema.

I had only just recovered from that, lying shivering and shaking in my bed and trying to push the memories of other hospital stays out of my mind, when (Oh bloody hell, not her!) I saw the Vampire Lady, dressed all in white, setting up her tubes and needles at my side. It was the one from the children's ward – she must have tracked me down somehow.

'Good-MORN-ing!' she sang, 'I-need-some-BLOOD-from-YOU-young-man!' Her greedy pea-shaped eyes glowed behind thick lenses. The look of pleasure on her face as her cold hands gripped my wrist and rolled up my sleeve frightened me more than anything else. It was only a small prick on the finger, but it was the way she got the blood that gave me nightmares for years afterwards: pressing the fingertip, sucking the blood up into a rubber tube, and then blowing it onto a piece of glass or into a bottle.

Half an hour later she was thirsty again. 'I-need-a-LOT-more! PLEASE-give-me-your-arm.'

Needles and syringes were stored in a kidney dish and covered with methylated spirits. The needles themselves looked big enough to drive a horse and cart through. It didn't take me long to learn more than I had ever wanted to know about them. Every morning before they were used, these needles would be sharpened with a flat file (Oh, that awful sound!) and by lunchtime they would be blunt again. As the needle was pushed through my skin and into the vein at the elbow joint, I could feel the skin tearing.

After breakfast they took more blood from me, stuck pins and needles into my arms and legs and filled me up with even more medicine. I needed two hands to hold all the pills and two bottles of water to wash them down.

Doctors came and went. A very elderly man was put into Mr Bell's old bed. He only lasted a few hours. I was beginning to understand why Mr Wallace didn't want that spot.

That night my mother finally caught up with me.

'Sorry, love, I've spent half the day arguing with the office staff. The way you were treated at the children's ward was disgraceful. They should have let you stay there instead of … here.' Mum looked around the room and pressed her lips together. 'Anyway,' she went on, smoothing my hair, 'I haven't finished with them yet, Kenny, believe you me!'

She had to leave shortly after that. My two older brothers weren't happy about having to get their own meals, she explained, and Mark, the youngest, was with a neighbour. She bent to kiss my forehead, joking about how lucky I was to be in a place where I would be waited on hand and foot.

Mum had her hands full, I have to give her that. Even at my age I could see how exhausted she was. She was about forty-seven at the time, trying to hold onto her three jobs – as a cleaner, waitress and shoe-machinist – as well as her four boys.

She had given birth to all of us at home. Steven and Ian had been the first two, then twins were born – or should I say stillborn – one inside the womb and the other outside it. 'Most unusual,' the midwife had said, and she must have been right because, as far as I know, their place of residence is still the University of Queensland. Anyway, I came along next in 1940, and Mark was born last of all. No girls, which was a bit sad for Mum, who always had little dresses prepared just in case.

Doctors, when they did their rounds, stood near the sister's desk. To pass the time I had started to listen to their discussions. I soon found out that if I kept my eyes shut they thought I was asleep and talked freely. I learnt a lot about my wardmates this way. What I hadn't counted on was hearing so much about myself.

It was during that quiet time between morning tea and doctors' rounds that I first heard my name mentioned. I kept my eyes closed and my ears open, hoping I'd find out when they were letting me go home.

'And the Hall boy, Doctor,' I heard the sister say, 'anything we can do for him?'

'No, I'm afraid not,' he sighed. 'Just keep him comfortable. We could lose him at any time.' (Lose me? In a hospital?)

'Why kids?' I heard her ask. 'It just isn't fair.'

'This boy has been very lucky, as a matter of fact. If you have a good look at his file, he should have died years ago. In and out of hospitals ... enlarged heart ... rheumatic fever ... even died once on the operating table when he was eight ...' (Died? Me? Why has no one ever told me about that?) '... and from what I can gather he had rather a bad reaction to the ether when they operated on his appendix. They lost him for quite a few minutes – who knows what kind of damage that would have done to his brain cells ... learning difficulties, years behind with schooling ...' They were silent for a while. 'At any rate,' the doctor continued, 'while he hangs on, we will learn from him. Maybe some good will come out of this in the end.'

Not one word about going home.

I hardly noticed when the doctor left. There was too much to think about. Strange, but the part about the 'learning difficulties' upset me more than anything else he had said. Missing out on the schoolwork wasn't my fault. And what about all the times I'd spent in the children's hospital? How come all the other kids were given lessons to do by the visiting teacher, and I wasn't? I knew I could catch up again if they only gave me a chance. I just knew it.

And as for dying? No way, not me!

Weeks began to blend into months. I was a bag of bones and my only friends were the spiders on the ceiling. I had a name for each one. Blood tests gradually slowed down to only one a day. This was surely a good sign. They even moved me out onto the verandah, with six other beds in front of mine, meaning those patients would die before me.

Outside the night sky was lit up with explosions and fireworks. The Brisbane Exhibition was in full swing, just yards from my bed yet a million miles away. How I envied those kids down there, with their fairy floss and toffee apples and money in their pockets for rides on the giant wheel. I could hear the music of the merry-go-rounds and the happy noises of excited children and I wanted to be there with them more than anything in the world.

I turned around to see Mr Wallace's bed being moved towards the sister's desk. He raised his head, took a good look around the ward, muttered a foul word to the nurses and died before they got his bed into place.

I was now fifth in line.

One morning I opened my eyes and saw a circle of six white jackets towering over me. They were all doctors, five males and one female.

'He still with us, Sister?'

My mouth felt dry and furry and my eyelids weighed a ton. Rough hands undressed me and I was too weak to protest. One by one each doctor examined me from head to toe, inside and out. There wasn't too much wrong with my hearing though, and their words sent me into a flying panic.

'He was out for how long?' asked one. (Out? Where did I go?)

When they had finished, they formed a tight little group at the end of my bed, shaking their heads, saying a few words, nodding. Then they turned around and faced the other direction before continuing to discuss me.

They reminded me of something I had once heard about emus – how, when they stick their heads into a hole in the ground, they think nobody can see them. The doctors seemed to think that by turning their backs to me I wouldn't be able to hear them. Most of what I heard didn't make sense to me anyway, except for the one thing they all seemed to agree on – that I wasn't going to live much longer.

Taking it in turns again, each one approached the bed, listened to my heart, then used a marking pen to draw a circle on my chest. Every circle had a number written in the centre. I looked like a board game.

'Sister, no one is to wipe these marks off. This patient is under our care.' The doctor who seemed to be in charge looked straight through me, rubbing his pointy nose thoughtfully. 'The six of us. Yes, we shall all work together on this one.' With that they walked away.

The circle system meant that each of the six would take a turn ordering daily blood tests according to the mark he had made the day before. Before leaving, he or she would leave a new mark in its place. Though I wasn't told what this was all about, I did overhear something about my having a 'floating heart', and having to keep track of where it had moved to each day.

After that I used to lie in bed and imagine my body all hollow inside, like a shell, except for this big red heart floating around all over the place. In nightmares I saw myself screaming with my mouth wide open, and my heart sailing up and floating out the window. Much later I learnt that it was the heartbeat, not the heart itself, that

No way, not me!

was moving, because of the rheumatic fever I'd had when I was younger.

After two weeks of this my fingertips, arms and legs were bruised and sore. Any movement I made was painful. The bedsores were becoming so bad that the sheets felt like sandpaper and I started to recognise that awful odour of broken weepy skin drifting up from under my bedclothes. I knew that I smelled as bad as the old men did now, and for the first time I wondered ... maybe the doctors were right after all? It was the odour of death.

The patients gradually accepted me. I realise today that some of them can't have been as old as I thought them at the time, but they were all grown men and to a boy of my age they seemed ancient.

They all knew me now, by name. Those who could leave their beds came to sit at my side and talk to me. Their families, when they visited, brought me fruit and sweets. One of the wives gave me a jar of home-made strawberry jam and her husband, from about ten beds away, yelled out, 'Don't swallow the seeds, Ken – they're hard to pass!' The whole ward broke into happy laughter for the first and only time that I can recall.

The days were long. Books were useless to me, not that anyone brought me any, but I quite enjoyed trying to figure out the comic strips in the newspaper. I learnt to read the expressions on the little cartoon faces, even though the words in the bubbles above them had no meaning for me.

My strength was slowly returning and one morning they moved my bed away from Death Row. After a while they allowed me to walk around a bit. It was my first chance to explore the ward in which I had lived for so many months.

There were beds lined up everywhere. I hadn't realised how many there really were. I found the bathroom easily enough, and the small kitchen where the tea and drinks were prepared. A small room leading off the larger one held a soldier in quarantine – he had caught some rare disease while he was overseas. When he died a few days later, it was all hush-hush and reporters were asking all sorts of questions.

Halfway down one side of the ward was a doorway with an exit onto the left verandah. I had been warned that it was strictly off-limits, so I didn't try to enter, but no one had said anything about chatting to the men through the open windows. The patients in this area seemed to range from fairly young to very old, but they had one thing in common – their strange habit of coughing and spitting into a mug. They all chain-smoked cigarettes, too, and listened to a battered old radio.

While one of these men was talking to me, he suddenly coughed into my face. Feeling the wetness there, I wiped it away with my pyjama sleeve. When I looked down there was blood on my sleeve. Matron was walking by and her face twisted with anger. She grabbed me by the ear and dragged me into the bathroom.

'Silly boy,' she hissed, 'those men out there have *tuberculosis*. It kills! Stay away from them!'

On another day, I was walking past those windows when I heard a hissing noise.

'Psst! Over here!' It was one of the TB men calling out to me. 'Hanging on the wall near your bathroom is a roll of fine wire – we need it for the radio.'

Getting the wire was easy. As I handed it through the window I felt like a burglar and wanted to giggle with excitement.

'Thanks, mate,' the man said between coughs. 'By the way, how would you like to hear the fight tonight?' Seeing the eager look on my face, he made the arrangements. 'Be at the door when the lights go out.'

And so it was that on 15 November, 1952, I found myself eating and drinking illegally with TB patients, and listening to Jimmy Carruthers take out the world bantamweight title. It was a night to remember.

Inside the ward was my home. The staff allowed me to make orange drinks or tea for the other patients and I made friends with a number of men. I would rather have had boys of my own age to talk to or play games with, but this was all I had, so I decided to make the most of it.

Some of the men used to pay me a small amount for doing odd jobs for them and with the money I earned I would enter the *Courier Mail* 'Spot the Ball' competition. In the newspaper was a photo of a football game, with the ball removed. You marked it with an X where you believed the centre of the ball would be, then placed it in an envelope, together with a sixpenny stamp for the entry fee. I also needed a threepenny stamp for postage. The nurses would address the envelope and post it for me, and sometimes I sent in three entries a week.

No way, not me!

Most times I didn't worry about getting the sixpenny stamp. I just put a coin straight into the envelope, and that must have been fine, because they never returned it – until the day that I put the X on exactly the right spot. Wouldn't you know it, they sent my letter back with the sixpence and a message that said, 'We cannot receive money in the mail.' They had even opened my envelope to get my address at the hospital, so they must have seen my correct entry form.

That week there were no winners.

When they published the photo it showed the ball exactly where I had marked it, and all the nurses felt sorry for me and were furious. They complained to the newspaper, saying I was a sick boy who had been treated unfairly, but they were told that I shouldn't have entered the competition anyway – it was for adults, not children.

Funny how you can be an adult in hospital and a child outside at the same time.

2. Pins and needles

As time went by, just like kids on a farm, I became used to death. I had no choice. It was all around me. Not one of my TB mates made it out of that ward without a ride on the covered trolley.

A man with a young family moved into 1A. He didn't look sick at all, but after some days he had trouble speaking, his eyes began to bulge from their sockets and his joints seized up. Tetanus claimed him.

My good mate, Old Christopher, was eighty-five. He was a lovely old man. The long hair hanging from his head matched the pure white of the beard that covered most of his face. He called me 'Penny', not 'Kenny' like the others did, and got me to sneak to the canteen to buy him clay pipes. When he lit them, he shook so badly that I would have to sit and hold his hand around the pipe until he was finished.

One morning Christopher's bed was empty and I felt like crying.

'What's up?' asked Nurse Cavendish, the one I used to call 'Bananas' for fun.

Pointing to his bed, I said, 'He's gone.'

'No, it's okay,' she told me, 'he's just having an operation on his leg.'

When Old Christopher returned, his right leg was missing, taken off at the knee.

Within days he was back to smoking his pipe. 'My leg is itchy, Penny. Would you scratch it for me?'

I didn't know what to do. 'But your leg is gone,' I whispered, afraid of upsetting him.

'I know, Penny, I know,' he sighed. 'But it's driving me silly. Go on, please scratch it.'

So sitting beside Old Christopher and scratching the sheet where the leg should have been became a part-time job for me. It earned me a shilling a go. Just one week later they took off his other leg, and he called me over.

'Hold my hand, please, Penny?' he begged me, and when I did, I saw tears running down from his pale eyes. 'I want to die. I don't feel like a person any more. What are they doing to me, Penny?'

I couldn't answer. His hands gripped mine like a vice. 'Light me the pipe, Ken.' It was the first time he'd ever called me by my real name.

Just a few hours later Old Christopher passed on.

A very strong bond had grown between two other patients who had previously never met. They taught me card tricks and made coins disappear into thin air. They were not afraid of dying except that it would break up their friendship. To solve this problem they made a pact that if one should die the other would join him right away. We all smiled at this sad but unlikely promise. But a day soon came when I was bringing one of them the cold orange drink he had asked for and found him staring at the ceiling.

'Mr Aspinall has gone to heaven,' I informed the ward sister.

'No way,' she said. 'I've just left him.' But she went to check him all the same. 'You're right, Ken.' Then she turned to Mr Ashford, his friend, and found him dead too. For weeks afterwards all the staff were talking about the 'Aspinall-Ashford Agreement'. No one had ever come across anything like it.

Mr Bones had been in 1A longer than anyone. His real name was something like Bowls or Bose, but somehow 'Mr Bones' just stuck. His bed was next to the door that led onto the back verandah and he couldn't breathe without his oxygen mask. Beside his bed stood a large oxygen bottle with a rubber hose attached, leading to the mask. At eleven o'clock one morning he asked me for a cuppa and when I brought it he told me to leave it on the locker to cool for a while.

I was returning to the kitchen when I heard a noise. Mr Bones had reached for his cup and saucer and brushed against the top of the oxygen bottle, which on this day was not level – part of it sat on the oxygen hose. The bottle toppled over, making a loud bang as it bounced off the painted concrete floor and rolled away. The hose curled around the bottle and pulled the mask from Mr Bones' face.

He was dead by the time I reached him.

My teeth had become very weak and one morning during breakfast I felt a dull crunch. One of them had crumbled. The doctors were worried that any dentist who saw what state my teeth were in would want to pull out the whole lot.

'He's not strong enough for that,' one of them warned. 'We'll have to make sure they only take out the broken one.'

In a wheelchair they carted me off to the dentist, where the sister had some trouble convincing the man to look at my chart before starting the job.

'Chart! What would I need his chart for, Sister?' he snorted, 'I've pulled out teeth before, you know.' But the sister won, and from the look on the dentist's face as he read page after page I could tell he didn't like what he saw.

'Open your mouth, boy, let's see what this is all about.'

After a lot of prodding and poking, he decided that pulling the broken tooth was out of the question until I'd had a three-day course of penicillin. As we left the surgery I heard him muttering something about 'what they've done to that child'.

But three days later, when the last injection was over and my veins danced with penicillin, Matron stood at the foot of my bed and frowned at the latest blood tests marked on my chart. She marched to the phone and cancelled my dental appointment on the spot. Her next orders were to the wardsman, who had already helped me into my wheelchair and was waiting for her go-ahead.

'We won't be needing you after all,' she told him. 'This young man isn't going anywhere for quite a while. We have a bed prepared for him next to Sister's desk.'

She couldn't be talking about me! I could walk ... I felt fine ... I could jump over the moon!

'Sorry, Ken, it's off to bed for you,' she said.

I was out of that wheelchair in a flash and like a racehorse I bolted for the door. 'Stop him!' somebody shouted and nurses came running. They were too quick for me. I was trapped. With a nurse on one side and the wardsman on the other, I felt like an escaped prisoner. Struggling was a waste of time.

'Now, come on! Grow up and behave yourself,' said the wardsman, giving my arm a good shake. 'What's the matter with you?'

'No!' I screamed. 'Let me go! I don't want to die!'

'But who said you're going to die?'

'It's that bed! Everyone who gets that bed dies!'

'That's not true,' he argued, but I knew better. I had seen it for myself, over and over.

'Yes it is! They all die in that bed. Ever since I came here!'

The big wardsman scooped me up and carried me to the bed.

Pins and needles

Before straightening up, he put both hands on my shoulders and looked me in the eye. 'Ken,' he said, 'my name is Allan and I'm going to make you a promise, my friend. I'll sit here with you every chance I get, and I'll make damn sure that you don't die while I'm looking after you.'

I trusted him. I had no other choice, and he had always been nice before. He pulled up a chair and chatted to me about all sorts of things, just to make me feel better.

But even having Allan beside me didn't help when it came time for my next blood test. It wasn't the Vampire Lady this time, just one of the everyday nurses, but I couldn't stop myself from burying my arms under the sheets as soon as she headed my way.

'Arm, please,' she said, as if she was buying a lamb chop.

'No!' I shouted.

'I beg your pardon?' Up till now I had always been helpful.

'You heard me, you ... *bastard*!'

It was a word I had never used before. It just came roaring out all by itself and somewhere deep inside it shocked me just as much as it must have shocked the woman. She sat there with raised eyebrows and open mouth. Allan, who had left his seat for a moment, hurried back to see what the problem was.

'Get – your – arm – out – now!' said the nurse through gritted teeth.

'No!' I screamed, liking the taste of the word. 'No! No! No!' It was so short, so easy to say – I could even spell this one without any trouble at all.

But the nurse got Allan to help her and I suppose that, even as my friend, he had a job to do. Between them they tugged and pulled until my arms were uncovered. They put a band around one of them and it cut in painfully.

'Now, pump your wrist, please.'

No way was I going to help. I went on strike again. I wasn't even going to do it for Allan.

Seeing that I wasn't going to help her, the nurse started tapping at the area around the vein. 'There it is. Right.'

The needle went in. My arm came up and hit her in the face.

'You silly boy, look at the needle – it's all bent!' She packed her things up and marched from the ward.

The ward sister, who must have seen part of this from across the room, called out to the other nurses. 'Get a screen around this patient. Any more trouble, strap him in.'

There were no visitors that afternoon, except for Allan who forgave me my bad behaviour and offered to be my slave. He said he'd get me anything I wanted. I'm ashamed to say that I told him to piss off.

When tea was over, the screen was still around my bed and though I couldn't see the other visitors, I could hear them asking where I was. I also heard the way their voices changed when they heard I was in that bed. I filled my lungs and shouted to no one special that I was going home with Mum. There was dead silence for a while.

When the bell rang at the end of visiting time Mum still hadn't arrived and I did my best to hold back the tears. Nobody wanted me; nobody cared. I made a secret plan to sneak out of my tent the minute the lights went out, but suddenly the screen moved and Mum was there. She bent down and gave me a kiss, then stood aside for Allan and the ward sister to enter the narrow space beside my bed. The three of them begged me to be a good boy.

'If you want to come home with me, love, you've got to help them, so they can help you,' said Mum, as if the others weren't even there. 'A funny thing happened tonight as I was leaving to come here. Darkie tried to get on the bus with me. He wants you home. I want you home. All of us love you.'

The strange thing was that I didn't feel sick. Weak, yes, and a bit tired, but not sick. The doctors didn't believe this. They talked of things like 'relapses' and other words I didn't understand and tried one thing after another to get the results they wanted. And after a while all the bedside discussions must have soaked into my brain, because bit by bit I had to admit that I was not feeling too well at all. I was sure that the pills were causing it, so I got up to an old trick, hiding them in my locker. That didn't last too long. I was caught out and soon the pills were replaced with vitamin injections. Bad deal.

Getting my legs over the edge of the bed was now impossible. My pillow was taken away so I was forced to lie flat out, and they were back to spoon-feeding me. I was too dizzy and weak to do much more than sleep the days away, but I woke up one morning to find a senior doctor and a group of interns ('learner-drivers', the nurses called them behind their backs) hovering around me, making notes and exchanging opinions. I felt like a bug under a magnifying glass.

'Anyone got a suggestion? We need to get his heart to pump.'

Pins and needles

'What about if we cut his left arm off, around here?' One drew a line on my upper arm with his pen. 'If we don't get the results we want, we could take off the other arm later.' (No arms!)

'What about the tuberculosis?' asked another.

'If we can get him past this main hurdle, then we can try to treat the TB.'

'Anyone got anything else to add?' asked the senior doctor.

'A leg, sir, could be better than an arm.' (No arms and no legs!)

'Possibly. The main thing to establish here is how best to reduce the strain on the heart. Amputation of limbs would certainly create a smaller area for the blood to circulate through.' They all stood there looking at me. 'Well,' he continued, 'I'll be seeing the mother this afternoon. Sister, have him ready just in case. The theatre will be on standby.'

That evening I had a surprise visitor. I'd had one or two visits from aunts and uncles, but my two older brothers, Steven and Ian, who were now nineteen and eighteen, must have been too busy with their apprenticeships to make it, and Mark, who was only a year younger than me, was kept away by Mum. This visitor was someone I had almost forgotten about. It was my father.

We hadn't seen each other for so long. We stared at each other for quite a while before any words were spoken between us.

'How are you?' were his first words to me in five years.

'Good, thank you,' I said automatically, wondering why he'd come.

'Anything you want? When you get out of here?'

'I'd love a piebald horse,' I told him, forgetting for a moment that I might soon be without arms and legs.

'Black and white is a piebald. It's yours.'

'You mean it?'

'Yes ... I'm sorry, but I have to go now. See you,' and with that my father turned and left. For all he knew, this might have been the last time he would ever see me alive. Come to think of it, that's probably why he came – to say goodbye.

After he'd gone it struck me that he had never even said my name. And he'd never once touched me. And the horse? I wasn't going to be holding my breath waiting, that was for sure.

It must have been the week for unusual visitors, because the very next day another stranger came to see me. He was a tall man dressed all in black, something that really stood out in a place where white uniforms ruled.

'They tell me your name is Ken,' he began, and I nodded, wondering who on earth he was. 'I believe you're going on a long trip. A one-way journey, in fact.'

Since I hadn't heard anything about these travel plans, I told him that I didn't think he had the right person.

'Can I sit down?'

'Not on the bed! Matron will go mad.'

'My name is Ryan. I'm the Methodist minister for the hospital. I came to tell you about this trip.'

Suddenly it started to make a bit more sense, but I still wasn't sure. 'Do you mean ... the trip we take when we die?' I had remembered some of the other patients being visited by men in black just before they passed away.

The minister's face brightened with relief. 'That's the one. What do you know about it?'

'Well,' I said nervously, 'I know they take you away on the trolley, with your face covered up.' This part always stuck in my mind, more than anything else. Besides, I had never seen where they actually took the dead people.

'Yes, yes – but that's only a small part. When you close your eyes for the last time, angels come and raise you up to heaven, where you sit and sing with God and live in peace forever.'

'But I don't want to go,' I cried, really getting scared now.

'What's going on here?' asked the sister, who was walking by.

'I don't want to go to heaven, Sister. I only want to go home,' I wailed.

Sister glared at the minister, who shrugged his shoulders and said he had only been telling me about the angels. He wasn't too happy when she asked him to leave.

For the first time since I had met this woman, I saw her smile. Ignoring all the rules, she perched on the edge of the bed and gave my hand a squeeze. 'You're not going anywhere without my permission.'

The doctor in charge of me had arranged to speak with Mum one night after visiting time. They disappeared into the hallway and when they returned the doctor went over to the sister's desk, where Matron was waiting. 'I have Mrs Hall's signature on the form '

Pins and needles

This was it! I knew this meant they'd be cutting off my arms and legs, or maybe even booking my ticket on the trolley. How could Mum just be standing there so calmly? Didn't she care?

'... so we can start on the new drug today.'

'What's it called, Doctor?'

'It's cortisone, Matron. They call it a miracle drug. That boy will be the very first patient in Queensland to use it.'

'Oh Lord, let it work,' breathed Matron.

I looked at Mum. She could tell that I'd heard so she just smiled and nodded.

'You're a lucky boy, Ken.'

Just a few days after starting the treatment my bed was moved onto the verandah again, well away from the sister's desk. What a relief! The new medicine must be working. I felt that I could even put up with the giant needles they kept pushing into my legs to inject the cortisone, if it meant getting better.

Three days before Christmas the staff started to put the decorations up. There was a special dinner planned for Christmas Day and everyone was cheerful.

'You can get out of bed today, young man,' said the doctor on his rounds. My legs were shaky and my whole body felt weak, but I was so happy to be allowed up that I didn't care. The doctor looked thoughtful. 'Tell your mother I'll want to see her tonight, before she leaves.'

They didn't know it, but I heard the whole conversation through the verandah window. 'Sorry, Mrs Hall, the new drug doesn't seem to be working. We don't want to stop it completely, so he'll receive it once a week at Outpatients. If I were you, I'd take the boy on a holiday. He won't see another Christmas. We are all agreed that this will be his last.'

Thirty-six hours before Christmas, I left ward 1A – and it wasn't by trolley. I was a bit sorry to be missing the big Christmas dinner, but the thought of going home was even more exciting. The nurses, sisters, and even Matron, kissed me tearfully. My wardmates wished me the best and shook my hand. Some of them cried.

At the front door of the hospital, Allan shook my hand and turned to Mum.

'I'm leaving too, Mrs Hall,' he said. 'I only stayed long enough to see Ken leave this ward on his feet. My new job is at McWhirter's, the department store in the Valley, driving a lift. If you ever get to that part of town, please come and say hi.'

A taxi pulled up at the kerb and Mum bundled me into it. 'Let's go home in style,' she said grandly.

3. The last holiday

Maroochydore on the Sunshine Coast was the spot Mum picked out for my holiday. She had always loved that place, had moved up there with her parents when she was only twelve, same as me. Myrtle Wittmann was her name in those days. She had gone to Nambour State School, made some good friends there, and on weekends helped her father who was building houses in the area. She told us kids that her parents had nearly been divorced because of it. Her mother wanted to move back to Brisbane, but her father had plenty of work up there and didn't want to leave. It came down to choosing between his wife and his business – and in the end his wife won. We often joked that Mum must have taken after Grandma's side of the family, because that was another woman who always got her own way.

Ian and Steven couldn't take any time off from their jobs, so it was only the three of us, Mum, Mark and me, who got to Roma Street station just as the stationmaster was calling 'All aboard!' The big steam engine gave off a loud whistle when we climbed onto the train.

I threw myself into the seat right next to the window before Mark could beat me to it and stuck my head out through the opening, enjoying the wind in my face and watching as city turned into suburb and houses gave way to fields. But soon the train picked up speed and the smoke from the steam engine became thick with coal dust, making my eyes water. With my eyes closed I leaned back on the slippery leather seat and listened to the wheels on the tracks talking to me: 'Clickety-click – clickety-clack – we're on our way – we can't go back.'

I was almost asleep when I felt the train slow down to just a crawl. 'Paper, paper!' somebody was shouting; it seemed to be coming from somewhere outside. There was a group of men standing near the track with tools on their shoulders. Suddenly two newspapers went sailing though the air and were neatly caught. Mum explained that this was the only way these men could get their daily news, but I thought they should go and buy it in a shop like everyone else.

The weather in Nambour was awful when we arrived. Big black clouds were hanging low in the sky and a huge downpour drenched us while we waited for the Maroochydore bus, which was late. The driver ignored Mum's request for help with our things, telling us to hurry up and just throw the bags in. He started to drive off before we had even sat down properly, so Mum let him have it. Rising to her feet and towering over him, she asked him his name, and her tone was not at all pleasant. He turned out to be Mike, one of her cousins, whose family owned the bus line.

We rode in dead silence for about twenty minutes, the rain pelting down and the wind growing stronger. Tree branches were scattered all over the road and now and then we had to swerve around them. Mike finally got up the courage to apologise to us and started up a conversation. After a while it turned out that he and Mum had sometimes played together when they were kids.

It was dark and gloomy and raining like anything when we pulled up at the Cotton Tree terminus, so Mike begged us to let him drive all the way to the small house we had rented. He even carried our bags to the door, but when he turned to help Mum off the running board she couldn't move. Her legs had 'turned to jelly', as she used to call it, and her mouth hung wide open. The front yard was alive with cane toads – big ones, little ones – they were everywhere we looked, glowing in the lights from the bus. To me it looked more like it had been raining toads than cats and dogs. At the count of three we made a dash for the front door, hoping we wouldn't trip over the ugly little creatures, or have one jump up at us. It was Mum and Mark who were scared to death, not me, but I had to go along with it so they wouldn't look so bad.

Mum made us change into dry clothes before we were allowed to look around. The house had been made into two flats and you could make out the join between them when you looked up at the ceiling in the lounge room. There wasn't all that much to see, really, just this half-lounge with a sink and small stove in one corner, two single beds for Mark and me along one wall, and a radio in the other corner. The one and only bedroom was taken by Mum. Although there was a tiny room with a bath, to Mum's great disappointment the dunny was outside, twenty yards away. No way was Myrtle Hall going to spend a penny out there in the dark!

The last holiday

Morning brought no change in the foul weather. We heard on the radio that there was a cyclone just off the coast, and even though we didn't want to be caught outside if it came in closer, we didn't have too much choice. We hadn't packed any wet-weather clothes – but there was no food in the house.

Twenty minutes later, soaked to our skins, we arrived at the local shops and bought food for two days and three potato bags to use as raincoats.

Five days later it was still raining. The rain must have made that house shrink, because I swear it got smaller and smaller every day, until we all agreed that if we didn't get outside we would go mad. Some beach holiday – we hadn't even seen the sea yet.

With the potato sacks over our heads we made our way towards the sand dunes around the Maroochydore Surf Club. Waves over nine feet high were exploding onto the beach. Foam covered the shore like froth in a washing machine, staying behind when the tide went out, and the wind blew it into ribbons that decorated the beach. Large rocks were revealed, some standing four feet high. If there was any sand left down there, we didn't see it. We weren't allowed to play near the water, of course, but Mum did let us mess around in the dunes further up for a while, where the sand was so soft that I sank in up to my waist. It was like quicksand.

On the sixth day the sun came out. I was ready for fishing, at the only place sheltered from the wind, a small wooden jetty at Cotton Tree, about half a mile from the mouth of the river. I had the time of my life.

Two days later a new cyclone arrived. By the time it blew over, eighty per cent of Maroochydore was covered in water. It was another three days before the first bus got through to Nambour, and the following day we had to go home to Brisbane.

We heard, much later, that January 1953 held the rainfall record for Maroochydore.

So much for my holiday.

4. Give the boy a broom

My regular treatments at the Outpatient's ward were finally coming to an end – not because I was cured, but because the doctors seemed to have given up on me. The results they wanted just weren't there. I still had a bad murmur, they told me (sounding like one of my teachers having a go at me for not speaking clearly). And the pains in the chest were there all the time, but there are some things in life that you just learn to live with.

'You do know that if the pain gets bad, it's dangerous?' asked the doctor with a frown on his face. He didn't like it when I just shrugged my shoulders, so he addressed Mum in a very firm tone indeed. 'Has this boy been told about his condition?'

'I didn't want to worry him,' she said in a low voice. That was pretty funny, really, because I had heard my health being discussed by doctors and nurses for years.

The doctor said it was time for me to stop the cortisone injections and take it in tablet form from now on. It was important to keep the drug in my system, he explained, as my body had become used to it and I would have problems doing without it. I was glad to hear that I would be having no more needles.

About a week after the injections were stopped, on a bright Saturday morning, Mum sat on the edge of her bed and asked me if I'd like to brush her hair. This was something she often did when it was time for a serious talk. She could sit still for hours while one of her sons lifted her long soft hair and pulled the bristles through the strands. I was always happy to brush Mum's hair – it was a relaxing thing to do and besides, if you were in for one of her long talks, being busy with your hands helped a lot. You also didn't have to look her in the eye, something that had saved me once or twice from getting caught out in a lie.

I started to brush Mum's hair, while she searched her mind for a suitable beginning, so I was daydreaming when she started and I missed the first few words.

'... Ken! Are you listening to me?' Her voice was strange. She sounded nervous.

Give the boy a broom

'Yes, Mum.' I stopped brushing and paid attention.

'I said your school days are over,' Mum repeated. This was not the bad news I had been expecting – if anything, it gave me quite a lift. (No more school! No more being laughed at and pushed around!) Mum seemed to take courage from my silence, because she went on to say, 'On Monday you start work at Doyle's. They make cane furniture.' I argued that I wanted to work with wood like my brothers did, not with cane, but once my mother had made her mind up, that was it. 'No!' she said firmly, 'and no more will be said about this matter. It's off to work with you on Monday and don't you *dare* let me down.'

Everyone you talk to always says that your first day at work is the longest day of your life. Well, this one was for me. The factory employed three men. I had a broom shoved into my hands and it turned out to be my only friend in that cold lonely place. All I had to do was clean around their feet as they worked and sometimes carry parts from one to another. I might as well have been invisible. The first man cut the cane, the second shaped it by holding it over a gas flame and the third wove the different parts into pieces of furniture. At three o'clock they all sat down and wove cane together.

Lunch or smoko, these men never uttered a word. They would take their seats, eat their meals, then light up a cigarette and that was it.

Friday at five o'clock I left for home, clutching my first pay envelope. Thirty shillings didn't last too long once Mum had taken her twenty-five shillings for my keep, which she said she would have to stretch into food and clothing for me. I was left with five shillings for myself and the first thing I did to show how grown-up I was was to buy a pack of cigarettes called 'Three Threes'. Nobody in the family made any comment about this, even though I had been expecting a lecture from Mum on account of my health problems. Smoking in those days was accepted as a part of life. Besides, she was a smoker herself.

Three weeks later Mum presented me with a wristwatch. It was the custom for every member of our family to get one when he entered the workforce.

The job at Doyle's wasn't difficult, but the boredom was killing me inch by inch. I had been cleaning up after the men for four months and wishing they would let me do some of the real work, which didn't look very hard at all. So one day at lunch time I approached the oldest one and very politely mentioned that I would like to learn the work. It was a big mistake.

'Learn?' he said at the top of his voice, 'your mother never said anything about you *learning*. It's not worth it for us to teach you, boy, with your bad health! Anyway, you had no schooling. I must say, you got a nerve! If we do put anyone on, it won't be you.'

With this I told my very first boss to get stuffed – and all three jumped to their feet. One of them reached for a length of cane but the youngest one held him back. 'No, brother! Don't cane him, just pay him off.'

I decided to try and find my own jobs from then on, to keep Mum from telling people what she always did when she thought I couldn't hear: 'Just give the boy a broom, he won't be with us much longer' or 'He isn't long for this world', and other whispered messages that all meant the same kind of thing.

My next job was at a joinery in Woolloongabba where they built wardrobe furniture from beautiful timbers like walnut and rosewood. In quiet times they made wooden toilet seats out of cypress pine. I loved the smell of that place from the first time I walked in.

Like my first job, it started off with sweeping and cleaning. The foreman pointed to a broom and told me to start at the front door, work my way to the back wall and then start all over again. Just before lunch the boss gave me a piece of plywood and a pencil. I was to go around and ask 'the boys' for their lunch orders, then take a box around to the corner store and be back before they stopped for lunch.

I scribbled down the orders as quickly as possible and collected the money. Outside the shop I looked at the list and was horrified to find that I couldn't read my own writing, so I made up an order from what I could remember and hoped for the best. Back at the factory the men seemed to accept my story of losing the list on the way to the shop, but I knew I wouldn't be able to get away with that a second time.

There had to be some way around it. The words I had written down had made sense to me at the time, but just minutes later were nothing but a jumbled mess that no one could have read. The only plan I could come up with was to take a small notepad to work with me the next morning, into which I had drawn tiny pictures of pies, sandwiches and cakes, and even a few symbols for the fillings. It worked. I would get the orders while the men were too busy to look up from their work, or if they did, I'd hold the notepad close to my chest so they couldn't see what I was 'writing'. Using a system of numbers, letters, lines and arrows, I managed to get the right lunches nearly every time and even managed to bring each man his change – though I mainly had to rely on the shopkeeper's honesty for this part.

For quite a while there were no complaints and I was feeling pretty happy with myself. I was thirteen years old, holding down a job, and most of the men were nice to me. Some of them were gradually starting to show me how the machines worked. I even got to put some of the toilet seats together for them and I did it well. Then one day a new lad started and took over these jobs and it was 'back to the broom for Ken'.

While I was cleaning around the compressors one morning, my hand was dragged under the four belts that spun around the twelve-inch pulley. When I got my hand back, the skin on my knuckles had been peeled back to the bone. Feeling very shaken, I let myself be taken to the office by one of the men. The boss took one look at my hand and before I knew what was happening he was pouring pure iodine into the open cut. Boy, did that hurt! I rose about two feet off my chair but clamped my teeth down onto my lip to keep from screaming out. Nobody was going to call me a coward!

As the boss was tying the bandage he said, 'Ken, can you spell and do maths?'

'Yes, sir.' I wasn't going to start admitting my problems just because he had me cornered. No way.

'What's eight times eight?' (Of all the luck! That was the only one I'd ever been able to remember – I don't know why. If he had asked me 'four times four' I would have been stumped.)

'Sixty-four,' I said firmly and the boss was satisfied.

'Look, we have room for two apprentices here, and I must say you are very good with your hands. So – I'm asking, would you like to be an apprentice wood-machinist?'

'Yes sir, I'd love to!' I was over the moon. Wood! That's exactly what I had always wanted to work with. The boss told me that I had to clear it with my mother but I didn't want her interfering again. This was my job.

One Tuesday a few weeks later I made my way to the college at the end of William Street in the city. At the front desk I was told to wait while they checked my name against the records, and their next words took the wind right out of my sails. 'Sorry, you don't have a Scholarship pass. You cannot start until you get it.'

To get my Scholarship I would have to sit for the grade seven examinations and do well enough to pass. This meant night-school at the same building on Tuesday nights until I was ready for the examination. At first I was a bit thrown by the idea of being in a school again, but then I told myself that this would be different and that it was my big chance to catch up to other boys my age in education.

So it was quite an exciting night for me when I first took my seat in the room along with twenty other pupils. A man of about twenty-eight with a soft voice introduced himself as Mr Smart, our teacher, which would have raised quite a few sniggers at my old school, but nobody moved a muscle in this one. He told us to fill in the forms in front of us with our names, the name of the school we'd gone to, what grade we had reached and what our past exam results were. We also had to write down the reason for leaving that school without doing Scholarship.

Looking hard at the paper, I knew it was a waste of time. I couldn't read more than a short word here and there.

'Sir,' I said with my hand up, 'can I take this form home?'

Mr Smart looked as if he didn't know whether I was joking or serious. 'Well, what have we *here*?' he said, his voice rising with disbelief. 'A *cheat*, maybe. Take it home indeed! Don't be ridiculous.' He left the room after that, saying he'd be back a bit later and I just sat there, feeling my cheeks burning because of the way all the other kids were staring at me.

Suddenly a quiet voice said, 'I'll help you.' It came from a boy sitting behind me, someone I had never even seen before. I thanked him and together we got the form done before Mr Smart returned.

The following week we were given two papers, one on maths and the other to be used for a composition on our last holidays. I smiled to myself when Mr Smart told us the topic, because for me it really had been my 'last holiday', at least going by what the doctors had told Mum.

Handing in the paper, I felt very confident. I knew I had done a good job.

Another week passed and our teacher announced that he had the results of our efforts in front of him. 'Mr Ken Hall,' he called,

Give the boy a broom

'please stand for me.' I did, and then Mr Smart asked me to do something really odd. 'I would like you to stand up on top of your desk where we can all see you, while I read out the results.' I climbed up and waited for Mr Smart to finish this job and it seemed that so far everyone had passed. Then he turned to me.

'Class, I want you all to meet Ken Hall.' I stood as tall as I knew how, my chest puffed out and my head held up high. I knew I must have topped the class and felt prouder than I ever had in my whole life ... until I heard Mr Smart's speech to the class. 'This is the world's only human baboon that you and I will ever know in our lifetime. His composition was the biggest heap of *shit* I have ever read. Did I say "read"? *I can't even read it!* His maths is a disgrace too – only three out of fifty. And I want to say this to you, Ken Hall: Don't you *ever* show your face around my class again! Class dismissed.'

While the others filed out of the room, I kept my eyes fixed to the floor, sick with shame and feeling as if I'd been kicked. My chest burned and my head was spinning from the shock.

When the others were all gone, Mr Smart told me to hurry up and leave so he could lock up. I heard the door slam shut behind me and, with my head down, I walked and walked without knowing or caring where I was going. It was dark and late.

My feet took me to the edge of the Brisbane River. I might have just kept walking right off the bank and into the water if I hadn't seen the outline of a man standing in the dark shadow of a building. He asked if I wanted to 'have a bit of fun'. This was the last straw! I had just been thrown out of class for being a human baboon and now here was some dirty stranger thinking I was only fit for the twisted games that Mum had warned us boys about ... I found myself charging at the man and calling him names as loudly as I could, but just when I was close enough to throw myself at him I caught a movement on my right and there in the shadows were two more men, so I changed direction and ran off the opposite way, not daring to stop until I was well out of their reach.

Puffing and out of steam, I found a quiet spot and sat down on the edge of the river. My mind was working overtime. Would anyone care if I jumped in and drowned myself? Slowly I stood up and saw, high above me, the last tram for the night crossing the Victoria Bridge. On top of everything else, I would now have to walk all the way to Coorparoo.

That gave me plenty of time for brooding on my way home. Committing suicide was not something I had ever thought of doing before, but it did cross my mind on this worst night of my life. I felt so worthless and unhappy that I didn't think there was much point in going on any more.

It was after midnight by the time I reached a place that I knew was only ten minutes from home. There, in the street light, a girl was walking towards the gateway of Dr James' house. She looked slightly familiar but I couldn't really place her. I wondered whether I should speak to her or just keep on walking, but before I could make a decision I had already passed her.

'Excuse me, would you have a light, please?' she asked. I turned and walked back. I lit a match for her, my hands shaking the whole time. Then she looked up at me with her head tilted to one side.

'Don't I know you?'

I told her that this was where I came to see Dr James, our family doctor. Her next question took me by surprise.

'What are you doing on Saturday night?'

I didn't know what to say because this was a totally new experience for me. We hadn't even exchanged names.

'Sorry, did I shock you? I didn't mean to.' She took a long drag on her cigarette and slowly exhaled the smoke in my direction.

She seemed to be waiting for an answer, so I told her I wasn't doing anything on Saturday and she said I should meet her at the same spot at six-thirty Saturday night. The gate creaked and she walked inside.

Two days later at work the boss sent me a message to come to his office. It wasn't hard to figure out what it was going to be about. He was probably going to tell me how disappointed he was about my not being allowed to go back to classes, meaning that I wouldn't be getting my Scholarship pass and that would be the end of my short apprenticeship. Well, I told myself as I walked into his office, at least I still had a job and that was the main thing.

The boss waved me into a chair and looked very serious. In his hand was a piece of ply, which seemed to interest him an awful lot, and after a while he asked the piece of ply to spell the word 'salad.' Then I realised that he must have been talking to me, so I begged his pardon and he repeated himself, laying down the wood and looking right at me. 'I want you to spell "salad" for me.'

'I can't.'

Give the boy a broom

'What do you mean, you can't?' His voice had a mean streak in it that I had never heard before.

'I can't spell, sir.'

'*Now* you tell me!' he spat. 'I just got a phone call from the college – a Mr Smart, it was. I didn't believe him at first, but now, looking at this so-called order that you wrote, I'm going to have to phone that man back and apologise to him. Have you got any idea how I *feel* about this?' (No wonder that bit of ply looked so familiar – it was the one from my first day. He must have found it somewhere with the off-cuts.)

It was pretty plain to me that he wasn't the least bit interested in how the whole thing had made *me* feel. Finally he threw something onto the floor behind my chair. 'Here, this is your pay packet. Collect your goods and leave *now*!'

Mum was in the kitchen when I got home and wanted to know what I was doing back so early. She hadn't known about the test or the apprenticeship, so I broke down and told her all that had happened. She crossed her arms in the special way that meant business and told me I was going to see the doctor, and 'furthermore' that she would be coming with me.

It was high time, said my mother, that we knew exactly what was wrong. By 'we' I knew that she really meant me. The doctor had a thick file spread out in front of him and step by step listed all the good and bad news.

I learnt, for the first time without overhearing it, that being born without tonsils and adenoids meant my immune system was 'nil', whooping cough had given me violent convulsions of the lungs, rheumatic fever had enlarged my heart, tuberculosis had weakened my lungs and St Vitus' dance was causing involuntary movement of my muscles. (Never even noticed that one before, but maybe it was something you couldn't see for yourself.) The doctor went on to explain that my appendix had 'cost' me a lot. He confirmed that I had died during the operation when I was eight, and the lack of oxygen had caused a small but very important part of my brain to be damaged. It was the part that controlled short- and long-term memory, which took away my ability to learn, as well as preventing my auditory memory from connecting with my visual memory, and so on. I didn't understand most of this, though Mum made a few notes so that she could go over it again with me at home.

The only good news was that I was still alive, and the doctor told us both how lucky I was that cortisone had come along just when I needed it most. He was very proud of having the first patient in the state to be using this American drug. He decided to put me back on the injections again. 'Just once a month you will get a small jab from a needle, my boy. When you think of it, that's a small price to pay for life. Anyway, a few years from now they may have a cure. Look – just get a job where you have no manual work, stick to it, and you'll be right. Any troubles, come and see me.' I had never heard of manual work so I asked him what it was. Turned out that it was the kind of job where you use your hands and your strength. I was to stay away from those and work in an office.

'But how can I work in an office? I can't read or spell.' This was getting me nowhere. We were going in circles here.

Mum had been sitting and listening, but now she was ready to have her say. 'Doctor, could you get Ken a job at the Xavier Home?' A special look passed between them.

He nodded. 'I'll try, leave it with me.'

I made myself a promise as we walked out of that surgery: *no one was going to know that I couldn't read or spell.* (I was able to write most of the letters in the alphabet, but without being able to spell there wasn't much point.) And another thing, the part about dying was wrong. I was absolutely convinced that I'd be an old man some day.

Maybe Mum and the doctor didn't realise it, but I knew exactly what sort of place the Xavier Home was: it was for physically and mentally handicapped children.

Early the next morning I spent a bit longer than usual in front of the bathroom mirror, looking at my reflection and turning my head this way and that way to see whether anybody would think I was handicapped. I was pretty sure that I looked normal, but I was so used to seeing my own face that it was hard to know for sure.

Then I took a walk up the long driveway of the Xavier Home in Coorparoo. Boys and girls of all ages were playing out the front. Very slowly and casually, as if I was just a visitor, I moved towards them. (No way, I wasn't a bit like them!) Their bodies were all bent and some of them couldn't even talk properly – they only grunted. Whatever the others might think, I knew this wasn't my world.

Give the boy a broom

Saturday night at six-thirty sharp I was ready for my first real date. I hadn't forgotten about it, whatever the doctor might have said about my memory problems.

With ten shillings lining my pocket, I made my way to Dr James's front gate and saw her walking down the steps. She (I still didn't know her name) was all dressed up in a long white gown, with black shoes and matching gloves. (Oh hell!) I was wearing my one and only pair of grey pants, with a white shirt that had two buttons missing and black shoes that had never been introduced to the Nugget tin. A horrible fear gripped my stomach as it struck me that she probably wanted to go dancing and I had never danced a step in my life. 'Hi, where would you like to go?' I asked, hoping I sounded a lot cooler than I felt. To my relief she wanted to go to the picture show at Stones Corner, if I didn't mind.

The whole evening was a bit of a disaster. Peg turned out to be quite different to what I had been expecting. For one thing, she remained seated while everyone else, including me, stood up for 'God Save the Queen', proving to me and the whole audience that she was one of those Mickey Drippings (which was what all of us Protestants called the Catholics) and quite a few of the patrons stared meaningfully at us until I just wanted to sit down and bury my head in shame. My next shock came when her hand crept into mine and she slowly lifted it into her lap, where she held it tightly. Don't ask me what the film was – I didn't know and I didn't care. For the next three hours I was such a bundle of nerves that sweat was pouring off me and I could hardly wait to get out of there and into the cool night air.

Then, on the tram home, Peg invited me to her twenty-first birthday party which was coming up soon, making me realise for the first time that this very beautiful girl was a lot older than me. When she asked me my age my throat closed up and my collar felt as if it was about to strangle me, and I lied, saying I was nineteen, but turning twenty in six weeks' time. No way was I going to tell her I was only thirteen. That only caused another problem, because she was thrilled and said we should have a party on my birthday, too.

But scariest of all was arriving at the James's place and having Peg drape herself over me so that I was pushed up against a rough old tree in a corner of the yard. She invited me to kiss her and made it clear that a peck on the cheek wasn't going to be enough for her, as she was 'a fully mature woman with *wants*'. Luckily, before anything else could happen, Mrs James called out from an upstairs window and Peg said good night, adding that she would see me again soon.

I didn't know whether to be glad or sorry about the whole damn thing.

Finding my next job was easier than I had expected. I knew what to look out for now, and my main goal was to keep my handicap a secret. Thomas Nursery Furniture was located between Ernest Street and Tribune Street, backing onto the South Brisbane wharves just down from the dry docks.

Noticing that all the employees read the newspaper during the twenty-minute morning smoko and again at lunch time, I started buying one for myself on the way to work each morning. I would perch myself on a wooden box, take out my sandwich and shake the paper open just like the others did. Copying their head movements, I would run my eyes up and down the pages, pausing now and then as if something especially interesting had caught my attention. The comic strips looked pretty funny, but I wasn't sure whether I should laugh or not. I learnt to glance at one of the other men and keep up with which page he was looking at, so that when he was reading the comics, I would be too. This way, when he laughed I could join in.

Before long I was given a three-foot ruler so that when I wasn't sweeping up, I could help put together the cots, high-chairs and play-pens. It wasn't as hard to master as I had thought it would be, but I had to study it carefully for a long time, trying to figure out how best to read it. There were three-quarters, five-eighths, seven-sixteenths and other complicated markings all along it, but to my surprise they all started making pretty good sense after a while. I found numbers easier to read and understand than words.

My urge to create something for myself out of wood had never been stronger and it nearly got me into terrible trouble one day.

Over the months I had noticed some of the men hiding timber for projects at home by sneaking it out into the back lane, lifting up a sheet of tin and placing the timber behind it. The only trouble was that quite often some of the wharfies came along and took it for themselves, much to the annoyance of my workmates. I wasn't game to take timber out of the factory itself, so I decided to be a 'wharfie' one night when the others had all gone home, and help myself to some of the stashed timber. My plan was to build a canoe at home.

Give the boy a broom

At six o'clock, with a thumping heart, I pulled out some planks from the hiding place, and by ten minutes past I was safely at the tram stop with ten lengths of timber at my feet. It had been so easy. Then I got the fright of my life: Mr Thomas, the boss, came driving up in his big black car and it was too late to hide – there was nowhere to go. My mind was racing and I thought about throwing myself face-down onto the footpath, but that would probably just make him stop to see what was wrong ... turning my back was another option, no, the boss was already beside me, I could see him behind the steering wheel ... but Mr Thomas just beeped his horn and drove on. Oh bloody hell, I'd be getting the sack tomorrow for sure.

In the morning he walked towards me with what I imagined was a pretty sour look on his face. 'Nice morning, son.' I nodded and waited for the crunch, but instead of sacking me, the boss just told me to hurry up and get ready for work because the bell would be going any minute. For once I was lucky.

My canoe looked great but wasn't much of a success. It kept rolling over and spilling me into the water. Dripping wet and mad as hell I took out my rage on Ian, who had been forced to drive me to Woody Point in his new car so I could try my canoe out. Two hours after I first launched it the damn thing still wasn't floating properly, and Ian looked so smug that I blamed the whole failure on him, accusing him of being jealous, and offering to knock his brains right out of his head. I meant it, too.

Ian told Mum that 'madness' wasn't the word for me.

The awful part about all this was that I really couldn't stop myself once I got into one of these rages. The slightest thing would set me off and the whole family had to suffer my bad temper. Weekends were always difficult because I was bored with push bikes but wasn't old enough to drive a car. Suddenly one day I felt like kicking myself for not having thought of the perfect solution to this problem earlier. It was so simple: I'd get a horse.

But Mum wouldn't have it. 'You can *not* have a horse, Ken. You don't know the first thing about them and you don't even have a paddock to keep one in.'

This made me very angry. I didn't think that she or anyone else had the right to tell me what I could or could not do, and told her so in my usual hot-headed way. She headed straight for the phone and called the doctor. I could hear what she said from the back door, where I stood and listened for a while before storming out of the house.

'Yes, Doctor, there is something terribly wrong with Ken. He has this thing about being right all the time ... he wants to fight everyone ... he just hasn't been the same since he came home from the hospital ...'

When I came back after talking to one of our neighbours who owned five acres of land joining onto our yard, Mum asked me where I had been, saying that Dr James was waiting to see me at his surgery as soon as possible. It was just too much. I did my block. And then I very smugly informed her that Mrs Hart had said I could use her land to keep a horse on, 'so there!' Turning my back on Mum, I went outside and started to plan where I'd build my fences.

Looking back, it must have been heartbreaking for my mother, who had worked so hard only to be repaid with such bad behaviour. It would be many years before we discovered the main cause of it. Cortisone turned out to have a number of nasty side-effects, and this aggressive attitude was just one of them.

One afternoon Mr Thomas ran into the factory, waving both hands in the air. 'Quick! Outside, everyone! A spaceship!' He hurried out again and we caught up to where he was standing in the middle of the road, pointing to something right above his head. There was not a cloud in the sky and what we saw amazed us all – a very small, shiny, cigar-shaped object, with smoke drifting out of one end.

'It's from Mars,' a woman shouted.

'She's right,' someone else said. 'They're coming, they're coming!'

The whole street had come to a stop. Cars, buses and trams just stopped dead in their tracks and people were gathering all around. Two men were on their knees, calling for others to join them in prayer. After a while the spaceship seemed to climb even higher in the sky and eventually disappeared from sight.

That night I told Mum what I had seen and she sent me over the road to tell one of our neighbours, a hero from World War I, all about it. Mr Jenkins had lost one of his legs while fighting the Germans and had been involved in the capture of the first German tank by Australians. (It had always thrilled me to know that this very same tank was on display at the museum right here in Brisbane.) Mr Jenkins had also seen the spaceship and we sat and chatted about it for a while, our eyes never leaving the sky for long, just in case it returned.

That night I dreamed of little green men from space.

Next morning at smoko we all shook out our newspapers and right there on the front page was a large photo of the sighting. I couldn't hold back my excitement.

'Men from Mars, Mr Thomas,' I said. 'They could be landing any time. They could land right here! What do you think, sir?'

'What *are* you on about, boy?'

'The story on the front page, sir.' I was feeling pleased with myself for being able to discuss one of the articles for once.

'Look, son,' said Mr Thomas, showing me his newspaper, 'my paper has been ripped. So would you please read me the story?' With this he nudged one of the other men with his elbow. 'Listen to this, John, Ken's going to read us the story about the men from Mars.' Now they were all looking at me.

'Come on then, we're waiting,' John said.

I didn't know what to do. Talking about it was one thing, reading it out loud was another. 'It's just a story about what we saw yesterday,' I shrugged.

'I've read it already,' John told me, losing his patience. He snapped his paper back to the first page. 'It says, "Ace pilot flies new craft over city and at the same time does a bit of sky-writing." You, my boy, can't read, can you? I've always had the feeling you were a phoney!' The room erupted with laughter. 'All this time we've had a dummy working with us.'

My world was shattered. Up till then I had been accepted, but I knew that everything had changed in the blink of an eye and there was no way I would now be able to stay. Taking a deep breath I asked Mr Thomas to have my wages ready for me that afternoon, as I would not be coming back. Not a single one of them tried to talk me out of leaving – if anything, they encouraged it. For the rest of the morning jokes were being made at my expense every few minutes. It was unbearable. At lunch time the men made it very clear that I wasn't welcome to sit in the same room with them, and at the first opportunity I sneaked into the office and put the clock forward by two hours. I would have done just about anything to make that terrible day end faster.

5. Horses don't care

To earn some extra cash for the horse I was planning to buy, I built baby cots at home from timber off-cuts I had collected. That wasn't hard; finding customers was the real problem. In the 1950s women seemed to go into hiding for most of their 'time' and I wasn't really game to approach ladies I suspected of being pregnant, just in case I'd made a mistake and they were only fat. So I talked Mark into writing a small advertisement for me, was lucky enough to find a local shopkeeper who allowed me to put it up in his window, and in no time I had plenty of orders to fill.

Although I had saved almost enough money to buy my horse, being without a job soon ate into my cash. And two other things still stood in my way: I had never ridden a horse and Mum was still dead against the idea.

The first problem was solved when Mum took me with her to visit a friend in the country one day. I remember not wanting to go, but she insisted that the clean country air would be good for me. When we got there I noticed a horse grazing near the house and immediately begged Mum's friend to let me have a ride. Of course Mum objected, but Mrs Sloane promised her it was a very quiet creature and I would be perfectly safe. To my delight, she had one of her boys saddle the horse for me. While I waited patiently for my first ride, Mum strode back into the house, saying she couldn't bear to watch me kill myself.

My foot slipped into the stirrup and without any problem at all I managed to pull myself up into the saddle. I had seen plenty of cowboy films and knew that the next thing to do was dig my heels into the horse's ribs. It worked. The horse moved. Trouble was, it took off so quickly that I didn't have time to steer it and it bolted for the cover of a huge mango tree where it parked itself in the leafy shade. I couldn't even get out of the saddle, being trapped by the branches all around me.

'Myrtle! Come and have a look at your son,' yelled Mrs Sloane. When Mum stuck her head out the door the two of them burst out

Horses don't care

laughing. I was furious. There had to be some way to get this horse moving again, so I broke off a small branch in front of my face. Before I could use it, the horse shot out from under the tree and took off across the paddock. I couldn't sit in the saddle properly because of all the bouncing and jolting, and horse and rider covered every inch of the property.

It was wild and exciting and even Mum's frantic shouting didn't spoil the ride of my life. Eventually things slowed down a bit and I was left to continue without an audience until it was time to go home three hours later. Naturally, I pestered Mum about letting me buy a horse all the way home.

Mark and I went with Mum to visit friends at Cribb Island one day soon afterwards. On the way home we drove past a riding school that had a sign out the front. I asked Mark what it said and he told me that you could rent a horse. Tugging on his sleeve, I asked if the sign mentioned how much it cost. 'Ten shillings for eight hours' was the reply, and my mind began to spin in circles. If I couldn't buy a horse, then at least I could rent one for a day – it was better than nothing!

Sunday morning I was on the tram heading into the city, then I took one to Newstead, and after that I had to hitch-hike. Four cars later I arrived at the riding school, but time was beating me – it was already one-thirty.

The horse they gave me was black, sixteen hands high, and even I could tell it was in need of a good feed. The saddle was tied together with string and the bridle had rope instead of leather for the reins. I sat in that saddle and kicked and kicked, but nothing happened. That mare just didn't want to move. She ignored me totally and kept her head down, munching grass.

The owner of the school walked over and held out a stick. 'Here, use this.' One look at the man with the stick was enough for my horse – she took off in a big hurry, poor thing. 'Be back by three,' shouted the owner. (Hang on, that's only an hour and a half for ten shillings, I thought. No way! I want my money's worth.)

When three o'clock arrived I was still riding around the Nudgee area, quite a distance from the riding school. It was too late to get the horse back in time and I was a bit worried about traffic, so I decided to ride home and take it back the next day instead. Simple as that.

It was late when I pulled my mount to a stop. The sun was going down and I still had a fair way to go. And a great big hurdle stood

What Next You Bastard

in my way – a *huge* hurdle, the Story Bridge, Brisbane's answer to Sydney Harbour's coat-hanger. Should I ride in the half-dark, or get off and try to lead the horse? I didn't like the idea of walking between all those cars, and the pedestrian walk on the side looked too narrow, so that settled it for me: I would have to ride across. As we moved towards the bridge, drivers stopped and watched in amazement. Some of them yelled out to me, 'Hey! Can't you read? No livestock permitted on the bridge!'

A quarter of the way across, the mare stopped. I could feel her body trembling, her metal shoes slipping on the hard bitumen surface. She didn't want to go any further. I dismounted and as my own feet touched the bitumen, my body started to tremble too. It was the bridge shaking as six lanes of traffic moved across it.

'Come on, mare,' I pleaded, pulling on the rope and trying to lead her. Drivers were leaning on their horns, getting more and more impatient. Finally she followed me, but I could tell she wasn't too happy. I couldn't blame her, though. I didn't like it much myself.

The sun was low in the sky by the time we reached the far end of the bridge and the mare allowed me to mount her again when she realised that the earth had stopped moving beneath her. We came to Mowbray Park, which must have looked very inviting from my tired horse's point of view, and I decided it was as good a place as any to leave her for the night. I removed the saddle and tied her to a fence, assuring her that I'd be back in the morning. There were still many miles for me to walk before I would reach home.

Nine o'clock the next morning I was standing in the spot where I had left the mare. Fresh manure was the only clue that a horse had ever been there. For two solid hours I searched the park and the surrounding area, but horse and saddle had disappeared. It crossed my mind that there would be one very angry horse owner out there somewhere, trying to decipher my address from the details I had scribbled on the form. For once I was glad that nobody could read my writing.

It took a long time, but finally I was given permission to buy a horse of my own. There were some conditions attached though. Part of the deal was that I had to go to the doctor for a check-up first, which was Mum's way of regaining some control over me. I knew this, but didn't mind if it meant reaching my goal.

The check-up itself was fairly straightforward, with Dr James giving me all the usual warnings, but the part that was really embarrassing was running into Peg, the receptionist I had once dated. She must have been working somewhere else for a while, because I'd never seen her since that night. Peg told me in no uncertain terms what she thought of me for taking advantage of her by kissing her, when I had lied about my age. And she promised to have her fiancé tear me to bits if I ever so much as mentioned that we knew each other. 'So get this – we have never met!' she finished, spitting the last few words into my face. It was fine by me.

The second part of the deal involved the loan of £7. Not only did I have to repay every single penny to Mum, I also had to 'pull myself together' regarding foul language and bad behaviour. Once again I agreed. *Anything* for my own horse.

She was called Tiny, was eight years old, stood thirteen hands high and had never been in foal. A bridle was included in the price. She was a real beauty, with her brown coat and lovely mane, and for the next three days we went everywhere together. On the fourth morning Tiny was gone. The gate was still closed, the fence wasn't broken, but for the second time I had lost a horse. I couldn't believe it. Mum and my brothers drove all over the south side for days on end without finding her. We even placed an advertisement in the newspaper, and two radio stations announced the details, but it was no good. Tiny had disappeared.

Some days later a man phoned me and said that he'd heard about my losing the horse. He offered to sell me another one for ten shillings a week and no deposit. Mum took over and made the arrangements and soon I found myself with a replacement for Tiny. I chose a taffy mare from the horses the man showed me and with her I received a saddle and bridle. The price was £15.

Riding seemed to come naturally to me, unlike certain other skills. Two weeks of riding by myself gave me enough confidence to enter my first competition at the Rocklea Showgrounds, where Taffy and I won our first blue ribbon for the walk and trot.

Whenever I could, I rode for miles and miles to forget my problems. Horses didn't care whether you could spell or not and I loved them for that.

Taffy and I were miles away from home one Saturday, riding along Bennetts Road in Norman Park, when we were stopped by a woman who was hosing her front garden. She smiled at us and remarked that we both looked thirsty, something I had just been thinking about. 'Why don't you hop down and have a drink? There's

What Next You Bastard

a bucket around here somewhere. I have a horse myself.' This made me wonder, as I'd often passed by the house and had never seen a horse around. I mentioned this to her. 'Oh no,' the woman smiled, 'I keep her way down the back. Really, she's not mine, but some months ago she just wandered into my yard and no one has ever claimed her.' With my heart pounding, I explained about losing Tiny and described her in great detail. The woman laughed in wonder. 'Well, I would say you've finally found her.'

This meant that I now owned two horses. The three of us entered one show after another, bringing home prizes and ribbons nearly every time. I had finally found something I was good at, and only wished that it was something I could do for a living.

People often came up to me and offered to buy Tiny, who was only a small horse, but very smart, with a big heart. She was so sweet-natured that she made parents want her for their children, but for a long time I resisted. Then along came a very spoilt teenager with a body like Marilyn Monroe, who pestered me at every show. She refused to take no for an answer and even offered me 'special favours' if I agreed to sell Tiny. I still said no. Then her father turned up and offered me £120. I accepted immediately. I had never seen that amount of money before. When her father walked away, I decided to go and claim my bonus from the girl. Why not? There had to be a first time for everything! I was a bit disappointed but not really surprised when she told me to get lost.

To this day I have never forgiven myself for selling that horse, because of what happened next. On the Sunday following, I noticed Tiny's rider losing at every event she entered. It wasn't the horse's fault, that much I could tell. The following week it was the same and then four months passed without any sign of them. I was worried about Tiny, so I tracked the family down and was horrified to see what they had turned my beautiful little mare into. She was kept in a stable with only a very small holding yard and her body had rolls of fat where muscle used to be. This meant she wasn't being exercised and when I saw the girl walk up to her, I could guess why. Tiny put her ears back and tried to bite, but stopped as soon as she heard me call her name. Her ears came forward again and she tried to walk over to me. The girl was furious. 'You bitch!' she screamed, hitting the poor animal with a stick I hadn't noticed her holding until it was too late.

I begged her not to do it again, but she reminded me smugly that this was now her horse, not mine. I was ordered off the property to the heartbreaking sound of Tiny being beaten and the girl shrieking that she wouldn't let her out until she behaved herself.

Just weeks afterwards I heard that Tiny was dead. She had attacked one of her owner's protruding breasts, tearing out a large piece of flesh that included the nipple. Her father shot the little mare that same day. I had always known that people could be cruel to each other, but witnessing such cruelty to an animal was new to me and it shocked me through and through.

I cleared my debts and with some of the money that was left over I bought myself another horse. Baby was enormous, more than eighteen hands high, and I had to stand on a fence to mount him. Chestnut in colour, built like a racehorse, and gelded, Baby had won six one-mile races during his career. I had plans to improve on that.

I had never forgotten the wild horses that I'd seen running around on White's Hill over the years and decided to try and catch myself one of their foals. It wasn't long before Baby and I tracked down the mob of brumbies, which was made up of six mares, three foals at foot, and one brown stallion. I wasn't going to be fussy about which foal I caught; any one of them would do. 'Charge!' I yelled, putting my head down and urging Baby forward into a full gallop. The brumbies took off in terror, but before long we were gaining on them.

We were just drawing up beside the mob, and I was about to sling my rope over the nearest foal, when I realised that Baby was trying to outrun them. He was ignoring my signals to slow down and soon we were passing the lead brumby. 'No, Baby, this isn't a race!' I sat up in the saddle and heaved back on the reins, but Baby had taken the bit ... and the clearing ended and we were headed full pelt into the scrub! I flattened myself and released the reins. Baby bounced from one tree to another. I felt myself being thrown forward with my arms in a diving position, and saw Baby's nose ploughing the ground. Then his head was under his body, his huge hindquarters on their way up and over. I was trapped by the stirrups and suddenly my body was pulled back into the saddle. But Baby's body was now rolling over me. My feet worked overtime – I had to get them out of the stirrup irons before Baby got up onto his feet. I felt the weight of my giant horse as he pushed all the air out of my lungs. Then I was free! And Baby was still rolling.

It was all over as fast as it had started. It had only taken moments, but time had slowed right down. We were both back on our feet now, dusty and exhausted. Amazingly, Baby was only missing a few hairs from his head. After checking him over, I gave myself a quick inspection too and found no broken bones, although I did have to wear a few nasty bruises for the next couple of weeks.

And the brumbies? Nowhere to be seen.

Jumping obstacles became one of my favourite sports. Teaching any horse, big or small, to jump a simple stick, a log, or a six-foot fence at the show, had a special feeling of danger about it. As rider and horse landed on the other side, the unexpected could, and often did, rear its ugly head. I loved it anyway! Much of what I learned I picked up from watching others. Some of it I was taught by an old hand who gave me lessons and advice on the dos and don'ts, but even there my stubborn streak got in the way more than once. Whenever I ignored his advice the results were disastrous. I still had trouble doing as I was told.

I spent six months training Baby for show-jumping. Everything went well while we were practising, but when the great day came for our first event, Baby had ideas of his own. As an old racehorse he just couldn't resist the challenge of beating every other horse around him, whether it was a race or not. Instead of waiting for his turn to jump, he ran flat out past the other horses.

I was dead set on making a go of show-jumping, so I bought another horse, a grey gelding of fifteen hands built like a tank. At only £20 he was a steal. He had been bred in the bush and there was talk that his mother had been a brumby. This horse would jump absolutely anything, but he had two small faults. First, you couldn't stop him until he felt like stopping – if you tried, he would lower his head until it was two inches off his chest and pull you out of the saddle. His second fault was that no one over twenty years of age could sit on his back. If he thought you were any older (and believe me, somehow he always knew), he'd try to buck you off; if that didn't work, he'd lie down and try to roll on you. If all else failed, he would bite and kick until you dismounted. Although I was tall for my age, I still had quite a way to go before turning twenty and Grey must have been satisfied with that, because I passed the test and was allowed to stay on his back.

Day one at Rocklea Showgrounds: Speed Test. Grey got a good start, leading all the way. He had only one speed – flat out! We were only a couple of lengths away from the winning post when a brown horse streaked past, leaving us in second place. The winner was called Dandy-Boy, and only a few weeks later he won at Eagle Farm Racecourse.

Later that day I entered Grey in the six-bar jumps. We stood and waited in the centre of the arena, watching the other five horses do the rounds. Not one of them had made a clear round without bringing down any hurdles.

Next it was our turn. I took my hat off to the judge and rode ahead to the first hurdle. As soon as he spotted the jump, Grey put his head down onto his chest, pulled the reins out of my hand, and went for that first jump like a rocket. Then the next one, then the next, until we had cleared all six – but he didn't want to stop! The hurdles at Rocklea were placed in a circle and before I could do anything about it we were jumping the first one again. We took home the ribbon for third place, which I thought was pretty unfair, but the judges decided against giving us first place because I couldn't hold my horse between jumps and because my dressage was no good. I suppose they would have preferred me to hold onto the reins rather than the saddle.

Over the next few years Grey and I did very well together. Sometimes we cleared the lot, other times we crashed straight through the hurdles, and still other times we never even got airborne – those were the times Grey tried to go under them. That horse was born to jump. Let out in his paddock, if the grass looked greener on the other side, he simply jumped the fence. When he was finished, he jumped back again.

Over the years I had a lot of offers for Grey. At one stage horse-dealers were phoning me twice a month, trying to part me from my horse. They were cunning people, those dealers. They often worked a scam with the pound-keeper where, if a horse they wanted could not be purchased legally, the pound-keeper would secretly open the fence of the yard or paddock where it was being kept and wait for the horse in question to wander outside onto the council ground. The horse would then be taken to the pound-yard and its description written down. Under the council by-laws, the 'stray' horse then had to be advertised once in the local paper, so that its rightful owner could collect it for a fee.

Trouble was, there was nothing to stop the pound-keeper from making a 'mistake' and incorrectly describing the horse and brand,

What Next You Bastard

making it impossible for the owner to recognise it. After a certain time the horse, wearing a new brand, would be sold at auction to the dealer for £1. The dealer would be able to sell the horse for £50 or more, and the money would be shared with the pound-keeper.

Such a move was eventually made on Grey. He disappeared from his paddock one night, and despite phoning the pound-yard daily with his description, the answer was always the same: 'Sorry, no horse of that description here.' It looked like I had to face up to it: Grey was gone.

But two hours after my last enquiry I had the local pound-keeper on the phone, ordering me to come straight over and get my 'bloody horse' before he shot it. Sure enough, when I arrived, there was Grey. 'That horse is mad! He's a killer! Next time he gets out I'll shoot the bugger!' I slipped onto Grey's back and started to walk him out of the yard, then noticed the look of disbelief on the man's face. He shook his head and told me that the horse had tried to kill him when he went to ride him. I wasn't surprised. That man was well over twenty years old and didn't Grey know it!

6. Palomino

Although horses were my great love, they weren't providing enough for me to live on. I dreaded the idea, but I knew I would soon have to get back into the workforce.

Mum came to the rescue again. She got me a job with a close friend of hers, Frank Snowdon, who owned and operated a business in Moorooka. It worked out well, because one of our neighbours, twenty-one-year-old Noel Goodwood, worked for Frank as well, and I shared the cost of the petrol for his old motorbike in return for his letting me ride the twenty miles each day on the pillion seat.

The firm employed five. Frank Snowdon's factory supplied wooden light-switch blocks and mains boards to homes and industries. I was to be under Noel, who would teach me all about the setting of the wood machines and how to work them. Most of the work involved running a three-sided planer, a docking saw, and a machine for drilling five holes in one movement. It was the kind of work I enjoyed most. At last, here was a place where a pencil was not wanted. I even made a new friend, a lad the same age as me called Clive Bowen.

We had all been working pretty hard by the time the Christmas holidays came around again, so when Mum suggested out of the blue that we might as well do something as a family we all jumped in with ideas. As usual, Myrtle came up with a winner: a camping holiday on the Sunshine Coast.

By Christmas Eve the car and trailer were packed and ready for an early start the next morning. Before the sun was even up on Christmas Day we were on our way to Maroochydore. The five of us sat quite comfortably in the Graham Page with Ian at the wheel. Daylight was just beginning to show through the tall buildings in Fortitude Valley as we passed through Brisbane. The streets were empty and the whole place seemed like a ghost town, the only noise the purring of the eight-cylinder motor.

As we turned left into Brunswick Street, the peaceful morning was broken by the sounds of squealing rubber and to our surprise we

What Next You Bastard

saw a fully laden wooden trailer heading straight for the big windows of McWhirter's department store on the corner. It took us a moment to realise that the runaway trailer was ours. By the time we stopped the car and jumped out, seven policemen had appeared from nowhere and the trailer was perched only a few feet from the windows. Talk about luck! We had bought the thing already painted and never thought to check what the tow-rod was made from. It was a four-by-two length of pine. No wonder.

While the rest of us waited, Steven and Ian took a taxi home, hopped onto Ian's motorbike and set off in search of a replacement tow-rod – not the easiest thing to find early on Christmas morning. They arrived back at the scene balancing a length of hardwood between them on the bike. It took a bit of time to fix the trailer on the side of the road, but we all pitched in – even the coppers got their shirts off and helped. With Ian's bike firmly strapped to the back, we set out once more.

After passing the last few houses of Chermside we were truly on the way. Just as well it was still so early, because the Gympie Highway was only wide enough for one car. Its gravelly edges were covered with tall grass that would have made heavy traffic dangerous. But buildings of any sort were scarce and other cars even scarcer – we were lucky to see one an hour. We passed an old DC3 plane in a paddock. Its wings had been removed, making it into a kind of caravan. We cracked some jokes about that, guessing how it came to be there and wondering who was living inside – a very old pilot maybe?

We had been travelling along quite happily for some time when we heard a strange noise coming from the back of the car. After pulling over and making a quick inspection we saw that the tow-bar was fitted to the car with only four tiny steel bolts, which also held the bumper bar on. Two of these bolts had snapped off and the other two didn't look as though they would hold on for much longer. Being Christmas Day there were no shops open other than the odd cafe with a petrol pump outside. But we were lucky – Bald Hills wasn't too much further down the road and we found a place open. We bought eight new bolts and kept replacing the broken ones every few miles.

We had almost run out of spare bolts when we came across a small store in the middle of nowhere. It was built entirely from corrugated iron and had a dusty billboard out the front. 'Home Made Chicken Pies,' read Mark. 'Can we get some, Mum? I'm starving.'

We made the necessary adjustments to the tow-bar and bought a pie each to eat on the way. As we rounded the corner we saw rows and rows of cages behind the store, filled with screeching pink and white cockatoos. Mum stopped chewing, swallowed a mouthful of pie and turned pale. 'Have you noticed the colour of the meat we are eating? I can tell you one thing – it's *not* chicken.'

More trouble. The Graham Page was boiling. Landsborough was a good hour behind us, ahead of us was new country. We couldn't, didn't dare to, stop. What if we never got going again? Steam was hissing out from under the long black bonnet and we all held our breath as that poor old machine chugged up the hill so slowly that we would have been quicker on foot. As we inched over the crest we saw the rainforest of Eudlo. There had to be water somewhere nearby. Ian killed the motor and let the car roll all the way down the hill until it came to a stop. Sure enough, just fifty feet to the side of the road we discovered a creek with water so clear you could see the large freshwater mullet feeding on the bottom. Saved again.

By the time we pulled into the camping ground on the Esplanade we were dead tired. The drive had taken us eight long hours but one look at that sparkling ocean with the sun bouncing off it and we were happy as Larry. There was a perfect spot for our tent right on the grassy foreshore under a big shady Norfolk pine. Then a drop of three feet down to the beach, and not much further to the surf. You couldn't ask for better than that.

It was lucky we came when we did, because three days later every single camping spot was taken and it looked like a miniature town had sprung up: Tent City. All one colour – grey.

Every morning we greeted the new arrivals from the night before and pretty soon my brothers and I had taken up a new hobby: 'bird watching'. Girls – they were everywhere, every shape, age and colour. Every tent seemed to have at least two of them. I spent hours and even whole days trying to win my first one, sometimes on the beach, sometimes in the sand dunes. And just when I was finally getting somewhere, there was always that one big hurdle: little sisters aged seven to twelve. You could never get rid of them – their high-pitched voices could be heard up and down the length of the beach. 'Mum, Ken and Margaret are kissing!' or 'Mum, Julie and Ken are holding hands!'

What Next You Bastard

Ice for the ice-box never lasted more than a few days. It was made from the water in the local tea-tree marsh and had its own special colour. Brown ice! As it melted it smelled of the dead leaves and rotting bits of fish in the marsh where it came from, but one thing about that ice, it had magical powers. I'll never forget the day when all three fish I had caught early in the morning and thrown into the ice-box were still alive and kicking at tea time. Flathead, trevally and bream – so lively that I swear I could have dropped them back into the sea and they would have swum away.

Mum seemed obsessed with freshness on this holiday: the fresh whiting cooked slowly in breadcrumbs for breakfast; the freshly baked bread served with ripe bananas and followed with juicy watermelons and rockmelons for lunch; more freshly caught fish with vegetables for tea. She even made us keep the side of the tent open at night so that the fresh salt air would fill our lungs while we slept. There was only one variety of freshness that she didn't take to and that was any kind of cheek from her sons. More often than not, I was the guilty one there.

The Maroochydore Surf Club was run by volunteers. Some of the boys lived as far away as Brisbane and often had to hitch-hike their way up to the Coast. One of their jobs was to keep a look-out for the sharks that worked their way along the coastline in great numbers and, to make money for the Club, the lifesavers sometimes put out a line in front of the clubhouse and set about catching a shark. The line was made from rope anchored to two 40-gallon drums; the hook was a steel rod that had been bent over, and for bait they used a shoulder of beef. It worked. One year, we were told, they caught themselves more than they had bargained for: a female tiger shark, eighteen feet long, with thirty-six babies inside. As they dragged her in, other baby sharks came swimming in with her.

The lifesavers displayed their shark catches, and charged visitors a small fee. The five of us had just spent a fair bit of time studying the latest shark display one night and were strolling along Beach Parade with no special plans for tea, when we caught the smoky, delicious aroma of roasting meat. It was coming from a caravan parked at the side of the road and the closer we got to it, the harder it was to resist. Mum must have felt like a change from all that fresh fruit and fresh fish just as much as the rest of us, who were just about drooling by now, because out of the blue she said, 'Why not? Five, please.' Leaning over the counter as much as we dared, we saw our very first hamburgers being made. The cook took five teaspoonsful of mince and placed them separately onto the hotplate. In his hand was a mallet of some kind and with this he started to belt the living hell out of that mince. We saw with our own eyes how it was possible to make a teaspoon of mince grow into the size of a saucer! At first we were dumbfounded, but one quick wink from the hamburger man and we all exploded into laughter.

As for night life, there was the 'Cinema/Theatre' and that was about all. Saturday night was the time to be seen there, because that was when the girls came out, meaning that going there any other night was nothing but a waste of time and money.

The Saturday night routine always started exactly the same way, with Mum announcing that there was 'no way in the wide world' that she would let me go to the movies with her and the others 'dressed like that'. I would tell her it was fine by me, because I wasn't going with them anyway, I was going by myself. At this point Mum would remind me that I had no money and that she refused to pay my admission to the theatre, and I would threaten to sneak in later when the lights were down. It worked nearly every time. Just before she and the others left, Mum would place ten shillings on the table for me, warn me to behave myself, and hurry out of the tent muttering things about my being 'the odd one in the household'. As soon as they were gone, I would take off my shoes, strip off my singlet and replace my shirt with the tails hanging outside my pants. Thick Brylcreem covered my hair (*'a-little-dab'll-do-you!'*) and I'd work the comb until it was slicked down in the latest brush-back style. Ready for action.

My timing was always carefully planned. There was a trick to this. You had to arrive at the theatre and buy your ticket, but stand out of sight at the back until everyone was seated. Doing this allowed time to check out the girls – who usually sat in twos or threes – before deciding where to sit. The moment the lights went out I'd make my move, heading for the prettiest girls I had spotted. The darkness of the theatre gave me courage to introduce myself to them, which I always tried to do before the film started. A few giggled and flirted with me, some pretended I didn't exist, and others gave me trouble.

One Saturday night in particular, the whole theatre was buzzing with excitement because of the James Bond premiere in which Diane

What Next You Bastard

Cilento had a part; Lady Cilento, her mother, was going to be present at the showing. There were quite a few important people in the theatre and everyone kept craning their necks to see who would enter next. I was standing in my usual position in the back, when I was astounded to see a very tall young lady appear through the doors and look around for a seat. Her waist-length brown hair flowed down over the bright yellow swimsuit she was wearing – that and nothing else, not even shoes! When she sat down by herself I couldn't believe my luck. My mind racing and my whole body breaking into a cold sweat, I tried to decide whether to wait until the lights went out, or make my move right away. It was too risky to wait; somebody else would beat me to it if I didn't hurry. To my relief she seemed quite happy to have me beside her and, with every eye in the theatre upon us, we exchanged names and made small talk until the audience was distracted by the late arrival of Lady Cilento, and the film could start. Paula was a very affectionate girl – she held my trembling hands during the film, which might as well have been in a foreign language for all that I could make of it in my condition. She confessed that she was hoping to be spotted by a film director and with one hand stroking my thigh, she leaned over and whispered something that almost took my breath away: she asked me to do her one small favour as soon as the lights came back on 'but not before'. I would have agreed to anything this girl of my dreams had asked.

Right on cue, when the lights came on for a short interval, I raised my voice and spoke the words she had asked me to, suggesting that the two of us go down to the beach and 'do it'.

Paula shot up out of her seat, gave me a look of absolute fury and disgust and screamed at me to get my 'filthy mind out of the gutter'. Then she struck me across the face with all her might before striding out of the packed theatre with its very attentive audience. With burning cheeks I slid down in my seat and managed to survive the next fifteen minutes until the lights went out again, then crept outside. I was just in time to see Paula with her arms around some grey-haired man in an expensive-looking suit, before she climbed into a big black Pontiac and disappeared into the night.

The next time I spotted a pretty girl sitting by herself I was a bit more careful. This one, at least, was fully dressed and didn't look the type to make a scene just for attention, so I sat down next to her and casually said hello. She had a lovely smile, but I didn't see too much of it because just then the lights dimmed and the film started. Now and then during the movie I made remarks about the characters or the scenery, but the girl said nothing at all. I leaned over and whispered that she could just tell me to leave if she didn't want to talk, but she just shook her head and smiled, keeping her eyes fixed to the screen. 'The shy kind', I told myself, and looked forward to the interval when we would be able to get to know each other.

Wrong. When the lights came on the girl opened her bag and took out a small notepad and pencil and wrote something down. 'Hi, my name is Betty, I am deaf and dumb.' It was lucky for me they were such simple words and that she had printed them in block letters, because otherwise I would have been stumped. When Betty handed the notepad to me I realised that I was now supposed to write down my own name, one of the few things I could write without disgracing myself. I didn't know whether to laugh or cry. Somehow I had picked the only person in the place who needed to communicate in writing.

I decided to give up on girls and give all my attention to horses again.

For some years a palomino brumby stallion had been roaming the district around Acacia Ridge. There had been many attempts to capture him since he was first spotted as a foal, but for eight years he had managed to escape all the best riders and horses. I had seen him when I was a little boy and even then he had a small herd with him. I was seventeen now, but one weekend when I was still just fourteen or fifteen I had been out riding with Dave Sharpe, who was so old he could have been around since the birth of Christ, and Fred Roman, a Native American, with jet-black hair and a nose like a tomahawk – top riders, both of them. By the time we had spotted the brumbies they had already seen us coming and were running like the wind as they cut in front of us. That palomino had taken one look at us and dug his toes in, leaving us covered in his dust. Dave rode over the ridge after the wild horse, not wanting to give up, but Fred and I knew it was pointless, so we had headed home and forgotten all about it.

And now, almost three years later, word was getting around that old Dave Sharpe had finally managed to capture the palomino and was keeping him in a forty-acre paddock. I heard that he had been left to run in the paddock for a month or so, but when Dave had

What Next You Bastard

tried to muster him back into the yard he had failed. He blamed the paddock: too many trees and underbrush. Help was needed and old Dave was looking for five riders to do the job over the weekend.

It was still dark when a group of us got to Dave's place. I wondered why so many riders were needed, but some of the others told me they had been here the last time Dave tried it and that I would soon find out for myself. It didn't take long for me to see what they meant – in the first three hours I saw the stallion no more than six times. Even though Dave had cut off his water supply three days earlier and had hobbled him, that palomino had somehow learnt to run, despite the pain he must have been suffering. He was still alert, but tiring from the effort and the lack of water. One moment I would catch a glimpse of him and the next he'd be disappearing into the timber. We chased him through the tall gum trees and almost had him a few times, but he still managed to outrun us at every turn. This game of hide and seek went on for so long that eventually we decided to give up the chase and wait for him to come to us instead. We had the water. He must have been able to smell it at the yards, where old Dave had turned it back on again in force. We kept a good distance and settled down to wait for something to happen.

Fourteen hours later it did. Half a mile from the yards this handsome piece of horseflesh went down on his knees. As we moved towards him he made a sad attempt to get back on his feet again, but his determination was no match for his exhaustion and raging thirst. Shaking with fear, he managed one small step and fell to the ground. We lifted his head with a halter, then tied a leather shoelace around his mouth to keep him from biting. With the hobbles removed, a chain had to be fastened to his off-front leg before we could untie the shoelace and force a bottle of water into the side of his mouth. All this time he was squealing and snorting, his eyes rolling around in his head, body covered in sweat. We stood well back to see if he would be able to stand up, and after a few attempts he did. Fred suggested letting a quiet mare run with him, hoping this would quiet him down and make him easier to control. Our job was finished for now.

We all went back to Dave's place two weeks later, to see what progress he had made in taming the stallion. It wasn't all that good. The mare had kept to his side, and he had been eating and drinking, but whenever anyone came near he panicked and tried to run. That's what happened on this day, too. He saw us coming and took a few long strides; without warning the chain snapped and wrapped itself around his near-side fetlock, pulling him down. His nose hit the dirt, his head went under his body and he rolled over. He lay there without moving a muscle and we all thought he'd killed himself for sure. But he wasn't dead, and no bones were broken, although he lay there with his eyes tightly shut, not making a sound. We got the chain off his leg and undid it from the off-side, then stood well back.

The stallion ran with the mare for many months and not once in that time did he lift his head. That proud manner of the past was nowhere to be seen. Even when the mare came into season he ignored her. The feed was lush, tall and green all around him, yet the palomino stallion was nothing more than skin and bones and all life seemed to have gone out of him. It was heartbreaking to see and we all felt guilty about our part in his downfall.

When Dave Farmer decided, after six months of this, to let him go, it took the horse three days to wander through the open gate and even then he would not run away. He just stood there, with his head hanging low, as if he had forgotten what freedom was all about. Dave felt so badly about the whole thing that out of pity for the horse he finally asked us to help him drive the stallion back to the waterhole where he had spent so much of his life before being captured. He had a drink and went for a swim and some of the fire seemed to come back into his eyes. Before I rode away I took one last look at the stallion. His head was raised high, nostrils sniffing the wind, his tail arched.

There was hope for him after all.

Work was going well. Somehow I had managed to keep my job with Frank Snowdon for much longer than I had expected. For one thing, no one worried about whether I could spell or not. As long as I was doing what I was meant to be doing, I was treated as an equal.

There had been some talk that the boss was getting a bit worried about a new invention he had heard about, a material called 'plastic', which might eventually replace timber and force him out of business. New ideas for the coming 1960s were being considered more and more often. England had seen change coming a few years earlier and had trained a new breed of manager for business. These men were now looking for work in Australia.

One Monday morning a tall lanky stranger was sitting in the office and Frank asked us all to gather around so we could meet him. Mr Booth was newly arrived in Australia and it was to be our job to make him welcome. Not only that, but Frank also informed us that, from now on, we would be taking our orders from this man.

Mr Booth proudly announced that he was a time and management consultant, whatever that was supposed to be, that he'd been working in this field for the last five years in England and that the way we did things here would soon be a thing of the past. He showed us his 'trusty stop-watch' and asked us to 'simply pretend' he wasn't there even when he came up behind us in the factory.

It took him no more than two weeks to catch up to me.

I was asked to turn my machine off and have 'a little chat'.

Mr Booth held up a questionnaire that I had filled in for him the week before and I knew I was sunk. 'Tell me what this *garbage* is all about, Kenneth. I can't make head nor tail out of it.'

Mr Booth didn't even give me a chance. He told me it wasn't good enough for him, 'nor the firm, for that matter', and gave me two weeks to find myself new employment. My famous temper took over and I delivered my fist into the soft stomach of Mr Trusty Stopwatch, with the message that he could 'stick' his job, I was quitting right now.

I stormed out of there with the man clutching his middle and wheezing, 'You can't do that to me ... you're fired!'

Enough was enough. I was fed up with a world where you were judged by your skill with a pencil. Just when everything was going well, along came another smart alec with fancy ways and education. What about the things that really counted, such as building things, making things, skills I knew I was good at? Frank Snowdon had never had any reason to complain about my work, but even though he wasn't there when I walked out that day, I knew that he would have backed up the so-called expert. They always did.

Anyway, I had burned my bridges by punching the man.

I felt like riding into the sunset and never coming back.

7. Heading west

The more I thought about it, the more I liked the idea. Why not find myself a job where I would be paid for riding – doing what I loved best?

Next time I was in the city I called into the office of a woolbroker and asked if there were any jobs available on a sheep station. The receptionist asked me my name and how old I was and seemed satisfied when I told her seventeen. I was in luck, she said, because Paul Wilkinson, the owner of Tudor Downs Station just outside of Julia Creek, was in Brisbane that day. She left the office for a moment and when she came back, told me to follow her.

The man looked to be in his late fifties, with ropy muscles and leathery skin the colour of old wood. He looked me up and down and asked me only one question: Did I know how to ride? I answered, 'Yes, Paul.'

My mistake.

'Now get this straight,' he told me firmly, 'if you work for me, the name is *Mister Wilkinson*, not Paul.' I couldn't believe it – did that mean he was actually going to hire me? His next words confirmed it. 'All right, then. Be on the train tomorrow.'

My God, it was almost too easy! Why hadn't I thought of doing this years ago? And then I remembered something. 'Mr Wilkinson,' I said, hoping I wasn't about to give him an excuse to back out, 'I can't leave tomorrow. You see, I've got some horses that I'll have to sell first. It might take me a couple of weeks.'

He didn't seem too annoyed, luckily, and after a moment he nodded and told me that my train tickets would be waiting for me here, at the office, and I should pick them up in exactly two weeks' time. He would be meeting me, he said, at Julia Creek.

Getting the job had been simple, but explaining it to Mum was another story. She asked me what they 'made' at Julia Creek and was horrified to hear that it wasn't a local factory, but a sheep station out west. We had one of our usual rows, with Mum reminding me that I was under the legal age for leaving home without consent and threatening to get the courts to stop me; and with me threatening to smash all the furniture in the house if she even tried to keep me from going. It ended with Mum ordering me out of the house, which was more or less what I had wanted anyway.

Poor Mum.

It didn't take the whole two weeks to find buyers for my horses. When I said goodbye to Mrs Hart and thanked her for the use of her paddocks, she told me she had been hoping that I might take the land off her hands. I explained that I didn't have the money to buy it from her anyway, but she said she was willing to offer it to me for the £16 it would cost to have the title transferred into my name. I was over the moon. I rushed home to tell my mother the good news, but she refused to consider it. Mum told me that I'd never be able to afford the rates on a five-acre block and, besides, who would want a block of land that size in Coorparoo? Maybe if I hadn't been in such a hurry to head out west I would have found some way of keeping the land, but time was running out and I had no choice but to let the matter drop.

Mum's biggest objection to my leaving was that I would be hundreds of miles away from a hospital, or even a local doctor. She had collected all available information on Julia Creek: it was over 1,000 miles by train north-west of Brisbane, being about 700 miles north to Townsville and then another 400 or so inland to the west. In fact, Mum knew much more about the place than I did – and every chance she got, she tried to talk me out of it. 'It's the back of Bourke, Ken, there's nothing out there but flies and dust.' I refused to listen. Then she tried another angle: if I would get myself checked by the doctor and *if* he said it would be all right, then she wouldn't stand in my way. For Mum's peace of mind I agreed, but I secretly knew that I would go no matter what the verdict might be.

The doctor wasn't too pleased with my health at all. He gave me all the usual warnings about the likelihood of my dying at any time and stressed how important it was to keep taking the medicine. I asked him if he could send my file to Julia Creek and promised that I would have myself checked over once a month by the doctor there. He asked me to leave the room while he spoke with my mother and twenty minutes later she reappeared with a long face. 'I can't say I'm happy about this, but if you really must go, then … all right.'

Heading west

She looked so small and defeated that I put my arms around her in a big bear hug. It was the first time in ages, and it felt good.

Seven o'clock in the morning found us saying goodbye at Roma Street station. As the train started to pull away from the platform, Mum was sobbing into her hanky and Ian was doing his best to comfort her. There was a big lump in my throat and my eyes were blurry with tears when I finally turned from the window and sat down.

The carriage was empty, except for a couple of women with small children right up the front and, sitting a few rows behind me, two blokes in their twenties. They nodded to me when I turned around.

I closed my eyes and drifted into sleep with dreams of becoming a cowboy.

'Nambour station, mate! Wake up, Nambour station!' I awoke with a jolt. The two young men were leaning over the seat in front of me and one of them was tapping me on the shoulder. 'Hey, mate, this is where you get off.'

'No, I don't,' I told them, sleepily, 'I get off this train at Townsville.'

'You sure, mate?' asked one of them. 'Better check your ticket.'

'Yes, I'm positive,' I said, although they had made me nervous now. I stood up to take my old wooden port down from the rack and noticed that the women and children had left the carriage. Opening my wallet, I pulled out the ticket and showed it to them. 'See? It says Townsville.'

'Sorry mate, the conductor told us to wake you at Nambour. Hell, mate! That's a lotta dough you got there – better put it back in your port.' He then introduced himself and his friend as Fred and Harry, who were travelling even further north than I was – to Cairns. We chatted for a while and when they returned to their seats, I fell asleep once more.

Next time I woke up, the train had come to a stop at Bundaberg station. Fred and Harry and their luggage were nowhere to be seen. I was alone in the carriage. That's strange, I thought, they were supposed to be going on to Cairns. My port was still up on the rack, thank goodness, but when I noticed that the catches were undone, my heart missed a beat. Sure enough, my wallet was gone. I walked up and down the length of the empty carriage and finally spotted it lying under one of the seats.

What Next You Bastard

Things could have been worse, I suppose. All the cash was gone, but nothing else was missing. I still had my ticket.

At Rockhampton all passengers were advised of a one-hour delay, due to trouble on the line – a cyclone further north, someone said. My stomach was rumbling and I realised that it had been quite some time since I had put anything into it. It felt good to be stretching my legs and as I walked around the area behind the station I collected a few empty bottles which I cashed in at the shop. There was enough for a small fruit slice and a bottle of Coca-Cola to wash it down.

By the time we reached Townsville, where I had to change trains, I was hungry enough to eat a draught horse. There was a three-hour wait for my train to Julia Creek and my stomach was really starting to complain. When I couldn't find enough bottles, I got so desperate that I pinched some empties from the stack behind a shop and walked in the front way to cash them in. It still wasn't enough for a proper meal, though.

And then, while I was walking along with my head down, a small piece of folded paper caught my eye – the colour of it looked familiar. It was a £1 note! Thank you, God! I marched into the nearest fish and chips shop and had myself a feast.

About 400 miles west of Townsville, the train arrived at Julia Creek station. It was very late and the station seemed deserted but, as promised, Mr Wilkinson was there to meet me. He introduced me to his jackaroo, Rod, but in the darkness all I could glimpse from under Rod's big hat was a mouthful of the whitest teeth I had ever seen.

The big LandRover bumped and jolted over the hard dry ground. I was sitting on a metal seat in the back and in no time I was covered in dust. Every rock we hit drove me out of my seat and made me feel like a human shock-absorber. I was in no mood for conversation, so it didn't bother me that the other two rode all the way in dead silence. My ears were ringing by the time we pulled to a stop, more than three hours later.

An iron gate had materialised out of nowhere.

'Okay, mate, get that gate, will you, this is home,' Rod ordered, spitting the words out as he wiped the dust from his mouth. I climbed down and opened the gate, looking around me as I did. (Did he say 'home'? No house to be seen!) Nine gates later, the LandRover lights showed the outline of a small house and when we pulled up beside it, Mr Wilkinson got out.

'See you boys in the morning, and Rod, have the horses saddled before breakfast.'

Rod turned the corner and this time the headlights lit up a tiny shack. 'This is it. Home sweet home. Grab your bag and walk up the steps. Open the door and then take the first room on your right, that's yours. I'll be five minutes behind you.'

My head started to spin as my feet touched the ground, my stomach cramping from lack of food. I made it up the steps and found my room, but had to grope in the darkness for the light switch. Where the hell was it? When Rod came up behind me I asked him and he laughed: 'Sorry – no light switch. See you in the morning.'

I felt my way around in the dark and had no trouble finding the bed. I almost fell over it, the room was so small. No sheets, no blankets and only a thin battered pillow that reeked of stale sweat. When I lay down on the mattress it gave off a foul decaying smell, but I was too sick and tired to care.

'Time to get up. Breakfast over at the main house in half an hour,' said a loud voice. He couldn't be serious. Could he? It was still dark outside. But Rod wasn't joking. 'Are you up?' he yelled again.

I muttered something to let him know I had heard and swung my legs over the side. The floorboards were splintery and cold and as I walked out onto the verandah of my new home, I heard a door slam shut behind me. There stood Rod, dressed in a riding outfit and looking every inch the cowboy or, should I say, jackaroo. It was my first real look at him, because it had been too dark the night before to see anything but those gleaming teeth. His straight blond hair was freshly combed and his bright blue eyes stood out against a face that was burnt golden brown from the sun. In one hand he held a big hat, in the other a bridle. He told me where to find the showers and pointed his hat in the direction of the homestead, saying that breakfast would be ready and I'd better get moving, because today we were going to be mustering.

I stepped down from the porch into the icy air, rubbing my hands together to warm them. Seeing my surroundings take shape all around, as the mist lifted and cleared, was like watching a curtain lifting on a stage. One by one the strange shapes took form and colour and I was able to make out what they were.

To my left was a two-storey house sitting on low wooden stumps. The whole house was built from sheets of galvanised iron, from top to bottom. A wire-netting fence enclosed the yard, which contained no more than four trees. The front of the house overlooked a tennis court, which had not seen a tennis ball for years. A strange-looking shed, covered with flyscreens, stood in the backyard, and beside it was a garage for one car.

Next to this was a windmill that stood about forty feet tall, with blades that must have spanned another thirty feet in diameter. Mist rose from the dam in the cold morning air, making it look so ghostly that I felt a shiver run up my spine.

Turning to my right I could see straight over the plains, with nothing but a sea of grass all the way to the far horizon. It was the flattest country I had ever come across.

It was easy to recognise the dunny, or outhouse, because they were always tall and narrow and made of tin or wood. When I got there, I found that it was the 'long-drop' kind, which got its name because the pit was so deep that people joked you could do your business, slam the door and be walking away before you heard it hit the ground below. I was about to find out for myself if this was true, or just another 'legend of the west'.

The showers were in a small hut that doubled as a laundry, going by the washtubs and boiler beside them. The warm bore-water stank as it sprayed onto the tin walls and the soap wouldn't lather. How was I supposed to get clean?

When I got back to my room I saw it for what it really was – a filthy broom-cupboard not fit for an animal. The mattress I had slept on was damp and badly stained, and tore when I tried to turn it over in the hope that it might be cleaner on the other side. I shouldn't have bothered. It was worse. Cockroaches scurried out of the stuffing and ran across my feet before finding a new hiding place in the cracked floorboards. The pillow I had buried my face in all night was black with dirt. Tears filled my eyes and I would have sat down and cried, but the only chair in the room had a broken leg and stood on top of a wardrobe that had a broken door.

What had I let myself in for?

There was nothing for it but to unpack my belongings and get dressed. I had brought a few changes of clothing, socks and underwear, a pair of riding boots and an old army hat. When I had put these away, I was left with my only other possessions: my wallet, my pills, two bars of soap, toothbrush and paste, a comb, one large jar of Brylcreem and – looking very out of place in these surroundings – a pair of rubber flippers.

Half an hour was almost up by the time I headed for the big house and hunger put a spring into my step. Maybe it was all going to work out fine, after all. A bell started ringing as I got nearer and suddenly Mr Wilkinson stepped out from the shadows and stopped me.

'Ken – it is Ken, isn't it?' I nodded yes.

'Well, Ken, while you're working for me, I don't want you coming around my house or my family. You will eat all your meals with the cook. You'll find the kitchen at the far end of the house. If you need to see me, you will tell Rod and he'll pass a message on to me. Do you smoke?' When I nodded again, he went on with his speech. 'Tell the cook and she'll give you what you want. Around here, payday is when you need cash, but tobacco, wax matches and papers will all be deducted from your pay.' It was quite a lot to take in, but Mr Wilkinson wasn't finished yet.

'Town is around a hundred miles from here. Every three months I go in to do some shopping – if you like, you can accompany me on that day. Most days we get up before the sun, work till twelve, have dinner and then return to work at two o'clock. No one works between twelve and two, except today, as we are mustering. Sunday is a day of rest. Remember your place around here and we'll all get on fine.'

And having said all that, my new boss walked away.

The cook was Mrs Brodie, with a Scottish accent and thick grey hair knitted into a bun. She called me 'laddie' and fed me a huge breakfast of mutton chops in gravy with fried eggs, buttered toast and a mug of tea. She couldn't get over my enormous appetite and when I told her how long it had been since my last proper meal, she took pity on me and kept the toast coming until I had to beg her to stop.

When Rod came into the kitchen I caught a glimpse of the dining room through the partly opened doors and saw a huge table with the family gathered around it. Mr Wilkinson sat at the head of the table, with a young woman, probably his wife, to one side. Next to her were two small children and on the other side sat a girl of twenty or so. Then the doors swung shut and Rod pulled up a chair next to me. He told Mrs Brodie to pack an extra lunch because Jean, the children's nanny, was going to be joining the muster. He was impatient for me to finish, so that he could get me some riding gear.

To my irritation, the boss told Rod to give me a small grey pony for my first day, rather than one of the full-sized horses, just in case I had lied about my riding ability. Riding him was awful. The pony was so fat that he couldn't keep up with the others, jig-jogging the whole way.

I was to ride along the boundary fence, far enough away from it to just keep it in sight. Any sheep I saw I was to get behind and push them towards the centre, where Jean would then turn them over to Rod. It sounded like fun.

Kangaroos were everywhere. For every sheep I found there were at least ten roos. I also spotted what I thought was a strange-looking black sheep, but as I rode closer I realised it was a big black boar. When it ran off, eight others came out of the long grass and followed it.

I had never seen so many sheep. They were mainly ewes and most of them were in lamb, which was why we had to move them to the far paddock. Wild dogs and wedge-tailed eagles were a problem here, Rod had told me. Dingoes ran all over the 100,000-acre property, but for some reason they kept away from that part of it, making it a safer place for the lambing season. When all the ewes were in their new paddock, drinking water from a bore-drain, we stopped for our lunch. They called it 'dinner' out here.

When we were finished, Rod said that the boss wanted me to show them the way home. I pointed in the general direction, but Rod said no, I was to lead the way and they would follow. It was some kind of test, I realised, giving my pony a good kick and sending him home. As the homestead came into view, Rod rode up alongside me and told me that I was to ride the fence of the paddock in which we had just left the sheep, every single day until the lambs were born. Tonight I was to leave the pony in the yard with some feed and, before breakfast, muster the horses in. After breakfast I was to get a water-bag and some lunch from the kitchen. After saddling a horse, I was to ride the fence and count every lamb I saw. If I saw any dead sheep, I was to count them as well. At this point, Rod leaned over and handed me a pair of fencing pliers. With these I was to repair any broken wire I came across. 'Oh, and by the way,' he said, 'the boss's horse is off-limits.'

Before it got dark again, I had a little time to walk around and explore the half-acre area that surrounded the homestead. In the large shed were a fuel truck, a Ferguson tractor, the LandRover, bales of hay and several rolls of fencing wire, some barbed and some plain.

When I returned to my room, Rod handed me a couple of sheets and blankets and a clean pillowcase. He told me that these were mine to look after and that he washed his sheets every second and fourth Sunday, so I was to wash mine every other Sunday. He held up something called a carbide lamp, explaining that there was no electricity on the property. He told me to pay close attention, as he was only going to show me once how to set it up. I was warned to be very careful, or it would blow up. To illustrate his point he told me about a bloke he once knew, who didn't light the carbide properly and it blew up in his face. 'They buried him with the shaft sticking out of his head,' Rod added, grimly.

That night we had mutton for tea. It was something I would soon get used to, as it was the only meat available on a sheep station. In the weeks and months that followed, mutton would be served for every meal: mutton chops, mutton stew, roast mutton, cold mutton sandwiches and mutton broth. You had to hand it to Mrs Brodie, though – she did her best to be creative, never serving the same meal twice in a row.

Before I left the next morning, the boss strode up to me and gave me a rifle and a box of bullets to take with me, telling me to shoot any dogs, roos or eagles I came across.

As I rode towards the paddock, the rifle felt heavy in my hands and reminded me of my very first experience with ammunition. I couldn't have been more than seven or eight years old the day I was in a bus shelter not far from my house, playing with a box of bullets I had found. Not having a rifle, I sat myself down on the slab floor and wedged the live bullets upside down into a crack in the concrete. Using a large hammer I smashed down on the shells with all my might. I managed to squash those bullets flat, but they didn't go 'bang', as I had hoped. Just as I was about to try another one, Mr Nunn from over the road came charging across, yelling at me to stop. When I ignored him and raised the hammer high above my head, he swooped down and snatched it from my hand, dragged me to my feet by my collar and sank his boot into the seat of my pants. 'Don't you know that bullets kill!' he screamed at me.

The rifle I was now carrying was a .22 bolt-action with a magazine for ten bullets; I recognised it as the same kind that a friend of mine had once owned. That same friend had shown me how to load and shoot the rifle, allowing me to fire two shots to try it out. When I reached the paddock I found myself no more than fifty feet from a huge red kangaroo. I reined my horse in and slowly dismounted, trying not to disturb the red.

I gave silent thanks to my old friend for showing me what to do, as I carefully slid a shell into the chamber, took aim, and fired the rifle.

Aiming at a live animal was quite different from shooting at a rusty tin can, but my arms were steady and my first shot brought him down. There was a small hole in his chest and when I bent down I could see fear written all over the poor roo's face. Blood streamed from his nose and he was making agonising noises as he tried to get back onto his feet. There was only one thing for it – I had to finish him off with a head shot.

Mr Nunn had been dead right. Bullets kill.

I didn't enjoy shooting the old roo, but if killing was going to be part of my job, then I just had to get used to it.

Back at the homestead Rod had another job for me, to be done three times a week.

We were standing in front of the strange shed with flywire all over it that I had seen on my first morning. (Was it really only yesterday?) Rod said this was called the 'butcher shop', then he handed me three knives, a hessian bag and an old bucket. Nearby was a small pen, where about twenty sheep were kept. Rod called them wethers, which meant they were castrated rams.

'Now watch me do this,' he said, 'because after today it's going to be your job. First you find the fattest one. If you're not sure, feel the stub of his tail – if he's fat enough, the bone will be covered. When you have the right one, you grab him by the head, swing him over onto his back, like so, then drag him over there.' Rod carried out these actions as he worked. 'Now bend his head back, take the knife and cut his throat. I think I better get you to do it, so you'll learn it right.' With this, he handed the wether over to me.

'Okay,' he continued, 'as you can see, this knife is sharpened, with a point. If you hold onto it, I'll put my hand over yours.' With the knife at the side of the wether's throat, Rod pushed it into the flesh, then with a quick motion, cut its throat. Hot blood was bubbling out, gushing onto my hands and pouring down into my boots. 'Quick, bend his neck more and put the point of the blade between these ridges, cut the cord and then break his neck.' As the blade hit the spinal cord, the sheep's body went into a mad kicking frenzy. We had to wait for those legs to stop moving or they could have injured us badly. 'Now take his back legs and put a small cut in behind the hocks, so we can hang him up off the ground,' Rod continued, hefting the heavy carcass onto a big steel hook on the wall. 'Next we cut a strip of skin from the groove between his hind legs, right down to the head. Now we skin him. If the wool is more than two inches long, we hang the skin over there. If the wool is too short, we burn it.'

Working together, we carefully cut the carcass all the way down the front, making sure that we didn't slice into any of the inside parts.

'Apart from the meat, we also keep the heart, liver and kidneys, and burn the rest. If you spill any urine from the bladder onto the carcass, burn the carcass and kill another one. Mr Wilkinson can tell when the meat has been contaminated with urine. Now. This is the last part to remove. Stick your finger in its bum, cut round it and pull it all out,' Rod said, grinning as he showed me how it was done. This part of the butchering didn't look too pleasant, but Rod explained that it was necessary, as it kept the contents of the bowel from falling down into the dangling carcass.

Finally he added, 'Before you leave here, you got to clean everything up. Then we'll take the carcass to the butcher shop and tomorrow, before breakfast, I'll show you how to cut up the meat for the cook.'

If someone had told me back in the city that I would be slaughtering sheep one day, I probably would have laughed at the idea. But here I was, second day on the job and already doing a man's work. Nobody could have called it fun, but there was something very satisfying about it all. I had no trouble accepting what had to be done. It was all just part of living in the bush.

When I did the job by myself two days later it took me over an hour to make my first kill. But as the weeks went by, I got it down to a fine art: four minutes flat.

And it didn't take me long to discover that, despite Rod's warning, the boss never once noticed if the bladder had spilled onto the meat.

Lambing season came around. Newborn lambs were on the ground and the ewes were doing fine. Soon I was checking fences only twice a week. Work around the homestead involved servicing the machinery, something I quite enjoyed, but best of all was being able to spend lunch hours on my own.

On fine days I had a quick meal and then walked down to the turkey's-nest for a swim. This was really just a waterhole, part of the run-off from the bore, and when I asked Rod why it was called the turkey's-nest, he said he didn't know – probably some turkeys had nested on the banks at some time.

On one of these occasions I had a frightening experience.

Although I usually swam with my flippers on, for some reason that I can't remember I took them off while still in the centre of the hole, where the water was at its deepest. Holding them in one hand, I started swimming towards the muddy bank. The flippers filled with water and the rubber ankle-strap twisted around my fingers, making it difficult to swim. It was too late to try and put them back on my feet, because by now they had got so heavy they were tiring me out and their weight was pulling me down.

My head went under the water and I started to panic. The more I tried to pull them off my hand, the worse it got. Treading water in slow motion, I sank to the slimy bottom, my lungs screaming for air.

Then, just when I thought I was done for, one of the flippers came off and it was just enough to get me back up to the surface, where I gulped in great mouthfuls of air and water. Doing the only stroke I knew, the dog paddle, I made it to the bank and collapsed in the mud with one flipper still twisted around my wrist and the other at the bottom of the turkey's-nest.

Never again would I go swimming by myself.

Driving the kerosene tractor was a job I liked. Dragging a small V-shaped tool called a 'delta' behind it, I cleaned out the bore-drains, always taking the .22 rifle with me. Wild pigs loved to lie in the bore-drains, but they also caused a lot of damage, mostly by blocking them. When this happened, water would spread over a wide area, sheep would get bogged in the mud and the pigs got themselves a free meal. Shooting pigs on this job could take hours. They seemed to be everywhere.

Emus were another target, mainly because they destroyed fences. These giant birds with their tattered feathers weren't able to fly or to jump over a fence, so they rammed it instead. I saw it myself, more than once: the emu lining itself up with the fence, running straight towards it and smashing into it with all its might, breaking right through the wire.

But kangaroos were the most serious threat to the sheep farmer. They lived on the best feed, which was needed by the sheep. Fences didn't stop them – they simply jumped over them. Sometimes they misjudged their jumps and ended up ploughing right through like the emus. When all was quiet, mainly at night time, they would lift the bottom wire or netting and go underneath. We all spent many backbreaking hours repairing fences. It was a never-ending chore.

Tudor Downs sheep station had its own routine and it took me a while to settle down and get used to the daily pattern of things. The hard work gradually built up the muscles in my body and even though I was still pretty lean, I seemed to be filling out in all the right places.

My days started very early and apart from those two hours in the middle of the day, when the sun was at its hottest, I was kept busy with all the different and necessary jobs on a property of this size.

After the first few weeks I no longer fell into bed straight after tea, too exhausted to keep my eyes open. Trouble was, this created a new problem: finding something to do to fill my evenings. It was no use relying on Rod's company because, as the main jackaroo, he was privileged to spend his evenings up at the house. From my bed I often heard their voices and laughter breaking the silence of the night.

There was no radio in my room and having no one to talk to was starting to get to me. Whoever had stayed in the hut before me had left a whole stack of short stories about cowboys in the back of the wardrobe. I asked Rod about them and his suggestion was that I burn the lot. He was only interested in one thing – his teeth. He brushed them before and after breakfast, before and after smoko, before and after every single meal. After tea he brushed them twice. Rod's teeth shone so brightly that he didn't need a torch at night, all he had to do was go around with his mouth open.

Anyway, I thought I might have a go at reading something, so I pulled one of the books out of my wardrobe and tried to make some sense out of the musty pages. But it was no damn good. I couldn't read more than a few words. In frustration I flung the book straight out the door.

After getting my address from the note I had sent her when I first arrived, Mum had sent me three letters, which I had more or less been able to figure out because, knowing my difficulties, she had kept the words short and easy to understand. I remember how scared I had been to ask anyone the address of the place, in case they found out that I couldn't spell; not only that, but if I got it wrong, Mum's letters would never get to me. What I had done to solve the problem was to look around in the shed for a box or crate with a delivery label on it, and copy it down when no one was looking.

Now I desperately wanted to write a proper letter back to Mum, but couldn't manage it. What I needed was something – anything – with writing on it, so that I could look for words that might help me with the spelling. The cowboy books were a bit beyond me, but an old newspaper I found under the bed was better than nothing.

After many nights and several attempts, I ended up with a page of scribble that would have to do. 'Deer Mum ...' Words I wanted to write but couldn't copy from the newspaper I guessed at, hoping that Mum would be able to work them out somehow. If nothing else, it would give her some reassurance that her son was alive and well.

The nightly boredom was really getting me down so one day I asked Mrs Brodie for any papers and magazines she didn't want. She was a very kind woman and must have suspected that I couldn't read too well, because she told me that she had plenty of books and then asked me if I'd like the ones with pictures in them.

Back in my room I made a start. It was like a huge jigsaw puzzle. If a picture had writing below it, I tried to match the words with whatever was in the picture. Trying to read my first picture-book was a nightmare: I'd slowly read each word until I came to one that stumped me, then go back through the pictures until I found the word, or something close to it. Just finding one single word sometimes took hours.

In one of her letters Mum suggested that I should get myself a dictionary, because it might help me. Mrs Brodie lent me hers for a while and I guess it was worth a try, but what Mum must have forgotten about was that you often had to know how to spell a word *before* you could look it up. After my next few attempts at letter writing, I got a reply from Mum: 'In your letter you say that you now have an Oxford dictionary. Please, son, do not use it for *every single word* you write! I am sorry to say that most times the words you use have nothing to do with the sentence you are writing ...'

Heading west

Using the picture-books had its drawbacks too. When I wanted to write 'the gun was *bigger*', I searched through the book until I found a drawing of a car, with the words beneath it saying 'the *big* black car'. But right beside that was a photo of a tall man, with the words 'standing on the corner was the *beggar* man'. Both words seemed to mean the same thing and more often than not I just copied out the one that sounded the closest when I read it aloud.

Despite all this, by the time I had worked my way through the picture-books, I usually had a fairly good idea of the storyline.

I discovered something else as well: there was always a good guy and a good woman, and the rest were bad.

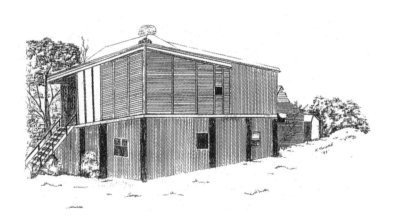

8. Jackaroo

It was a very hot day, about a hundred in the shade. I was riding the furthest paddock when I noticed a busted fence in the far corner. Tying my horse to a prickly acacia bush, I set about making repairs. Sweat was pouring off me, the grass was burnt black and flies covered my back, some even trying to get up my nose. One of the little buggers flew down my throat and I tried to cough it back up, but all I managed to do was empty the contents of my stomach instead.

Ugh!

What I needed was water. I reached for my saddle-bag and was disgusted to find there was a big hole in it. All the water was gone. The mare must have punctured it while rubbing against the prickles on the acacia. There was nothing to do but finish the job on the fence. By the time it was done, the sun was high in the sky and my throat felt like sandpaper.

All the waterholes had dried up and the horizon was hazy from the extreme heat in the air. When I saw the outline of the homestead my hopes lifted – until I realised it was nothing but a mirage. My mount was feeling the heat too, as she stumbled across the patchy ground, tongue swollen from thirst. I knew how that felt – mine was the same. Normally I would have given her a drink of water from my hat before heading for home, but on this day we both had to do without. To spare her, I got down and walked.

Two trees stood about a mile to my right. Good. At least we might get some shade until the sun dropped.

About halfway to the trees I tripped over the carcass of a sheep and when I got back on my feet I saw it – a hole – three feet or so in diameter. It held a few gallons of muddy water and was partly covered by another two dead sheep that were black with blowflies and crawling with maggots. I was too dizzy and thirsty to care. With the lid of my quart-pot I scooped the thick soupy liquid into the not-so-clean handkerchief that I had spread over the bottom half of the pot, watching as, drop by drop, the water filtered through. To hurry it along I found a twig and stirred the mud. It was pointless. The few drops I managed to collect only seemed to swell my tongue even more.

'Baa ...' Just a few feet from me was a ewe with a lamb at foot. Taking a mighty leap I brought the ewe to the ground, turned her over and milked her. The milk was much too hot to drink, so I made my way across to the shade of the trees, dragged the saddle off the horse and waited for the milk to cool down.

Clouds were building up. Soon the sky was so black that I couldn't even see the sun. So, with the milk in my stomach, I headed for home. My poor horse was so tired that she was shaking, head down and blowing air out of her big nostrils. When we neared the small dam that was just a few miles from the homestead, her stride picked up as she smelt the water. Somehow she even whinnied.

Storm clouds were building up in the south and at the same time my stomach was beginning to churn from the tepid sheep's milk and the murky water. I had to dismount for a toilet break, but the mare was too impatient to wait for me. She headed directly for the dam and when I caught up with her I walked straight in, not stopping until the water was covering my lips and trickling down my scorched throat.

It was heaven.

Finally arriving at the homestead, I was amazed to find it deserted.

The gathering storm looked pretty nasty and the mare bolted towards her mates.

I fell onto my bed, wanting nothing more than to sleep off my exhaustion, but the thunder and lightning put a stop to that idea. I sat down on the verandah steps instead, enjoying the cool wind and the electric fury in the sky. Lightning was hitting the ground on the horizon and with each strike black smoke appeared.

Suddenly Rod came running from the main house, yelling, 'Quick! Help me get the water-truck ready – the back paddocks are on fire!'

The horizon was covered with smoke. As we were getting ready to leave, two station managers from nearby properties arrived at our homestead with a couple of men, and a vehicle loaded with, of all things, booze. There were bottles of overproof rum, some whisky and dozens of bottles of warm beer. It seemed an odd thing to carry to a fire. The boss, and a couple of visitors he had been entertaining, emerged from the house carrying even more bottles, loaded them into the LandRover, and the convoy went out to do battle.

What Next You Bastard

When Rod and I pulled up with the water-truck we realised that the fire was actually on the adjoining property, Marland Station, which had a frontage of three miles, all of which was burning.

Our only defence, once the water had run out, was to beat the flames with a long stick that had a square flat piece of hide attached to one end. It was a losing battle from the start. Mr Wilkinson and the other landowners joined their jackaroos, but dashed to the vehicles every now and then for another swig from a bottle. Before long they were spending more time drinking than fire-fighting and when the rain began to pelt down they left it up to nature to do the rest.

Three hours later, most of the fire was out and so were most of the men, Rod included. The other two station hands and I were the only ones sober enough to drive home.

So that was the day I got to drive my very first motor vehicle – the LandRover.

Over the next few days I began to suffer terrible stomach cramps. At first I put it down to the after-effects of my day in the paddock without water, or the night of the fire. But when the cramps continued into the following week, I started to worry that my old health problems might be catching up with me.

They were more severe at night than during the day, for some reason, maybe because my days were so busy that I didn't have time to stop and think about them. But alone in the hut, I would be sitting on my bunk with one of Mrs Brodie's picture-books when out of the blue one of these stomach cramps would double me over. They were always followed by the shakes. Even rolling a smoke was impossible; the hand holding the cigarette paper would shake so much that tobacco would spill all over the floor. It was the only thing that kept me from chain-smoking.

Sleeping was almost impossible, and when I woke up my mattress would be soaked with sweat; my body would be bent and every one of my joints would be aching. Only two things helped me through these long evenings and gave me a strange sort of relief: trying to read – which took so much concentration that for a time it took my mind off the pain – and the carbide lamp – flickering in the breeze by the open window, the fumes from the burning carbide gas had a certain soothing effect as I breathed them in.

For months I hadn't had any medication and I knew that I needed it. But Julia Creek Hospital was a good three hours' drive away.

Jackaroo

One Sunday morning, while resting, I was surprised by a strange voice. 'G'day, mate, my name is Mr Wells – old Paul told me to see you. Can I sit down?' We sat on the verandah steps and he told me he was an insurance salesman from the State Government Office. He asked me if I had any life insurance and seemed pleased when I said that I didn't think so.

'Good,' he said, 'Paul thought not. He told me that you would want to be covered and it would be all right to sign you up. You don't mind answering a few questions, do you? Righty-o, then. Paul has given me your name, age and birth date, so let's start with question one. Ever had rheumatic fever?'

'Yes,' I replied.

'I'll just write "no", it's a silly question,' Mr Wells said. 'What about TB?'

'Yes,' I said again.

But the insurance fellow just rolled his eyes and sighed. 'Never mind,' he said, 'I'll fill this in later – just put your name here. No need for a medical or anything like that, and Paul will give me a cheque and dock your pay.' He gathered up his papers, told me he would see me again next year, and left.

The great day came: I was off to the big smoke, Julia Creek, with the boss. For the first time since my arrival I would be able to do some shopping for things like pants and shoes, and I wanted to see a doctor about my medicine, which had run out after the first month.

Rod had filled the fuel tank on the LandRover the day before, but only halfway to town the motor started to run like a hairy goat. We had to leave the choke fully pulled out just to keep going – when the motor was hot, it ran better. I remarked to Mr Wilkinson that it was 'running a bit like the tractor' and he immediately realised what the problem was: Rod had used the wrong fuel – power kerosene.

Wrong fuel! Just the thought of Rod-the-Perfect doing something wrong at last made me feel good. I started laughing. After a moment the boss joined in, and we spent the next few miles driving in a comfortable silence. I almost got up the courage to ask him why I had to stay away from his wife and children and the nanny. Being away from home, I was missing my family and longing for some company. The words were on the tip of my tongue, but they never came out. It would be better to keep my mouth shut, I decided.

Instead I asked the boss if I could have some of my pay, so I could

What Next You Bastard

buy a couple of things. He was very sorry, he told me, but all my money had gone on the insurance payment – although anything I needed to buy, I could ask the store-owner to put on the Tudor Downs account for me.

The township of Julia Creek was so small that it took me less than ten minutes to walk all the way around it. After getting my supplies, I visited the local doctor and asked if my doctor in Brisbane had written to him. He had. But the man wasn't interested. 'Look at you,' he said, 'you look healthy to me. It would be a waste of time for me to check you out. If you get sick, come and see me.' No amount of protesting made any difference. 'On your way out, tell my wife to charge this to Mr Wilkinson.'

At the hospital they refused to see me, telling me that I would have to visit the doctor at his surgery – which I had just done. Nobody wanted to know my problems, so I spent the rest of the afternoon in the bar of the Gannon Hotel, where Bill Gannon, the owner, was happy to serve me beer on Paul Wilkinson's tab.

'Damn dogs!' The boss had just finished counting all the sheep that had been killed during the past few days. He had seen the dingo that he believed was responsible many times. He had set traps and put out poison baits, but this dog was too clever. 'Come on,' he said, 'I'm going to show you where I saw this dog and all next week I want you to ride out here and see if you can find him.'

We arrived at the place where the dog had been spotted last and the boss was disgusted to find that all his traps had been dug up, with dingo tracks all around them. Then we saw him. He was huge! But before we could even take aim, the dog had disappeared again. 'That's it!' the boss screamed in fury, 'I'll give you one week to search for him, Ken. If you don't get him, I'll bring in a dogger. In fact, I'm so fed up that I'll pay £50 a dog to anyone who can get rid of these damn pests for me!'

Next morning I was out early.

I rode all over the paddock, but never once sighted the dogs. All I found was a group of three fox dens dug into the ground beside a little gully. It would be hard to hide anything here. I dismounted for a bite to eat and noticed hair – a lot of hair – lying around the dens. It looked and felt just like cats' fur, but there were no bones to be seen. I thought it was strange, but soon put it out of my mind. I had other things to think about.

At one o'clock in the morning I woke with a toothache so bad that I went to the main house to wake the cook. My moaning and groaning brought the nanny instead. She inspected my mouth and told me that she could easily fix the problem for me, and what she needed for the job was a long needle. Now, needles are *not* my favourite things in life, pain or no pain. Jean found what she needed and held it into a flame until the end was glowing a bright red. She ordered me to open wide and explained that this was going to kill the nerve that was causing the pain. No way was I going to let her near me with that thing! At this she lost her patience, telling me that she didn't have all night, and giving me a lecture about looking after my teeth. 'If you had teeth like Rod's,' she said, 'you wouldn't be in this mess.'

Jean's only other idea sounded a lot more pleasant: she took a bottle of Mr Wilkinson's overproof rum and poured a large glassful. I was to fill my mouth with it, keeping the rum on the tooth as long as possible so that it would eventually deaden the nerve. It worked. The whole side of my face went numb and my lips were burning as if I had just eaten a whole plateful of hot peppers. With each swig of rum the pain lessened, until sleep got the better of me and I passed out with my head on the kitchen table.

Just a few months later, Rod had problems of his own. The dentist told him that the excessive brushing had taken all the enamel off his teeth and that they wouldn't last much longer!

Sundays were our days off, but there really wasn't much to do. We couldn't just jump into a car and go to the theatre or watch football or a cricket match. But there was target shooting! It was something useful and at the same time kept us amused. We used to place empty .303 shells and .22 shells on the fence that circled the turkey's-nest, then, from a distance of a hundred yards or more, would shoot them with our rifles. We became very good shots, but none of us was ever able to out-shoot the boss. His eyesight was incredible.

I finally found myself a friend. He was a third-year jackaroo, on loan to us from Marland Station, our nearest neighbours. The two station owners had a custom of loaning each other their workers and James was going to be with us for a few weeks, after which I would be sent over to Marland for a while to help with their work. James was nothing at all like Rod, thank goodness. He spent time

What Next You Bastard

with me, rather than at the house, and for the first time I had someone to talk to.

James was slightly older and shorter than me, with curly brown hair and eyes that crinkled up in the corners and almost disappeared when he laughed. His one great love was shooting. He had his own .22 semi-automatic rifle, an army-issue .303 and a .22 Hornet. I bought the Hornet from him for £7 and we spent every spare moment we had shooting.

James and I decided that it would be handy to have a pistol, so that we could shoot while out riding – whenever we saw dingoes or wild pigs, we would be able to ride right up to them and shoot them from the saddle. So James bought an old single .22 rifle from Mr Wilkinson and cut it down to nine inches. It would have to do.

Next time I was sent to check a paddock, I took the 'pistol' with me. A feral cat was running along the track in front of me, so I urged my horse into a gallop, took the pistol out and loaded it on the run. As I came closer to the cat, I leaned over the horse's shoulder and fired. Four things happened all at once: there was an almighty explosion; the cat flew into the bush unharmed (I think); I flew backwards out of the saddle; and my horse bolted all the way home without me.

James just about killed himself laughing when I told him.

Next on the list was his .22 semi-automatic rifle. We discovered that by 'sweating' a piece of nail onto the trigger-adjustment screw, we had a fully automatic rifle. There was one slight problem, though – its magazine only held ten rounds. To improve on this we joined four magazines together and put it to the test. Our target was a big old sow, sleeping under a tree. James lined up the sights and pulled the trigger. That pig never had time to blink an eyelid before collecting the better part of forty bullets in her hide. This exercise revealed that we had another problem to deal with: once the trigger was pulled, you couldn't stop it from firing until all the bullets were gone.

This was very expensive shooting! Back to the drawing board.

We worked on the .303 next, cutting it down until we were left with a twelve-inch barrel. At nine o'clock one night the job was finished and James and I decided to check the results. There was no one in the bunk-house, as Rod and the four extra workers that Mr Wilkinson had hired were all up at the main house, playing cards in the kitchen. We knew that nobody would be worried by the sound of a gunshot – it was a common enough event on a property like this one. We turned off the carbide lights and it was pitch black outside. James poked the sawn-off rifle out the window and squeezed the trigger.

The blast was deafening.

'I'm dead! I've been shot!'

One of the workers had been sitting right outside our window. His hair was smouldering from the long flame that had sprung from the rifle barrel and he was now jumping up and down and howling. James dropped the rifle onto the floor like a hot potato and we watched him run off into the darkness, like a human torch.

Our ears were ringing with a high-pitched noise, but when we had recovered enough to follow, we found the man sitting in the shower with water pouring down over his fully clothed body. He was still shaking with fright, but apart from having a new hairstyle didn't look too badly hurt. He had lost at cards and had come back to the bunkhouse for a quiet smoke! He got a lot more than he had bargained for.

The time came for me to leave Tudor Downs and help James at Marland Station. As I arrived there, the station manager and his wife were just leaving to drive into town for supplies, because the monsoon rains were due in the coming weeks. They had left it too late. Only a few hours later a heavy downpour set in, stranding them in Julia Creek and leaving those of us at the Marland homestead with only enough food for two days.

Apart from James and myself, there was one other person on the property, the caretaker, Bob. He was in his late seventies and lived in a small hut by himself.

For two solid weeks the rain pelted down, making it impossible to do any of the usual work around the grounds. The telephone wires had been damaged by flooding and the three of us were completely cut off from any outside contact.

James and I were bored. Our only entertainment came from fooling around with our guns, but pretty soon even that lost its appeal. There was nothing but crows to shoot at, and before too long we had used up all our ammunition, anyway. Bob wasn't impressed when we suggested killing the hens for meat, especially as they provided our only food. For every meal we had eggs – boiled eggs, fried eggs, scrambled eggs, poached eggs. After two weeks of this, the air in our bunkhouse was so foul that we agreed not to smoke in case lighting a match caused an explosion. We had another problem, too: all three of us were beginning to suffer from severe diarrhoea, spending hours at a time in the long-drop. But I was the only one who was starting to pass blood as well.

The rains finally stopped and the sun came out, making the muddy soil steam and the air thicken with humidity. It took the manager and his wife another four days to get back and when they heard about my condition they told James to drive me into town and leave me there. When I recovered, I was to make my own way back to Tudor Downs, since I was obviously not going to be much use to them at Marland.

The doctor at Julia Creek told me that the hospital was full. His only advice was that I should buy myself an apple, grate it and eat it, but that I shouldn't drink water or eat anything else until my condition improved. He warned me that it could take a week or more before I was well enough to return to the Wilkinsons.

I booked myself into the Gannon Hotel and when the owner became suspicious about my long periods in the bathroom, I found myself having to explain what was wrong. It was all very embarrassing. But Mr Gannon just nodded sympathetically and told me to sit on the bed and wait for him to come back.

'Drink this, son,' he said, handing me a large beer-glass full of some disgusting-looking black liquid. It'll make you sleep, but when you wake up, you'll be fine.' His words were kind and warm and I couldn't help trusting him completely. I polished off the glass and gave it back. The taste wasn't nearly as bad as I'd expected, in fact, it was surprisingly good. 'Lay down and I'll see you later,' Mr Gannon said.

Six hours had passed and darkness had fallen over the town by the time I stirred.

At the bar Bill Gannon told me he was glad to see me 'back from the dead'. He said that he had asked the cook to leave a meal for me in the kitchen, so I should go and have a shower and he'd be seeing me in the bar later.

That strange-looking black drink must have done the job. Not only was I feeling a lot better by the time I had eaten my first proper meal in nearly three weeks, but the diarrhoea had stopped and I was no longer passing blood. When we chatted in the bar afterwards, and Bill Gannon learnt that I'd been born in Coorparoo, he asked me whether my mother might be Myrtle Hall. I was amazed to hear that he had known her for years. Unfortunately the bar became very crowded just then and so I never found out how or when they had met.

Bad news was waiting for me when I got back to Tudor Downs a few days later, after hitching a ride on the mail truck. They weren't going to pay me for any of the time that I had spent away from the station, because I hadn't done any work at Marland. The boss wasn't interested in hearing any arguments on the subject.

My attitude towards working for the Wilkinsons was never as keen after that.

The windmill that stood forty feet tall came to a sudden halt one day. The rod that lifted the pump up and down had broken.

Rod and the boss winched the tail around to keep the blade from turning while trying to make repairs – something that was necessary from time to time – but on this particular morning the blades kept moving in the wind, regardless. They ordered me to climb up there and tie the blade off with a chain to keep it still. No amount of protesting could get me out of it: I told them that I had never been able to stand heights, my nerves were no good when it came to things like that and, above all, I was dead scared. Rod said he wasn't going because he was the foreman, and anyway, he had some paperwork to do later and just couldn't afford to get his hands dirty. The boss told me that he was too old to do things like that any more, besides which, I was the only one who would be able to fit through the manhole in the platform.

'Just do it!' he spat, when I still didn't move.

Taking a deep breath, I started to climb the rusty ladder. My hands were clammy with sweat and my feet were shaking with every rung that took me further up. That climb seemed to take forever! My eyes were closed because I couldn't stand to see the ground so far below me, and it wasn't until I bumped my head on the underside of the platform that I knew I had reached the top of the ladder. Opening my eyes, I looked up and saw the narrow opening that I was supposed to squeeze through. I also saw that for this next part I would have to take my hands off the rails and lean back a good foot or so before I would be able to get my arms above my head and through the hole. The whole structure was shaking in the wind and I was dead sure that I was going to fall at any moment. My whole body froze. I couldn't move.

'For chrissakes move, Ken! We haven't got all day!' Through half-opened eyes I made out a tiny figure that looked a bit like Rod, only smaller. He was walking around in circles, kicking at the dust with his heels. I shouldn't have looked down. It made me feel worse.

And then I saw the way the boss was glaring up at me, his hands on his hips, and knew that I had no choice but to give it my best shot. Somehow or other I managed to squeeze the upper part of my body through the gap and lever myself onto the rickety wooden platform, where I crouched on all fours. Being so close to the spinning blades as they cut through the air was scaring the hell out of me: one wrong move and I'd be sliced to ribbons! Impatient shouting came from below, but this boy wasn't going to move till he was good and ready!

Gusts of wind were making my shirt flutter backwards and forwards and after a while I noticed that there was a kind of pattern or rhythm to them: some gusts were weaker and some stronger. If I could just grab one of the spokes during one of those weaker gusts, then maybe …

Having some sort of plan to work to made me feel a bit better. The wind had dried the sweat from my body and I was as ready as I would ever be. Backing up to the main frame, I held onto it with one hand and with the other leaned out to grab at a spoke. At my first attempt it ripped me away from the mainframe and would have lifted me right off my feet if I hadn't let go in time. Next try I grabbed it on its way down and held on for a moment and I felt it slow down slightly. I kept this up, grabbing at a spoke again and again until the shaft slowed down enough for me to keep it from turning. The moment the windmill stopped, I swung the chain through a gap in the spokes and tied her off.

No cheers from below. Instead I heard Rod shout, 'Okay, Ken, you can come down now and help.'

The thought of having to brave that rusty ladder again was just too much for me. I refused to come all the way down to help them fix the broken pump, because I knew perfectly well that someone (meaning me) would be sent back up again when it was done.

Now that the blades were still, the platform had stopped shaking and so had I. For the first time I noticed the view. It was magnificent! I could see for miles in every direction. Hearing squawking noises somewhere behind me, I turned and I spotted a number of crows in the distance; they were flying in circles and I could just make out a couple of dingoes jumping around and playing in the grass beneath them. (Someone told me, much later, that dingoes did this to get a meal of grasshoppers – as they ran through the grass they disturbed the grasshoppers, making them leap into the air, where they were snapped up by the pouncing dogs.) Knowing how keen the boss was to find the dingoes, I called out to him and pointed out where I had seen them, but all I got was a dirty look and some angry words about 'getting one job done at a time'.

Dingoes were now killing sheep at the rate of twenty a night. They had their own little tricks, these cunning animals: first they got the sheep moving, then they herded them into a single line. As the sheep panicked and ran, the dogs would run up behind them and bite a huge chunk of flesh out of the groin, bringing the sheep down in agony. At the end of the run the dogs would eat either the first or the last they had brought down and the rest were wasted, killed just for the fun of it.

Paul Wilkinson didn't find it funny at all. He was toying with the idea of buying some cattle to run in the back paddock, but they would cost him £4 a head and the last thing he needed was to lose them to dingoes. It was time to call in a dogger.

The dogger turned out to be a professional dingo catcher in his late eighties. We all sat around the kitchen table the night he arrived, comparing notes on the most likely place for him to start his search.

I had already tried more than once to earn the £50 per head that the boss had offered for every dingo brought in, but they were always too quick for me. From my day on the top of the windmill, I had learnt that circling crows might mean dingoes on the ground below, and a couple of times this led me on the right track. But the one time I'd had one in my sights and pulled the trigger, wouldn't you know it, the bullet was a dud and the dingo got away before I could reload.

Anyway, the dogger asked me how to get to the back paddock, which was where most of the slaughtered sheep had been found, and then he wanted to know if there was any shelter in that area. There was, I told him, an old boundary rider's hut. The old man seemed happy with that and asked Mrs Brodie to get some rations together for him, enough to last him at least two weeks, because he would be leaving before sunrise. The boss said he could sleep in the bunkhouse with us boys for the night and asked how long he thought it would take to find where the dingoes were living.

'If I can find the place where they feed their young, they won't be far away,' said the dogger. When asked how he could do that, he smiled. 'Easy. They love cats. What I look for is cats' fur.' Without thinking ahead, I blurted out that I knew of such a place, and the dogger said that he wanted me to go with him in the morning, to show him where. Me and my big mouth! The boss agreed, eager to settle this business once and for all.

We were up and on our way before dawn.

In the dogger's battered old truck we drove to the spot where I had seen the fur. 'They're here, m'boy,' he said softly, 'I can feel it.' The old man took a shovel and dug up the three fox dens. He removed eight dingo pups and slit the throats of seven of them. The remaining male pup he tied to a steel chain and set traps all the way around him. When we returned the next day we found a bitch in one of the traps, shot her and reset the trap. Next day, another bitch. The dogger nodded wisely, 'You can count on it, boy, the next one will be the dog.' He was right. The following morning the largest dingo of the pack was howling in the trap.

The boss handed over £550 in cash – £50 a head for each of the eleven dogs, just as promised. The old man thanked me for making his stay such a short one, but didn't offer me any of the money. Even the boss knew perfectly well that without my help that dogger could have been out there in the heat and dust and flies for weeks, maybe months, searching for the right spot. But it didn't make any difference to him. Once again I found myself wondering why I bothered to stay.

The dingoes were gone for the time being, but in their place we had a new problem: the snakes were in plague form. The boss had already placed iron sheeting around the base of the house to keep them from going underneath, but somehow they still managed it. They were attracted by the cool darkness under the floorboards and the whole family was terrified by the thought that the snakes might find their way inside the house.

Jackaroo

So now we built a false wall with a small hole in the middle of it and placed a saucer filled with milk on the ground in front of it. From the kitchen table, where I sat and waited with a shotgun, I watched as one snake after another entered the hole, then shortly afterwards slipped out for a drink. While its head was in the saucer of milk, I aimed and fired at it from the kitchen, smashing the plate and the snake with a single bullet. Good target practice.

Then there were the cockatoos. We'd had very dry weather for a while and in the space of just a few days cockies in their hundreds had settled all around the homestead in search of food. Their screeching was deafening. Mr Wilkinson couldn't stand it any more. He marched up to me and thrust a double-barrelled shotgun into my hands. 'Shoot the bastards!' he yelled. 'I can't even *think* in my own house with all that racket!' At least two hundred birds were walking on the ground, clustering and flocking together. As soon as I pulled back the two hammers on the shotgun, they scattered and rose into the sky. They had reached about twelve feet by the time I fired both barrels together.

Not a single bird fell. I couldn't believe it. I watched them fly away from where I was lying in the dust. The force of the two barrels had thrown me flat on my back. When I got up on my feet again, I wiped what I thought was sweat from my face, but my arm came away red with blood. My whole face was burnt from the gunpowder. When I inspected the shotgun, I realised it was so old that the firing pins were worn down.

Foxes were next on the list of pests. One night I was so irritated by their endless barking, which was keeping me awake, that I took a spotlight and a gun and went out after them. Six foxes were lying on the ground where I had shot them before I noticed what beautiful pelts they had. For the first time in ages I thought about my mother: she would love a fox-fur coat! The next day I shot a scrub turkey and poisoned it with strychnine and was delighted to find eight foxes with perfect coats the following morning. While I was skinning them I was so busy congratulating myself for coming up with such an easy method of hunting – no messy bullet-holes! – that at first I didn't even notice the terrible smell. I stopped and sniffed the air, then smelled my fingers, and, oh boy, did they stink! There must have been some sort of gland in the foxes making the rotten smell. Skunks couldn't have been any worse.

Soap and water were not enough to remove the odour from my hands. It was making me sick and I just couldn't carry on. Mum's coat would just have to wait.

Things were starting to change. Cattle had been ordered and around the homestead a new cottage was being built for a married couple. The man was to be a cowboy and his wife was to work around the house. A few weeks later I started to notice that the boss's attitude towards me was definitely changing as well. Maybe it had something to do with the fact that he'd found himself another new worker, a lad of twenty or so called Sam.

Unlike Rod, Sam was a true cowboy, with his twenty-gallon hat, fringed shirt and riding boots with three-inch heels. Leather chaps covered his long thin legs, and I heard that he was an experienced cowhand, having spent the previous year in the Gulf, working on cattle properties. This was to be his first job on a sheep station, but the Wilkinsons were becoming more and more interested in cattle, so I supposed he would be pretty useful around the place.

I had the feeling that my days were numbered, although this time it had nothing to do with reading or writing. Somehow, knowing this made it a bit more bearable when the time came.

We had been planning for some time to attend the Kynuna Rodeo. Everyone from Tudor Downs would be going and it was something to look forward to. Kynuna was a small town of only sixty people and they held a rodeo every year. Sam had been entered in the saddle rough-ride and we were all keen to see how good he really was.

The boss sent me to check the back boundary on the day before the rodeo as it had been some time since it was last done. When I reached the dam I dismounted and took a drink of water. It had a bad taste. I got back on my horse and rode on, but after about twenty minutes I doubled up with sharp pains in the stomach. I couldn't continue while I felt like this, so I turned around and rode back to the homestead. Clutching my stomach, I returned the horse to the yards and made a dash for the long-drop.

Rod was waiting for me when I finally came out. 'Mr Wilkinson is not too happy with you,' he said. 'In the morning, have your port packed. He'll find you a new job when we get to Kynuna.'

I was glad that it was over. Any pleasure I'd had from working here had died quite some time ago. Early in the morning the boss summoned me to get my final pay. Neither of us was smiling.

'Look, boy, *you* really owe *me* money because of your insurance policy. I'm ready to overlook that, so I've made out a very small cheque for you. Just hand it over at the hotel in Kynuna and they'll cash it for you. And when we get to town, I'll get a new job for you with one of my mates.'

9. *Kynuna*

Ten in the morning found us in Kynuna. What a strange place. There wasn't much to it at all – just the local racetrack, the showgrounds where the rodeo was being held, and a dusty collection of old buildings.

Paul Wilkinson was already parked outside the Kynuna Hall when Rod and I pulled up in the LandRover. He told me to book myself into the hotel and that he would see me that night after the rodeo. That was it. No handshake. Nothing.

The Blue Heeler Hotel was bursting its seams from the rodeo crowd which had brought business in from miles around. There was standing room only at the noisy bar, where the managers, a young man and his wife, were trying to keep up with the drink orders. They were amazed when I told them I wanted a room, telling me that they had all been booked out right after last year's rodeo. My disappointment must have shown on my face, because they said they would let me spend the night on the lounge room floor, even offering to keep an eye on my bag until I came back that night.

Close by was the general store. When I stepped inside it was like stepping into a world that I had only ever seen in the movies: clothing that seemed to date back to the 1930s; food in containers from the same era with prices to match; and shelving that reached from floor to ceiling, overflowing with outdated items and knick-knacks. It was like suddenly finding myself in a maze. I was so busy looking around at everything that I nearly jumped when a friendly voice said, 'Can I help you?'

'Not really,' I said, but after a while I thought it might not be such a bad idea to ask this man if he knew of any jobs in the area.

'What's your handle, boy?' (My handle? What the hell was that supposed to be?) 'Your name, boy – what is it?' When I told him he said, 'Well, Ken, my handle is Tom Pattel and I believe I can help you. Have you ever worked with sheep? Good! Over at the hotel ask for Darryl Carey, and when you see him, tell him I sent you.'

Kynuna

Back at the hotel I asked around and was told that I would find Darryl Carey at the bar around seven o'clock. To fill in the day, I wandered across to the rodeo which was in full swing. The only familiar face I saw was Sam's; he had just won the Saddle Bronc and was busy being mobbed by the only two unattached girls in a hundred-mile radius.

By six o'clock it was dark and the hotel was so full that patrons were hanging from the windows and ceiling. Further up the road at the hall it was a different story altogether – and a different class of people. The men were all dressed in suits, the women in long ball gowns and even the children were all dolled up. When I entered a hush fell over the crowd and the atmosphere turned cold. 'You there!' A hand came down on my shoulder and pushed me backwards through the doors. 'May I suggest you get a suit before you return?'

When I returned to the hotel a two-up game was just starting out the back. Twenty or more men had formed a circle and were placing paper money on the ground in front of them. 'Come in spinner!' called the man in the middle, tossing two pennies high into the air. All you had to do was bet which way up the pennies would land. I had never played before, but it looked so easy that after watching for a while I decided to join in. I was very lucky, managing to turn my ten-shilling note into £40 in the space of a single hour. I quit while I was still ahead and pushed my way through the noisy crowd to the bar.

Darryl Carey, when I found him, turned out to be quite a likeable guy in his mid-twenties. His sandy hair was neatly combed back off his face and he looked me up and down over the rim of his beer glass. After asking a few questions about my experience, he hired me on the spot. 'Be here Monday morning at seven and I'll pick you up.'

While sitting at the bar with a cold beer and thinking about my new job, I overheard part of a conversation that was taking place behind me.

'Yessir! Born in Pommy-land, came out to Australia last year, age twenty-two ... name is Hall.' At this I pricked up my ears. Another Hall! When I swung around I saw two men, one of them wearing a police uniform with three stripes on his shoulder – must be the local cop. And he wasn't paying attention to the man who was talking. He was staring at me instead.

'You there! I want you outside!' he barked. I obeyed instantly and followed him outside onto the dusty road. 'You're new around here and I don't like people I don't know. So tell me all about yourself, name and age first.'

A notepad came out and a pencil moved quickly over the pages during the whole five minutes it took to tell my story.

'You got a job with Darryl Carey – well, that's good. We'll be seeing a lot of each other. Okay, son, you can go and finish your beer now,' the cop nodded, sounding a lot friendlier than before.

But before I could make it back to the bar, Rod stopped me. 'Mr Wilkinson wants me to take you to see him now.'

We arrived at the hall and Rod spoke to the doorman who reluctantly allowed me to go inside. All I could see was a floor jammed with couples trying to dance the foxtrot. While I searched for my old boss I noticed that most of the women were very young and the men were old, like Mr Wilkinson. The music stopped, couples moved off the dance floor and I spotted him.

'You wanted to see me,' I said.

'Yes, Ken, have you got your bag with you? Hang on – first I'd like you to meet your new boss. This here is Mr Mayes. You'll be working for him,' he told me, indicating the elderly fellow beside him. Well, I thanked him very much and told him that I already had a new job, and Mr Wilkinson was furious. 'But what about Mr Mayes?' he demanded.

'No, *Paul*, as I said, I've got a job.' Saying his first name felt good and there was nothing he could do about it now. His face turned red as a beetroot and he opened and closed his mouth like a fish but no words came out. His friends were shocked, muttering things like 'the cheek of that boy' and 'it was Paul's place to get him work'. But I knew that it would have been the same kind of conditions as before: lots of work, poor treatment and very little pay. I went back to the hotel.

It was well after the ten o'clock closing time, but behind the front doors the serious business of drinking rolled on. 'The Pom' was sitting alone, so I pulled up a stool beside him.

'Hi. My handle is Ken Hall,' I started, liking the way I was able to use my new expression. 'I overheard you talking to the sergeant before. Is your name really Hall?'

'Certainly is,' he said cheerfully.

I ordered two beers from the barman. 'My great-great-uncle was

Sir Benjamin Hall from England,' I told him proudly. 'I believe the clock Big Ben was named after him.'

The stranger was astounded. 'It's a small world! He was my great-grandfather. I only found out recently when I had my twenty-first. Until then I never knew I'd been adopted at birth. On the day of my birthday I learnt the truth, so I packed my bag and came out here.' For a moment he was silent. 'If you don't mind, let's talk about something else.'

To my disappointment, I never saw him again.

Waking up in the corner of a hotel lounge on a Sunday morning, with a hangover the size of Tasmania, is not something I would wish on anyone. My head was pounding and I felt dizzy. The smell of frying bacon, mingling with stale beer fumes and the stuffiness of a room packed with dozens of sleeping bodies, was suddenly too much for me. I made a dash to the bathroom and when I came back found Darryl and the sergeant sitting in the bar with the managers.

'Well, we got us a live one here!' said the sergeant.

Darryl looked up. 'That's my new man. By the looks of him he's not fit to work for a week. Barman, two hairs-of-the-dog – one for me, and one for my new man.' I watched the barman mix Worcestershire sauce, an egg, curry powder and alcohol in a tall glass. 'That's the ticket,' Darryl laughed, 'a drink that will kill the dog that bit you the night before!'

Lifting the glass to my lips I took a careful sip. It was revolting.

'Like this,' said my new boss, throwing back his head and downing it in one gulp. 'Come on, you can do it!'

It was barely halfway down before it was on its way up again.

Monday morning I handed over Paul Wilkinson's cheque, which barely covered my two nights' stay in the hotel. Without my winnings from the two-up game I would have been flat broke and starving.

Darryl picked me up in a dusty old utility and we headed for an 80,000 acre property called Tinvale Station, north of Winton. It was only half an hour's drive from Kynuna, something that cheered me up quite a bit. Darryl's parents, Mr and Mrs Carey, were lovely people and the only thing they had in common with Paul Wilkinson was their rule of keeping jackaroos out of the main part of the house.

Everything else was different.

Mr Carey walked me over to my quarters, a long building with eight rooms, and invited me to choose whichever one I wanted. He added, very kindly, that this was now my home and that if I needed anything at all, I had only to ask.

Two days later I still couldn't get over the difference. Here I felt like a member of the family. Nobody ever told me to do something, they asked: 'Ken, can you do that for us?' or 'Would you mind ...' And most of the time they actually thanked me for whatever I had done for them. It made me want to do more and more.

Another thing that made working for the Careys so much better was my friendship with Darryl, as well as living so close to a town. The two of us spent most of our nights at the pub in Kynuna and I soon got to know all the locals. The managers of the hotel were from Townsville, I learnt, here to make a quick buck and return home to build their dream house on the coast. Old Tom Pattel from the local store let me put anything I wanted on the books, to be paid off later. I bought shirts from him for only five shillings and they were so well made that I was still wearing them five years down the track.

The local police sergeant came to the hotel each night to check on after-hours drinking. At ten o'clock sharp he would put his head through the door and yell, 'Out! Time to go home!' and then walk down the street. Five minutes later he'd slip in the back door and join the others at the bar until two in the morning.

One night I offered to pay for the sergeant's beers. 'Yes, my friend,' he said between sips, 'and what can I do for you?' I explained that I would like to get a licence to drive a car and a truck. His beefy red face made his crinkly white hair look like one of the Careys' sheepskins. 'I have seen you driving a car and a truck in town, yes?'

'Well, not actually here in town, Sergeant,' I protested, 'only on the property.'

'Yes, I have, my boy,' he replied, with a twinkle in his eye. 'See me tomorrow when you come to town.'

Sure enough, the very next day I had my licence, which allowed me to drive every single vehicle on the list. There had been no test of any kind. I couldn't believe my luck. Back in Brisbane I would have had to sit for a written examination, something I would have failed for sure. My driving wasn't all that bad – I just had trouble changing gears. Now I was able to drive Darryl home after a heavy night in town. I never allowed myself to get drunk, not after seeing what it

Kynuna

had done to my old man, and Darryl could be a bit of a handful when he drank, so it was something that suited us both.

Christmas was coming up again. My job at Tinvale was still going well, but I was starting to feel a bit restless. I wanted a break from the dusty dry town where the living was good, but one very important part of life was missing – female company. The Kynuna Ladies were not an option, even though they could be found living all around town, sometimes in mobs of two hundred or more. 'Kynuna Ladies' was the name given to the local wild goats. The only eligible human female was the fifteen-year-old daughter of the local drover, who was carefully watched every minute by her family. Young men from miles around came to town with dreams of winning her, but they always returned to their properties empty-handed.

I was sitting at the bar one night, drinking beer with a stranger by the name of Kevin. He told me that he was a cattle buyer for a Brisbane abattoir and he lived in Greenbank, which wasn't too far from my home. He was happy to have found someone who knew where he came from and was especially interested when I told him about the brumby stallion I had helped to run in that area some years before.

'Who did you run the brumbies with?' Kevin asked me.

'Fred Roman and old Dave Sharpe,' I told him, and Kevin grinned from ear to ear.

He shot out his hand. 'Shake it, mate! I ride with that pair whenever I'm not working! What did you say your name was? Look, I want you to tell that story to the people at the bar. They don't believe we have brumbies around Brisbane.'

With the story told, we sat and talked some more. Kevin kept shaking his head and saying what a small world it was. Then he turned to me and said he was heading back to Brisbane in a couple of days, as soon as he could find someone to share the driving with. Would I be interested? You bet I was.

The Careys were quite happy to give me some time off over Christmas and two days later I was on my way home. We left early in the morning in Kevin's battered old car, which was soon full of dust of two kinds – bulldust from the stories we told each other and bulldust from the road, which was so narrow and corrugated that the car seemed to be breaking up beneath us. The shock-absorbers were useless.

What Next You Bastard

Kevin had done all the driving during the day and when it started to get dark he suggested I get some sleep, as I would be driving soon. Sleep! He must have been joking! The back seat was full of his belongings and there was nowhere to stretch out. I tried resting my head on the passenger-side door, but it bounced all over the place. There was no other choice but to try sleeping sitting up. My eyes had been closed for what seemed like hours but I was still awake when the car stopped.

'Okay, Ken, it's your turn to drive. Did you have a good sleep?' my mate asked. I didn't want to offend him, so I said that I had. While Kevin slid across into the passenger seat, I stepped out into the darkness to water a couple of bushes and was amazed at the complete blackness of the night. I had never seen so many stars shining so brightly and the sight of them almost took my breath away. Back in the car, I settled myself behind the steering wheel and shut the door.

'Kevin? Is it in gear, or what?' No answer. Kevin was dead to the world.

This was going to be a bit tricky, I realised. The gear-column was up on the steering wheel and all I had ever driven so far was a car with a floor-shift. I tried to remember Kevin's hand movements during the gear changes and decided to give it a try. Pushing in the clutch, I turned the key and the motor started. So far, so good. When I put my foot on the accelerator and eased off the clutch, the motor roared but the car didn't move. One more try and I found a gear. We were on our way. It was only then that I noticed something important was missing – the road! I couldn't see it anywhere. There was a very good reason for this: I had no lights. Fumbling around on the dashboard, I finally found a switch and was relieved to find that when I pulled it up the headlights came on. But there was still no road in sight. Stopping the car, I climbed out and had a look. There it was, about twenty feet off to my right. Kevin was stirring, so I quickly got us back onto the road and before long I heard him snoring again.

I had just driven through a small town when I noticed something strange in the distance. A few miles down the road, heading towards us, were about ten sets of bright spotlights. The road was narrow and when I pulled over to the side for a better look, the movement woke Kevin, who had been asleep for three hours or more.

'What are you stopping for?' he said angrily.

Kynuna

'Look,' I pointed, 'those lights – what are they?'

Kevin moved like a bolt of lightning. He shot out of the passenger's door, ran around the front of the car and threw himself behind the steering wheel. He drove as far as he could off the road. A strange rumbling noise was growing louder as the bright lights came closer.

'Down! Get down, it's a road train!' yelled Kevin, but it was already too late. The trucks were upon us so quickly. Gravel and dust was being hurled at us like some furious hailstorm or sandstorm that had sprung up out of nowhere. Our windows were all down and, as I ducked for cover, I was hit twice by flying stones. There was a terrifying racket as the body of the car was pelted. And then, when it was over, the silence surrounded us once more. It had seemed like a long time, but was really only a few seconds.

Kevin and I sat up and surveyed the damage. It was hard to believe, but no glass had been broken – though Kevin wasn't overly pleased about the new dents he would surely find in his paintwork the next morning. He explained what had happened. There had been three Mack trucks in the convoy, three of the new 'road trains' – semi-trailers each pulling two dog-trailers, which were flat trays with wheels but no sides. Each road train had 60 wheels and weighed between 80 and 120 tons. The drivers of these monsters had made it very clear that any cars on the road would have to make way, because they wouldn't. And it was almost impossible to pass one without receiving damage to your car – usually the windscreen, but often much more. There was only one way to deal with the situation – as soon as you saw them coming, you got as far off the road as possible.

Well. I guess I was still learning something new every day. Kevin took over the job of driving again, just in case, but the only other obstacles we came across were a kangaroo or two, every thirty or forty miles.

It had been a long drive, more than twenty-four hours, and I wasn't sorry when Kevin dropped me off at a service station in Sunnybank early the next morning. A quick phone call to my surprised mother and I was home in Coorparoo again. It felt good to be back, even though it would only be for five weeks.

Darkie was howling and barking from the new garage that Ian had built under the verandah and when I let him out he flew up at me and knocked me to the ground. He showed me how much he'd missed me by licking me all over, and finally gave me his seal of approval, lifting his leg and christening me.

There was some mail for me – a letter from the State Government Insurance Office, informing me, Mum said, that in the first week of January I owed them my next payment. She wasn't happy about this at all. My only concern was how I would manage to pay the damn thing, until I remembered the pay cheque Mr Carey had given me before I came home. I still hadn't opened the envelope. When I did, I nearly fell over. I had been expecting only a small amount, especially after the Wilkinsons, but I was rich! Now I'd be able to pay the SGIO bill, and board for Mum, and still have enough for a deposit on a car.

Mum was as cautious as ever. Before I did anything, she begged, I ought to see the doctor. I promised that I would, but only after Christmas.

The neighbourhood hadn't changed much in nearly two years, but the people living in it had. All my old mates were busy with work, or with women. Everywhere I went it was the same. 'Sorry, mate, not tonight. I'm going out with my girl.' And any girls I met were either too busy or just not interested. Mum talked us all into going to Maroochydore again for a few weeks around Christmas, but even up there I wasn't much luckier. Parents remembered me from last time and refused to let me take their daughters out.

On 4 January, 1959, we celebrated my nineteenth birthday with a couple of cold drinks and hamburgers on the beach. Mum and my brothers sang 'Happy Birthday' and it was great having family around for the occasion. I couldn't help thinking how different it all was from my eighteenth, which the Wilkinsons hadn't known about, and wouldn't have cared if they did. Even Christmas at Tudor Downs had been a day like any other for the jackaroos, except that Mrs Brodie served us the family's leftover plum pudding for afters.

Back home in Brisbane again, I went to the bank and paid my insurance bill, ignoring Mum's warnings that the company was 'taking money falsely'. But I did keep my word about going to the hospital for a check-up.

To everyone's surprise, the doctors were very pleased with my condition. The pains I had been suffering were from gout, one of the side-effects of the cortisone. There was no sign of the tuberculosis – my lungs were 'marked' but seemed to be getting stronger, and there was only a small heart murmur.

Kynuna

'Doctor,' Mum said innocently, 'Ken would like to take out life insurance on himself. Would this be possible?'

'No, Mrs Hall, not at all. I'm sorry to say that the life span for your son is not great,' he replied. And when Mum revealed that I had been sold a policy while out in the bush, without any medical, he shook his head at me and sighed. 'All I can say is, save your money son, forget about the insurance.' Turning to Mum once more, the doctor described some of the reports that had recently come in from America about the nasty side-effects of cortisone, which nobody had known about. His descriptions of aggressive behaviour and moodiness and 'always being right' made Mum and me glance at each other knowingly. When he told of several American patients who had become so addicted to the drug that they had even killed to get it, we were horrified.

The doctor's advice to me was to go out west again, which he believed was the safest place for me. I would be better off away from the influences of the city – on that he was very clear.

With the money I had left, I put a deposit on a car that Ian had spotted for sale in the newspaper. Having life insurance made it possible for me to get finance from AGC, and the paperwork would be ready within a week.

It was an early model Holden, interestingly painted black, cream, green and chocolate. There were only a few miles on the clock, no rust and no dents. I fell in love with it at first sight. So did the local girls. At first I thought I had suddenly become irresistible to the opposite sex, with dates every night and pretty girls all in a row, but then I realised that it was not my body they were after, but a taxi.

One afternoon Ian needed some goods from the local store, so I generously offered to take him in my pride and joy. We came to a corner and I took my foot off the clutch and slammed it down on the brake pedal.

'Where the *hell* did you learn to drive?' exclaimed Ian, gripping the dashboard. I told him it was out on the farm, so then he wanted to know who had taught me, rolling his eyes when I said that no one had.

'Look, stop here and move over. You need a few lessons,' he declared. Actually, it was only one, but he corrected my most dangerous fault. Instead of using my left foot on the brake, I now knew to shift my right foot from the accelerator instead.

What Next You Bastard

Holidays were over and I was heading west again. Driving around in my local area hadn't been too much of a problem, because I knew my way around and was able to recognise the more familiar street signs by sight, but finding my way out of town and into the right direction for Kynuna was more instinct and guesswork than anything else. Now and again I had to stop and ask for directions, but the further west I went, the easier it became.

I had just driven through Roma, a small town about 300 miles from Brisbane, when a very fat policeman waved me over and ordered me out of my car. While he searched the inside, he asked me where I'd got the car from and refused to believe that it was mine. He was taking me in, he said.

At the local police station I was accused of stealing the car from Townsville and told that I was going to be charged with theft. They also said they knew who I really was. My licence was in my port in the back of the car and it took a lot of persuading before anyone bothered to check it out.

'Come off it! We've caught you red-handed!'

I explained that I was on my way back to work in Kynuna, and that I was known to the police there. That raised a smirk or two.

Four hours later I was called to the phone. They wanted me to speak to some person at the other end. The caller asked my name, place of employment, the name of my boss and also the name of the Kynuna racehorse that had recently run in a Mackay race. Luckily for me I remembered the local horse that had won in Mackay some months before, and within minutes I was free to leave. No apology, just: 'You can go.'

As I was walking out the door the policeman who had been questioning me said, 'Hang on, let me have a look at that licence again. You can't drive all them! Back inside.' And with that he crossed out all but the car, truck and motorbike endorsements.

Mr and Mrs Carey were away when I got back to Tinvale, so I spent more time than before in Kynuna. I did what everyone did when there was nothing to do – sat in the hotel bar every night and every weekend, talking. Everyone in town knew everyone else's business. I heard that Darryl had patched up his differences with Roy Lloyd, whose family had once been very close friends of the Careys until a mysterious feud had separated them. The bartender said it was one of those 'on again, off again' friendships that you sometimes come across in isolated areas. Inside the pub they were placing bets on how long the truce would last this time around.

One of my regular drinking partners was an Aborigine by the name of Two Left Feet Peter. I always stuck to beer myself, but his favourite 'poison' was overproof rum. His skin was so dark that it looked more blue than black and he had been born with two left feet, but boy, could this man run! He was as fast as an emu! Peter himself didn't know how old he was, but I would have put him in his early eighties, at the very least. We became good friends.

Some members of Two Left Feet Peter's tribe were camping beside the creek on Kynuna Station, the very spot where Banjo Paterson's song 'Waltzing Matilda' was written – or so it was believed by the locals. (This was one story you could really find yourself in trouble with. Many families living around Winton and Kynuna had their own ideas of exactly where the famous billabong really was, but the boys from Kynuna Station made sure their version went through – with their fists!)

Peter took me to meet some of his tribe. When we arrived at the creek I saw two girls, about sixteen years old, run down to the dry creek bed, sit down, and with their hands scoop up the fine sand and place it between their legs. I turned to Peter and asked him why they would do such a strange thing.

'Protection, mate,' he grinned. 'Stops all the men from rootin' them. Most of us we get drunk, so them girls makin' bloody sure nobody will try doin' it to them.' I was sure the idea worked very well.

It was a special day for Peter. He was meeting his cousin and other relatives who were on walkabout from Darwin. I was strolling along with him when we came to a group of ten or twelve people dancing in a circle. They were dressed only in loincloths. Peter started to sing as soon as he recognised his people and piece by piece threw off his white man's clothing and joined in the circle.

Not wanting to be in the way, I moved to one side and watched quietly as they danced and sang. None of the words meant anything to me, in a language I had never heard before and would never hear again, but I could sense the happiness of the reunion. After a while I sat down and enjoyed just being there. Smoke from three small ceremonial fires drifted in and out of the dance, and the Mitchell grass quickly turned to dust under stomping feet.

Tucker. Dancing was hard work and now it was time for food. There was snake, goanna, scrub turkey, and something I'd never seen anyone eat before – witchetty grub. They held this wriggling, fat, white thing that looked like a caterpillar or giant maggot by its tail end, bit its head off, then sucked out the insides before finally eating the rest of it. It made me shudder just to look at it, so I closed my eyes for a moment.

'You eat, you not get sick!' Standing in front of me was a smiling woman with only one tooth in the middle of her mouth. Her skin was wrinkled and she looked about seventy, though later I learnt that she was only forty-eight. Between her fingers the old woman held the tail of a goanna. 'Eat!' she urged me, nodding her head up and down. 'Like fish.' Not sure whether to believe her, I peeled back the blackened skin and took a small nibble of the white flesh. She was right. It did taste just like fish, and was very good.

While all this had been going on, I never saw any sign of drink, but now wine and rum appeared from nowhere, and the women got up and left, heading down to the dry creek bed for the sand they would soon be needing.

Waking the next morning, I found myself under the big tree opposite the hotel, and to this day I have no idea how on earth I got there.

It was race day. Two Left Feet Peter often did odd jobs for the locals and this time he had been paid to look after a small plane at the end of a runway, right on the edge of town. For this he received one small hip-bottle of rum in advance. 'Now, Peter,' said the owner of the light aircraft, 'I want you to keep the Kynuna Ladies well away from my plane.'

'No worries, boss,' said Peter, tripping on his way out of the pub and falling down the steps. Everyone laughed.

'He's drunk!' yelled the bartender. 'He'll go to sleep on you, Mr Smile!'

But Peter was already getting up from the dirt. 'No I won't, boss.'

'You'd better not,' replied Mr Smile, 'or I'll skin you alive.'

Just on dusk Mr Smile was seen running all around town in a rage, looking for Peter. 'I said I'd kill the mongrel and I'm going to do it right now!'

A crowd gathered behind the angry man, who had returned from the races to find that Peter had gone to sleep on the job, just as predicted, and the Kynuna Ladies had eaten most of the aluminium skin off his plane. I thought it would have been interesting to see

Mr Smile trying to catch Two Left Feet Peter when he had woken up, seen the trouble and started running!

Peter avoided town for a long time after that. He had good reason to. Mr Smile had paid some of the locals to give him a good working-over when they found him.

10. Droving

Australia's first world championship rodeo had just been held in Winton, about a hundred miles to the south-east. Most of us went along and watched as Roy Lloyd won the American Roping Saddle event for 1959. Because he was a local Kynuna boy, the whole town was proud as could be.

The truce between the Lloyds and the Careys was still holding good, much to the amazement of everyone, and most nights Darryl and Roy could be found sitting together at the bar, trying to outdo each other in the drinking stakes. Trouble was, the more these boys drank, the more abusive they got, and it was nothing unusual to see them throwing punches at each other before the night was over.

One weekend things really got out of hand. The two had been drinking since ten in the morning, and it was getting pretty close to three when it all started happening. It was on for young and old! Roy Lloyd threw his bar stool aside with a big crash and strode out of the pub, yelling abuse at the top of his voice. He screamed to no one special that he was going home to get his rifle, so that he could shoot 'the Carey bastard'.

Darryl didn't take any notice. He just sat there and kept right on downing his beers, one after the other.

Around six or seven, when it was dark outside, I was sitting next to Darryl and having a drink myself. As I lifted the glass to my mouth there came a loud bang. I got such a fright that the glass slipped through my fingers and smashed on the floor. Everyone was out of their seats and rushing to the front door. A .303 rifle had been fired outside the hotel.

Roy Lloyd was stumbling down the road, yelling, 'Darryl Carey, come outside. I'm gonna shoot you!' About a dozen people crowded in the doorway and watched Roy fumble with the rifle, trying to reload it. Darryl stepped out onto the hotel verandah, took one look at Roy and rushed him, knocking the rifle out of his hand. What a brawl. They punched and bit and kicked and gouged each other's eyes as they rolled in the dusty street. The whole town gathered around them, egging them on and calling for more. I stayed up on the verandah with the publican, well out of the way. Fighting wasn't my cup of tea.

A few minutes later the sergeant came running down the street and saw the rifle lying in the dirt. He yelled to a man in the crowd, 'Get that rifle and get it out of here!' The man just stood there. The sergeant stopped running, turned and looked directly at him: 'Move it, or I'll have you, too!' The man soon picked up the rifle and put it out of harm's way. When the sergeant got close enough to the boys, he grabbed Darryl, but Roy was still throwing punches, so he tried to hold them both apart. He wasn't doing too well and the drunken crowd around him wasn't making it any easier. Looking around for inspiration, he saw me standing on the verandah.

'Ken Hall! In the name of the Queen, I call for you to assist me!'

What? Who the hell did he think I was? No way was I going to get *my* head kicked in, thank you very much! I just stood there and pretended I hadn't heard him. It was all over a few minutes later, anyway. The sergeant had sorted them right out.

'The pair of you, go home!' he ordered, sounding tired and disgusted at the same time. Then he looked up to where I was still standing. 'And you, Ken Hall,' he shouted, 'just you stay right there. If you so much as *move*, I will book you!'

Bloody hell. How come I was the one in trouble?

Puffing and panting, the sergeant climbed the verandah steps and stood so close to me that the sweat dripped from his nose and splashed onto my cheek. His face was bright red and his body was shaking with exhaustion, or anger, or both. 'If you ever again refuse to come to my aid when I call you in the name of the Queen, I will put you away in jail in Townsville. Get – the – message?' One of his big red fingers dug painfully into my shoulder with every word.

I was too shaken and too ashamed to do more than hang my head and whisper, 'Yes, sir.'

The publican stepped up and put a friendly arm around my shoulder. 'Look, Sergeant,' he said, 'the lad would not know the law.'

'Well, he does now – I hope.' He gave me a nod, then announced it was time for a drink.

We sat inside for a while and neither of us mentioned the incident again. By the time we had put away four beers each I was starting to feel a bit better about myself. No one likes to be thought of as a coward. Before he left the sergeant said, 'I think you'd better camp here for the night, Ken.' Whether he was concerned about my driving, or about Darryl's condition, I wasn't sure, but I had a strong feeling the sergeant believed this business between the two boys was a long way from being settled.

Darryl came to town early the next morning and took me back to Tinvale, but something had changed between us and the easy friendship we'd had for so long was never there again. I began to worry that I might even become a target myself and hated the idea of being involved in such a senseless feud.

Even Mr Carey, who had always been so kind to me, was beginning to change his attitude. Late one night an electric storm came and went. In the morning I went to the stable and did my usual duties and everything looked fine. On my way to the kitchen for breakfast, I saw Mr Carey. He asked me if I had fed the horses and fowls and I replied that I sure had.

I was just finishing my breakfast when he came in with his hands on his hips. 'Tell me, where do you keep your *eyes*, Ken? I want you to go down to the stable and have a look.' He had such a strange expression on his face that I jumped up and hurried down to the stable. I couldn't believe what I saw. The big tree that grew between the fowl pen and the stable was lying on the ground, flattening the pen and part of the stable wall.

'Pack your bag. We don't need you here any more,' Mr Carey said, before striding back to the house.

That tree and stable had both been standing when I was there at daybreak. I would have sworn it! Taking a closer look, I saw that the trunk had been split down the middle and the wood was burnt. It must have been struck by lightning during the night, but taken some time to burn through enough to make it fall over, sometime between my early visit and breakfast time. And now Mr Carey was accusing me of lying about getting my chores done. It was too much for me. I threw up my arms and walked away in disgust.

So much for being a member of the family.

The only job I could find was at a property halfway between Kynuna and Julia Creek. The people who hired me were a young married couple, Don and Alice Gaffney, who lived in a small caravan and had been hired to build a very long fence for the Bourkes, who owned the land. I had heard some talk in town that it was really Mrs Bourke who owned the property. There was also a story about her being one of the first women ever to fly all the way from England to Australia by herself, though I never dared to ask her if this was true or not. On properties as big as these, keeping a small plane was nothing unusual, but these people had more than just one. There were three or four different kinds of light planes in the front paddock and both husband and wife seemed to spend more time up in the air than down on the ground.

Except at night.

Mr and Mrs Bourke liked their grog and had noisy arguments about it. Mrs Bourke would hide it from her husband, and he from her. Each had a personal supply of beer bottles that the other wasn't allowed to touch, but if one ran out before the other, the search would be on. Many a night I heard furniture and glass breaking up at the house before a hidden bottle was found. One night the fighting was worse than ever. Nothing her husband said or did was going to make Mrs Bourke reveal her latest hiding place.

'If you don't tell me, I'll chop up one of your planes,' he threatened.

'Go on, chop it up! I don't care,' she screamed. I heard the back door slam, and when I came out in the morning I saw that he had kept his promise and cut the smallest plane up with an axe. Not long afterwards he bought her a new one, though.

The fencing was all done by hand. Don Gaffney and I dug the holes with a crowbar and a post-hole shovel. Mr Bourke had one very strict rule – all posts had to be three feet in the ground. Trouble was, some of the holes took us a full day to dig, on account of the stony soil. When it was impossible to get down more than two feet, we would fill it with water and leave it to soak until morning. Now and then, despite everything, the hole was still too hard to dig, so Don would send me home early and work on it by himself.

We had been working on two post-holes at the side of a creek bed one afternoon, when we struck solid rock at two feet. As usual, Don told me to go home, but after a few minutes I decided to turn around and go back. I might as well watch him and learn how it was done. What I saw took me by surprise. He had taken out his cross-saw and was cutting about twelve inches off the bottom of the post, chopping the end into small pieces and placing them into the hole. I thought it was pretty clever of him, but made myself scarce before he realised that I'd seen him.

What Next You Bastard

My sleeping quarters were in a shed, but I took my meals with Don and Alice Gaffney in their caravan. That night at the table I raised the subject, mainly because I wanted Don to know that I wouldn't mind helping him with those difficult posts.

'You know those posts we can't dig the holes for?' I said. 'Why don't we just cut a foot off the bottom and put it in the hole with the post? Then there'd still be three feet of post in the ground.' I expected him either to let me in on his secret or laugh at my small joke, but I got a lecture instead.

Alice just frowned, but Don lowered his spoon and spoke carefully. 'Now get this straight, Ken! While you work with me, you don't cheat. If the post is to go down to three feet, then that is the depth we dig to. So, please, we will have no more talk of that kind.'

Biting my lip, I said, 'Okay'.

The Bourkes wanted the best. This fence was to have twenty steel posts between each pair of wooden ones. Fencing was an art, they told us more than once. A good fence was a straight fence – it looked better and did a better job. This one was so straight that you could kneel down and shoot a bullet from one wooden post to the next without clipping any of the steel ones in between.

Mr Bourke loved to fly low over his new fence, checking that nothing was crooked. If he spotted a post that was out of line, he would buzz it until we got it right.

'Oh, it's glorious up there!' he sang. 'Next time I go up, lad, would you like to come?'

'My legs aren't long enough,' I told him, 'I like to keep them on the ground!'

'Johnny Pens is looking for men in Winton,' the sergeant said. 'He does a droving trip, cattle I believe.' It was worth thinking about, as there were no jobs vacant for jackaroos. So I took myself off to Winton the very same day and signed on.

Johnny Pens was a fullblooded Aborigine. He was known for his skill with horses and cattle and could be trusted with large herds. His wife and his mother would be coming along to cook for the men, and one of his cousins, a girl in her twenties, would be riding with us. Her name was Meg. Johnny was offering good pay and all we had to do now was wait for the go-ahead from the cattle-owners.

The Tatts Hotel in Winton was a faded old building where I took a room for a couple of days until everything was ready. Across the road a bit stood the newly built North Gregory Hotel, where you could buy any meal you wanted, from sand crabs to fresh fish, or even French cuisine, whatever that was supposed to be – but there was one problem. You had to wear a suit and tie before they'd let you in. Too bad.

When word came that the trip was definitely on, we headed back to Kynuna, where we were taking over the herd from another drover. I made arrangements with the sergeant to leave my car at the police station until I returned, and was ready to start my new job. A cowboy at last!

A rickety wagon with two horses attached was standing outside the hotel when I arrived. The three Aboriginal women were already sitting in the back and pretty soon Johnny Pens turned up with two men who had just come back from Cloncurry. I was expecting to ride a horse, not sit in a wagon, but we were all told to pile in and Johnny, being the boss, took the reins. We set off. There was a terrible smell coming from the two white drovers and it took me a while to realise what it was – stale rum. They reeked of it.

We had been travelling for a while, and were moving into heavy scrub country with dry creek beds and very little grass, when I saw the first few cattle. They were being herded by a lonely-looking cowboy, and the boss wasn't very happy at all, saying that they should have been in more open country.

'Okay, we here,' he said, jumping down from the wagon. 'You men innerjuice yourselves, an' Meg, get them some horses quick.' The two drovers were called Dave and Bert and seemed quite proud of the fact that they had recently been kicked out of Cloncurry by the police. I didn't dare ask them why.

Meg returned with three horses, fully saddled. 'Okay, you three fellas, get out there an' help keep them buggers together,' Johnny ordered. 'We got a count to do before we take over that bunch.'

The horse she gave me looked all right, but as I went to mount it I saw the big toothy grin on Meg's face and made up my mind to take extra care. Undoubtedly, being the 'greenest', I was getting the worst horse. I wasn't too wrong at that. As soon as I slipped into the saddle, the horse went stiff. Kicking it would probably have sent me flying through the air, so I sat quietly for a minute, working out the best way to handle him. Young Mrs Pens came over and told me that this horse wouldn't move unless I was holding a stick, then sent the now sulky-looking Meg over to a tree to break off a small branch for me. Her grin was gone now that the fun was over.

From what Mrs Pens had said, I thought I would have to use the stick, but my horse made sure that I never had the need to. One look at it, and he was on his way, always keeping one eye on the branch in my hand. Whenever I shifted it from one hand to the other he got nervous, stopped paying attention to where he was going, and ran into things.

Eight of us were holding the herd together. Johnny and the leader of the other team made a kind of gateway with their two horses, and as the herd passed through it, started counting heads. Each of the two bosses was carrying small white pebbles in his pocket. Whenever he counted fifty head, he would drop one on the ground beside him. Doing this would give them each a total and make sure that the counting tallied up. The rest of us were ordered to work the cattle through this gateway at a speed that made counting possible – something that sounded pretty easy, but wasn't, because of the scrub. Four times the counting had to be restarted because cattle kept getting around behind the bosses.

I had never seen cattle of this breed before. They were built like racehorses and seemed to run like them too. They were very toey, putting their heads down and charging at horses and riders for no reason at all.

Two hours later we were finished. Two of the drovers from the other team rode past me on their way home. 'Well, mate, they're all yours. Glad I'm not in your boots,' said one of them. When I asked why, he told me that the cattle had stampeded every single night since they had left the station more than a week ago, adding that it wouldn't be long before they killed someone.

'What breed *are* they?' I shouted back, but they were already out of earshot.

'Zebu – that's what they are,' Johnny yelled, 'an' there'll be no sleep tonight less we can get this mob outta the scrub.' But it was already too late. It was nearly dark and we were still a long way from clear land. Word was passed around that we would be camping just on the edge of the scrub country and we would all be keeping watch.

'Okay, Ken,' Dave said, 'go and have a feed. When you finish, Meg will give you a night-horse and I want you straight back out here. And by the way, Johnny said I'm in charge when he's not

Droving

around.' I just nodded and turned my horse around, but Dave had more for me. 'Oh yeah. Tonight we're all gonna sing, and there'll be no smoking, you hear? Those beasts are edgy. They'll stampede at any excuse.'

At the camp I went to dismount, but the damned horse saw my stick moving and shot out from under me. I hit the ground with a thud. The three women said nothing until I was back on my feet and then they called me over and gave me a bowl of stew. I was too tired to enjoy it. My eyes were having trouble staying open.

'This fella, he's our best night-horse,' Meg told me, handing me the reins of a small white horse. My legs were bruised from spending all day in the saddle, and the skin was raw. The hairs under my long pants had been rubbed into little knots and were slowly being pulled out in clumps. I had been told to shave them off, but had forgotten to do it.

Back in the saddle once more, Meg gave me my final instructions. 'When it gets real dark, jus' you give 'im his head an' he'll look after you. Don't try an' steer the bugger cos he kin see better'n you. An' when you see that Bert, you tell him come in for his tucker.'

I was just heading out when the older Mrs Pens yelled, 'Stop, stop! You gotta sing, fella, start singin' real quick!' I only knew a couple of songs, so, feeling a bit silly, I rode towards the herd, singing, 'I've got a lovely bunch of coconuts ...'

This was my first night-horse. I could remember hearing stories about these unusual horses that were used to working in the dark. In daylight they were pretty hopeless; they couldn't see. Not that they were a special breed of horse, but just one horse out of a hundred seemed to be different in this way. I remembered that in Brisbane I had once heard of a white horse with pink eyes that kept falling over or walking into things during the day, but at night could be ridden through the bush at top speed. And I also remembered once seeing a cart-horse wearing sunglasses. His owner had cut the ends off beer bottles and fitted them into a leather frame that sat over the horse's eyes. The horse worked hard while he wore them, but when they were removed he couldn't see more than two feet in front of him. Not all night-horses have pink eyes, though; most of them have normal-coloured eyes.

Bert was easy to find. I stopped singing when I reached him, but he told me to keep it up. 'For Gawd's sake, don't stop, mate. ('I've got a lovely ...') If you do, ride away from the herd and start singing again, then ride back to them easy-like. Have you worked cattle before? No? Hell! Boy, ride with me – you sing while I talk. Look how they're lying there – see their front legs? One leg's out in front, the other one's under them. That means they're not ready to camp for the night. With their legs like that they can be up and in a gallop in one stride. Any minute, they can go. There, see that cow with both her front legs tucked under her? She's ready to settle for the night. Okay. Work that area between Johnny and Dave, and don't stop singing, Coconut Boy. I'll leave you to it.'

I was pretty sick of singing about coconuts anyway and that last remark settled it. But the only other song that sprang to mind, mainly because I was thirsty, wasn't much better. I had always been a great Slim Whitman fan, and liked his songs, though I bet he would have been very ticked off by my out-of-tune version of his 'Cool Water' song.

Right now all I hoped was that those poor beasts out there weren't going to notice the difference and charge at me. It went something like this: 'O Dan can't you see / That big old tree / Where the water's runnin' free / (Cool water, cool water) / As free as can be / Cool water, c-o-o-l w-a-t-e-r ...'

Once my eyes got used to the dark, I was surprised by how far I could see. Over to my right, the glow from the campfire helped me to keep my bearings as I slowly rode along. My horse was like a robot. He worked close to the herd and could obviously see it better than I could.

Every now and again some of the cattle would jump to their feet and make a short run, stop, look around, and return to the herd. And every time they did this, the pony under me would dive after them, usually without any prompting from me. It was a long night and I would have really enjoyed a smoke or two, but because it unsettled the cattle it wasn't allowed. I did have a bottle of cool water, though!

Towards morning many of the cattle were rising to their feet and wanting to graze. The idea soon caught on, and before I could do much about it, most of them were on the move. I tried to push them back. Did I say I pushed them? It was my pony, who seemed to know every move they were making, and kept well in front to stop them stampeding. And though it was still quite dark, not once did he lose his footing. I started to wonder why the boss even bothered to put a rider on this clever little horse, seeing that he was the one

Droving

doing all the work. We were like a concertina – push one lot back and another lot would be moving out. We were so busy that the time slipped away and before I knew it the sun was up.

Half-dead in the saddle, all I wanted to do was lie down somewhere and sleep. Quitting even crossed my mind. If this was droving, I'd had it! I had almost made up my mind to walk off the job, when Meg rode up to relieve me.

'Go get somethin' to eat an' catch some sleep, Coco Boy, you deserve it. I'll wake you up in two hours.' (What? I wanted to sleep for a week, at least!) But Meg must have noticed how bushed I was, because she added something that suddenly made me feel ten feet tall. 'You done the best last night, Coco. You never lost none. All them other buggers, they lost heaps, so now they have to go find 'em.'

Getting off the horse was hard enough, but sitting down was impossible. I was so saddle-sore that I could only stand or lie down, nothing in between. I was looking forward to having a wash after the long dusty hours on the horse, but when I asked young Mrs Pens about it, she just rolled her eyes and said she could tell I was new to droving. The only time I would get a wash, she said, was when we got to the dam, more than three days away. She pointed to the back of the wagon and told me I would find a basin of water with a piece of soap there, which I could use for my hands and face before a meal, but I wasn't to throw any water out because it was for everyone to use.

After breakfast they let me sleep for a bit more than two hours, flat on my back on the hard ground, with my spare clothes rolled up as a pillow under my head. It seemed like only minutes had passed before I was told to get up and help with the herd again.

The wagon was packed and my horse was waiting for me. As I gritted my teeth and pulled myself onto his back, old Mrs Pens handed me a newspaper parcel, which she told me to put into my saddle-bag. It was tucker for my lunch, she said.

The herd was already on the move, and when I caught up with the men Dave told me he wanted me 'pushing the tail' until I learnt more about droving. 'Where's your whip, boy?' he asked. When I replied that I didn't have one, he looked shocked. 'No bloody whip? Where the hell did they find you? Here, take mine. You do know how to use one, don't you?' Dave shook his head and clicked his tongue when I said that I didn't. 'Look, just keep those tails moving. I'll send Meg back to show you your job.' With that he rode away.

While he was getting Meg, I tried out the leather whip. I gave it a good swing, but all that happened was that it wrapped itself around the back leg of my horse. Next try, it went under his tail and he didn't like that much either. With my third attempt, I managed to wrap the thing around my face. Meg gave me lessons as we rode along, though, and pretty soon I was starting to master it – even getting to the stage where I could crack that whip above my head, or land it on any part of a slow-moving beast. We didn't stop for lunch, eating on horseback instead.

We were headed for Julia Creek, which wasn't more than 150 miles or so, but to keep the cattle fat, we couldn't drive them further or faster than about three or four miles a day. It was very slow going. And there was no stopping until it was time to make camp at about five or six o'clock, just before the sun went down. It always surprised me how quickly it got dark in this part of the country. One minute the sun would be shining, next thing it would be night-time. Now that we were moving through open land, the herd was easier to control, but we still had to take turns watching them at night.

The boss told me that I would be on watch from midnight until two-thirty, so I'd better get some sleep. I was to wake Bert after that, and he would take the shift until dawn. He said that Dave would be taking the first watch, then it would be his turn, and that he would then wake me for mine. Each night, said the boss, I was to make sure that I knew where everyone was sleeping, so that I didn't wake the wrong bloke.

It was very dark and even though we sat facing the campfire, whenever the Aborigines spoke all I could see was their big strong teeth and the whites of their eyes. They shone in the night, and I couldn't help remembering Rod at Tudor Downs.

The first few nights I lay awake for a while, but I soon trained myself to get as much sleep as I could, as quickly as I could, because some nights the cattle were restless and it took all of us to hold them together.

After four days of droving we reached the dam and I jumped in, clothes and all. It felt great. At last I was able to strip out of my filthy gear and give it a good wash. Acacia bushes make very good clothes hoists so, having spread my things out to dry, I splashed around in the lovely cool water for a while. Further along was Meg,

Droving

taking a bath and washing some clothes. Though I tried not to stare, it was pretty difficult to ignore her. Her firm breasts jiggled as she scrubbed and rinsed away the dirt from the drive.

Johnny and his family just rode straight past the dam, not stopping for a dip. This surprised me a bit, because one way or another, they seemed to be wearing clean clothes every second day and I'd had the impression that being clean was important to them. It suddenly dawned on me that the old woman was probably saving the water from the dishes until she had enough for the family to wash with, though it wasn't something I was ever likely to know for sure.

Dave and Bert didn't bother with a bath either. All Dave did when he reached the dam was dismount, fill his hat with water and pour it over his head. Then he rode on. Bert stopped, took his boots off, soaked his feet for a minute and then rode away. Next time we came to a dam it was the same pattern. You could smell those two men for miles up wind – their clothes were so stiff you could almost hear them creak when they moved.

Meg was waiting for me one night when I came back from my watch. She had stripped off her clothes and all I could see in the moonlight were her pointed breasts and her silky dark skin. She flashed her white teeth and whispered that I should follow her. A small distance from the camp was a smooth patch of ground, where she had spread a blanket on the grass, and soon she was pulling me down on top of her. We rolled around for a while, quietly exploring each other's bodies with none of the awkwardness I had felt with girls in the past, and then Meg said she felt like talking, asking me to tell her about myself.

Then it was her turn to talk. I learnt that Meg had been born in the Winton area and never been to school. She had been taken away from her parents at an early age, she told me bitterly, and been put to work on a station. She thought she had been about eleven at the time, and had her first child at twelve. When she noticed how shocked I was by this, she said that she'd had nine babies in total, but the white bastards had taken them all away from her right after birth. She had never seen any of them. The government had put them all into homes, she sobbed, and all she wanted was to get her babies back.

I felt sorry for her, and said so. Then she told me that I was the only man who had never tried to take her by force. Her first boss had been sixty years old and hadn't taken 'no' for an answer, treating her like an animal whenever he felt like it. Meg was sure that it was only because she was black. 'White girls, they lucky,' she sighed. 'They get to keep all their babies an' live in a proper house. They kin go any place in the world they want an' do what they like.'

And then Meg reached for me and, with a playful smile, said, 'Come on, Coco Boy – make me feel white.'

What was that? I sat up in fright, still on the blanket, with no clothes on. It was morning, and someone was throwing pebbles at me. It was the old woman, and she wasn't very happy.

Meg avoided me all that day and even that night at the campfire she turned her back to me, keeping close to Dave. She was making it very clear to everyone that she was staying away from me and I couldn't help wondering why. She had been the one to approach me, not the other way around. I got the feeling there was some jealousy on Dave's part, especially when every now and then he gave me a dirty look. And after that first time, Meg disappeared with Dave every night, not returning till morning.

It had taken us nearly eight weeks to bring the herd to Julia Creek, and on the last day of the trip, Johnny Pens came up to me and remarked what a nice morning it was. I agreed. The sun was just coming up, turning the sky a rosy pink and making the earth look new born.

Then he told me that tomorrow, after handing the cattle over, he would be taking on a new lot, on a drive that would take six months. 'Dave and Bert, they'll be stayin' with me,' he said. 'But, mate, I'm real sorry, but I can't keep you on – the women, they think you could be trouble. I'll get you back to Kynuna an' then you'll be on your own.'

Johnny put out his hand and I shook it.

'No hard feelings, mate,' he grinned.

11. Art of the game

There was no work in Kynuna, so I collected my car and drove back to Julia Creek. I parked behind the Railway Hotel and, after walking around town for a while, entered the bar. A hush fell over the room, just like in the westerns I had seen at the movies. More than a dozen pairs of eyes bored into mine as I looked from one face to another, wondering what the hell was going on.

Behind the counter stood a barmaid, with long black hair falling down around her shoulders like a veil. She couldn't have been more than eighteen, and I couldn't see all of her, but from the waist up she was gorgeous. We stared at each other for a moment and then she broke the spell, asking if she could help me.

I said I'd like to book a room, please, and she said she would have to go get the boss, but after taking a couple of steps she turned back. 'Did you want a drink first?' I ordered a beer and as she pulled it she kept staring at me in a funny way. Then she left the room to get the owner. During all this, the men at the bar hadn't spoken a single word. They seemed to be frozen in time, like statues, not even moving a hand to lift a glass to their lips. Up and down went their eyes, until I felt like saying 'Boo!' just to get a reaction.

The girl returned with the owner, a barrel-shaped man in his late forties. 'Will Bright is the name,' he said gruffly. 'You wanted to book in, did you?' I nodded. 'You're new in town, aren't you?' he asked.

'That's right, just got in from Kynuna.'
'Born there, were you?'
'No, I ...'
'Looking for work, are you?' interrupted a stern voice from behind me. When I turned around, I found myself looking at the long arm of the law. 'There's a strange car parked around the back. What's your name and is it yours?'
'Yes it is sir. My name is Ken Hall.'
'Where did you come from tonight?' he asked, his eyes narrowing with suspicion.

'Kynuna,' I answered.

'Got your licence?' I handed it over and as he checked it, he asked, 'Did you give anyone a lift?' After a moment he seemed satisfied and handed it back to me. 'I'm sure it's not him, Will,' the officer said. 'Look, son, a young bloke broke out of the Townsville lock-up this morning and was seen heading this way. He is very dangerous,' he announced to everyone in the room, 'so if anyone sees a stranger, let me know right away!' Then he nodded to Mr Bright and left the hotel.

'So – how long did you want the room for?' the owner wanted to know. I told him that I couldn't really say, but probably until I found myself another job. Mr Bright asked me if I could ride and I explained about the droving trip I had just done with Johnny Pens. 'Look,' he said, 'I can most likely get you on another droving trip. Whaddya reckon?' I thanked him, but said I'd have to think about it, because my backside was still pretty raw from the last one. At this, he smiled. 'End of next week a fellow will be here, goes by the name of Big Red. I'll tell him you might be interested. Here's the key to your room.'

It was the strangest thing. As soon as that key passed into my hands, the bar came back to life as quickly as if someone had flicked a switch. I had been accepted.

Johnny Pens had been true to his word and with his money lining my pocket I knew I would be all right for a while in that department. I ordered another beer and the girl called me 'sir' and asked me if I wanted to put it on my bill, or pay now. Taking a sip, I said, 'The bill', and wondered why she blushed whenever I looked at her. Her name was Nanette, she told me, then looked down at the floor as if she had said something embarrassing.

'Three beers down here, love,' called a big man sitting at the bar. Then he caught my attention by throwing his hat onto the floor. 'You want a drink, boy?' I walked up and showed him that I already had one, and he moved over to make room for me. 'Alex Rudd,' he introduced himself, telling me that he had been born in Julia Creek and made his living from working the shearing sheds. He was also a bareback riding champion, he informed me proudly. 'Hey, Bill!' he shouted. 'Over here! Like you to meet Ken. By the way, Ken,' he grinned, 'it's your shout.'

Bill Kumfer, better known as Old Bill, was a smiling man in his late sixties. He was the local taxi driver and kept a small office next door to the billiard parlour, just down the road a bit.

Art of the game

We sat and talked for a while like old friends and when the hotel doors were shut at ten o'clock, we all stayed on, drinking for a few more hours. When I finally went up to my room it was very late and I was looking forward to sleeping in a comfortable bed for the first time in weeks.

Sitting on my bed and removing my boots, I thought I heard the door hinge squeak and looked up to see the door to my room slowly being pushed open. Before I even had time to wonder who it could be, Nanette was standing in the doorway with another girl, this one a skinny blonde. Both were giggling behind their hands.

'Ken, this is Kym – she's a barmaid, too,' Nanette said, pushing the other girl forward so that I could see her. 'See what I mean, Kym?' Then they both yelled, 'See you later,' and ran down the corridor laughing. What sort of place was this?

In the morning I slept in and missed breakfast, so I walked across to the Bluebird Cafe where food was available any time you wanted it. After a short stroll around the block I decided that nothing much was happening in town, and made my way back to the Railway Hotel. The bar was open, but only one customer sat at the long counter. Nanette and Kym were working at opposite ends.

'A beer?' asked Nanette the minute I walked in. She called Kym over to pull it for me. Both girls leaned on their elbows and stared at me while I took a long swallow and then Kym put her head to one side.

'You're right, Nanette, he does have really sexy brown eyes.'

'Told you, didn't I? He's got that come-to-bed look, you know?'

I felt my cheeks grow hot and didn't know which way to turn, but just then Kym was called away to serve the other customer. Before she left, she said, 'Call me *any time*.'

But it was Nanette who interested me, not Kym. Very quietly I asked her what she was doing after work.

'Me?' she said, with a grin from ear to ear. 'Going out with my boyfriend!'

Old Bill could be found playing billiards at any time of the day at Roy Hampton's Billiard Parlour. Taxis in Julia Creek were not exactly in great demand, and his phone often sat on its dusty shelf for hours or days without ringing. The wall between his office and the billiard parlour was pretty thin, so Old Bill never had to worry that a call might come without his hearing it. On the other side of the parlour was the barber shop, followed by the SP bookie's room, which was also owned by Roy Hampton.

Hanging around the billiard table with Bill made a nice change from hanging around the hotel bar, so while I waited for Big Red to come to town, I learnt how to play.

Bill's shiny round head, with its horseshoe-shaped ring of grey hair, looked just like one of the billiard balls as he bent over the table and scattered them in all directions. He seemed to enjoy teaching me the 'art of the game', as he called it. As the days passed, he showed me how to set up my opponents to a stage where I knew I'd be able to beat them.

In this quiet town you had to find your entertainment wherever you could, and I guess that fleecing the out-of-towners was Bill's favourite sport. The taxi meant that Bill knew every time a stranger arrived in town; he would pray for them to enter the billiard parlour and when they did his fun would begin.

'Stranger in town, mate?' he'd say, after watching the fellow knock a few balls around for a while.

'Yeah.'

'Got time for a game?'

Naturally, Old Bill was too smart to show how good he was straight off. After losing a couple on purpose, he'd say something like, 'Damn! That's twice you've beaten me. I'll have to try and concentrate a bit harder. What about we play a game for dough, say ... ten shillings? How about it, mate?' And then Bill would let the stranger win the next three as well, with the money on the table now at £3.

'Oh, jeez, mate,' Bill would sigh, shaking his head sadly, 'you're too good. I'll have to pull out.' But as the stranger started stuffing the notes into his pocket, he'd suddenly say to him, 'Look, I prob'ly need shooting for what I'm gonna say, but I have to have a shot at getting me dough back. Double or nothing.'

Right on cue would come the reply: 'Put your money on the table, old man.'

Having hooked the stranger, Bill would proceed to pocket one ball after the other with ease, cleaning up nicely. Now and then an out-of-towner might have suspected that he'd been had, but he always felt sorry for the old man, who looked even older while he was playing. I'm sure he would have made more money from billiards than from driving passengers around in his battered taxi.

Art of the game

To my frustration, news came that the droving job was on hold for a few more weeks, and I found myself with nothing better to do than spend my time improving my billiard game. Bill never asked me to play for money, but before long we started taking turns at playing the strangers. At least my time at the tables was paying off – not surprising since I often spent eight hours a day practising my moves.

One Saturday I won over £100, though it wasn't all from billiards. I'd been doing what I usually did after a game, which was to march up to the SP bookmaker's room, look at the board and run my finger down until I found a horse starting at seven to one. The horses' names and all the other writing looked like double-Dutch to me, but the numbers were pretty easy to figure out, so I'd simply point at the board and put £2 on for a win. Then I'd go back to play another game, bet another £2 on a horse, and so on. It made it all the more exciting to be betting with my winnings from the table. By the end of that Saturday, seven of my bets had come home at seven to one, leaving me with £100! I was rich!

My car had been running well and one day three youths from town came to offer me a job. They wanted to go to Townsville for a week and would supply all the petrol and meals if I would drive them there and back again. It would make a nice change of scenery, I decided, and old Bill wasn't interested in being away for that long, so I wasn't pinching his business. The four of us piled into the car and set off.

It was dark by the time we arrived in Townsville and as we drove through the main street a man rushed out of the shadows and tried to flag us down. We just ignored him. A little further along a couple standing on the footpath called, 'Taxi!' It happened again and again, and it wasn't until I actually saw a taxi driving past that I realised what the problem was. The car I had bought in Brisbane was an old Townsville taxi! This explained a few things: the unusual (I had thought) paintwork of black, cream, green and brown, and also why the police had twice thought I was from Townsville.

We were all very tired and hungry after the long drive, so when I saw a cafe that seemed to be open, I pulled up to the gutter. As the boys got out a woman jumped into the back seat. 'Main Street, please, number forty-two.'

'Hey! What do you think you're doing, lady?' I said. 'Would you please get out of my car?'

'This is a taxi, yes?' she argued, not budging from her seat.

'Just take her, Ken,' one of the boys laughed. 'We'll order for you, so's you can eat when you get back.'

'Okay, lady, but you'll have to show me the way.'

Over the next week, whenever the boys wanted extra cash, I'd find myself driving around at night, taking fares. If you can't beat 'em, join 'em, as the old saying goes. There was no meter in my car, but everyone always seemed to know exactly how much they were supposed to pay, and it was an easy way to make money.

Townsville in 1959 was a bit of an eye-opener after being so long out west. Rock and roll fever had spread like a bushfire and some of the sights amazed me. Girls wore full-skirted dresses, with a froth of six to ten petticoats bouncing as they skipped along. The widgie hairstyle and the crew cut seemed to be as popular with the girls as with the boys, and from their lips came the words to Elvis Presley's 'Love Me Tender' and 'Every Day Love Gets a Little Closer' by the Everley Brothers. You could be standing anywhere, and girls would burst into song.

The three boys were making the most of their holiday in the city and their behaviour was very different to what I was used to. One of them wasn't successful in picking up girls on the street, so the rest of us were talked into going in search of a brothel. We were directed to the outskirts of town, where a row of five huts stood about eight feet off the ground, on tall wooden stumps. This was where the whores conducted their business. The routine, we had been told, was to drive slowly along the front of the huts, where the women stood in their open doorways with a bright light behind them. While the rest of us waited in the car, this one boy jumped out and ran up the steps of the nearest hut. The other two rolled their eyes and suggested that we all get comfortable, it was going to be a long night, but he'd hardly said the words before his mate was bounding down the steps and climbing into the car again.

His £2 had been well worth it, he assured us with a wink and a grin.

But most of our nights were spent parked on the top of Castle Hill, looking out over the city towards Magnetic Island. The moonlight glittered on the dark ocean and we sat and smoked and talked about faraway places we'd never been to.

It had been a rainy week, but on our last day we all agreed to go for a swim before driving back to dusty Julia Creek. As the three

Art of the game

of us walked down to the beach we noticed a small black dog already in the water, splashing around, but before we even got our feet wet, it just disappeared right before our eyes. One minute it was happily doing the doggy paddle, next minute it was gone. And, oh hell! Not far from the spot we'd last seen him was a dark fin heading out to sea.

No way! was the unanimous decision. The swim could wait till another time.

The car was packed and we were ready to leave. I noticed that the differential was leaking oil, so I made a quick visit to the Holden dealers. They replaced the gasket, and two hours later we were on our way back to Julia Creek.

We were about halfway there when the differential started making a noise. Pulling over, we found that the nuts and bolts around the housing of the diff were loose, causing all our oil to run out. It seemed the dealer hadn't tightened the bolts when the new gasket was installed.

No tools to fix the diff, two hours from a town. All we could do was sit on the side of the road and wait for help to come along. When it came, four hours later, it was in the form of a mail truck on its regular run. We were lucky – the driver had tools with him, and even some oil to replace what we had lost.

Back on the road, I was surprised but pleased to find that the noise had stopped, but less than twenty minutes later it more than made up for its short silence. The diff started to howl. We saw that it was full of oil and was still working, so we carried on anyway. In each town we approached after that, people could hear us long before they could see us. When we finally crawled howling into Julia Creek, I dropped the boys off and took the car around to Colin Mars Motors to see what he could do.

Word came that Big Red's droving trip was put off for another three weeks and I was starting to wonder if he really existed.

In the meantime I made a new friend, Alan Buck. Though he was in his sixties, we got along very well and when he suggested that I move out of the hotel into his place, I jumped at the idea. Alan had bought himself a small block of land in town and a caravan to live in that was big enough for both of us. And board was cheap – all it cost me was a bottle of rum when Alan got thirsty, which wasn't really all that often.

Two days later Alan's nephew, who was about my age, arrived in town and moved in with us. His handle was Jim Buck.

Jim Buck and I became good mates. We shared everything equally: meals, money and girls. Until one night, when walking to the local picture show, we noticed a small item lying on the footpath. We took turns kicking it along in front of us like a football, until Jim Buck finally bent down and picked it up. It was a bundle of notes, £65 all told.

'I'll put it in my pocket and we'll split it in the morning,' Jim grinned, but halfway through the movie he started feeling very sick, leaving me to watch the rest of the film by myself. 'Sorry, mate,' he told me, both hands clutching his stomach, 'I'm off to bed.'

I got home that night to find that my good mate had done the dirty on me. He was nowhere to be seen, and neither were the new blankets, shirts and travelling clock I'd just bought the week before.

Old Alan landed himself a job sixty miles away and asked me if I would drive him there. He would pay me, he said. When we got there he gave me a cheque and said I'd be able to cash it at the Bank of New South Wales in Julia Creek. But next morning when I handed it over, the teller frowned and asked me where I'd got it from. I explained that it was from Alan, the old man who lived in the caravan behind the post office. With this, I was told that it couldn't be cashed until the next day, and that I would have to leave it there in the meantime – something I didn't understand, because all my other cheques had always been cashed straight away.

That night as I walked through town, I heard, 'You! Be at the bank when the doors open in the morning!' It was the teller. Things were getting stranger and stranger. At ten the next morning the bank opened and when I entered, I almost fell over the bank manager, who was standing just inside the door.

'Young man,' he growled, 'don't you *ever* do this sort of thing again!' He pushed the cheque into my hand and wiped his fingers on his vest. 'We call this fraud! Do it again and we will call the police. Now, please leave the bank.' I glanced at the cheque and saw that it had pen lines drawn all over it, and some sort of scribble, but couldn't make out what was wrong. Arguing with the bank manager was useless. He insisted again that the cheque was a fraud and ordered me off the premises. It would have to remain a mystery for the time being.

Wedding photograph of my parents, Stanley Augustus Hall and Myrtle Sophia Hall (née Wittmann) in 1932.

At about six months old in 1940.

Family portrait around 1943 (*left to right*): Ian, Mum, Mark (baby), me, Dad and Steven.

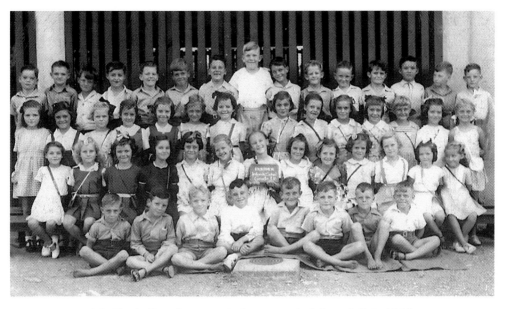

My Grade One class, age six (*top row, sixth from left*) in 1946.

At age ten, with my younger brother.

At age twelve, just before being admitted to Ward 1-A in 1952.

Early 1953 on my 'last holiday' at Maroochydore.

With Mum and my little brother in cyclonic weather.

Surf Life Saving Club at Maroochydore, Queensland in 1953.

Age sixteen: too old for bicycles, too young for a car—
(*below*) one of my first horses, the unstoppable Grey, in 1956.

At nineteen, just after returning from the west in 1959, with my first 'Whippet' utility.

> TUDOR DOWNS
> JULIA CREEK QLD
> 1957
>
> Dear Mum,
>   I Hop this letter fin us well I am
> OK the days are Hot at [night] I slep [with] no
> Blan on the [bed]
>   THE BOS Seems to bee a good man the [farm]
> is 1,00000 aer Big lots of Room Hear, Plesont
> Dinner.
>   We fed of How the Son and [farm] before dark
> time. I Have been too ked slep to cat
> Thy only Ked the longs one
>   MUM I sed [wen] to where can you [send] us get
> me some ONE I PUT ON FIST
> Work Hear I rue a long way for cooprow. Two
> baly at Home. No [one] Hear at Nyt [when]
> when it Comes ONLY SLEP TO DO.
> IT IS SUNDAY NO WORK HOP you can read
> my letter Hop to Hear from us [soon]
>
>   LOVE KEN xxx
> PS NO PLAIN FELCODE SEA DOC [soon]
> go to towne soon

One of my letters to my mother from Tudor Downs, 1957.

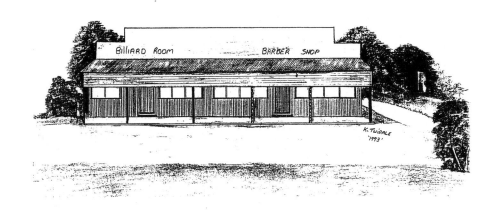

Four sketches by my daughter, Kim Twidale, who accompanied me out west in 1993, revisiting places from my days as a jackaroo: (*facing page*) my room at Kilterry; (*top*) Julia Creek; (*centre*) Tatts Hotel, Winton; (*bottom*) shearing shed at Kilterry.

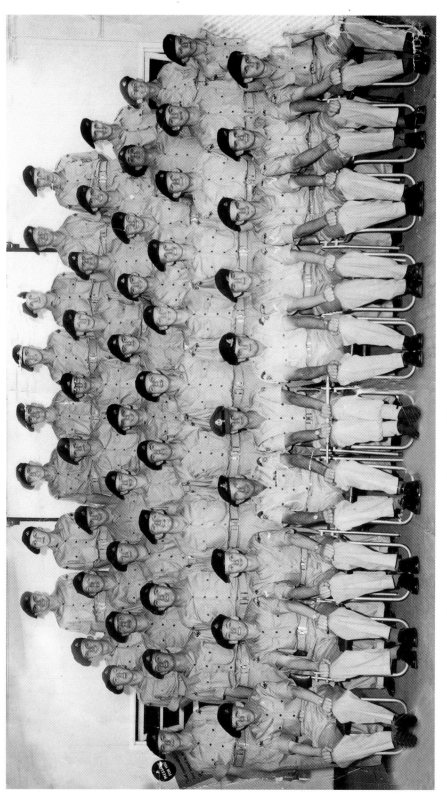

One of the boys. National Service, 1959 (*second row from back, fourth from left*).

Tug-o'-war (*third from left*).

The proud soldier, Wacol Army Barracks.

Me with a mate, two of the last intake for Nasho.

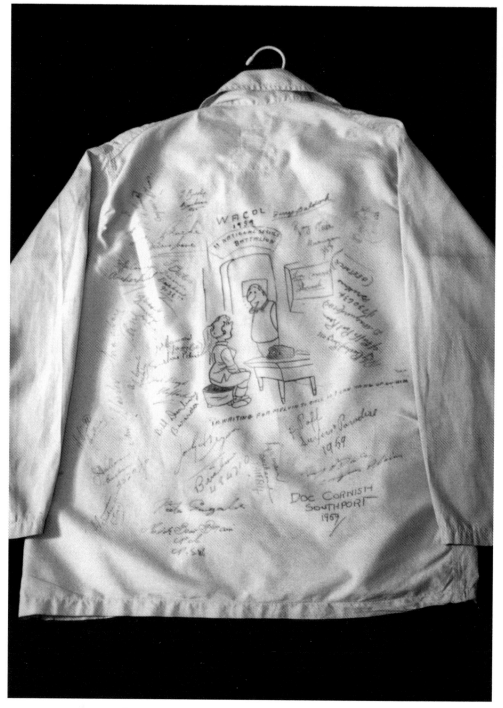

My pyjama top from National Service, signed by my mates on our last day, 1959.

Grandad George Wittman with Mum in Hervey Bay in 1961.

At the beach, age twenty.   At Jan's place, Mitchelton, 1962.

North Stradbroke Island in 1963: (*above*) accommodation huts;
(*below*) workers beside the dredge.

(*Above*) 'The Old Girl', aka The Dredge; (*below left*) the dredge's nozzle, which draws in the sand; (*below right*) a view over the island.

Photo booth portraits, Janice at 15, me at 19.

Our wedding photo, 14 March 1964: Kenneth William Hall and Janice Shirley Hall (née Greer).

In the saddle, 1965.

Art of the game

Now that Alan wasn't around, I booked myself into the Railway Hotel again and settled down on a stool. Nanette was working the bar and stood watching me while I downed a beer.

'Damn those sexy eyes of yours!' she said after a while. 'Can you pick me up at nine in the morning and take me somewhere?'

At five to nine I pulled up out front and she climbed in. I asked her where she wanted me to take her, but all she said was, 'Out of town, I'll tell you when to stop.' We drove for a few minutes and then Nanette said, 'This'll do. Just stop under that big tree there.' I cut the motor and started to get out of the car, but she stopped me. 'No, let's stay in the car. Ken, please look at me.'

Looking at Nanette was easy, something I had no trouble doing. She leaned over and brushed my mouth with hers, lightly, like a butterfly. Then she pulled away and started telling me about her boyfriend, who was really her fiancé, because they'd been engaged for a year and a half, and not once during that time had he ever made a pass at her. Nanette was afraid that maybe there was something wrong with her, that maybe men found her undesirable for some reason.

'Bloody Kym has all the fun, you know. She has it all the time. It's not fair!' she cried. I guessed she was looking for reassurance or she wouldn't be telling me all this, so I didn't waste any time showing her how attractive and sexy she seemed to me. Nanette seemed happy at my eagerness to please her, letting me kiss and fondle her, while she bit my neck. But just when I was starting to get somewhere, she shouted at me to stop and pushed me away so roughly that I cracked my head on the side window. 'No, no,' she wailed, 'this is wrong! Please, take me back.'

'Why?' I asked, feeling pretty frustrated. One minute I was up in the clouds, next thing I was down in the dumps, all without warning.

'Because I'm getting married in two weeks,' Nanette sobbed. I didn't say anything, just put my hand on the ignition key, but she stopped me. 'Please, wait, I'm sorry, I know I shouldn't have ... look, I know!' she said, brightening up, 'when we get back, I'll get Kym to do it for you.'

'Forget it,' I said, turning the key and bringing the motor roaring to life. To top it off, there was now a loud knocking noise coming from under the bonnet and in my mind's eye I could see the pounds flying out of my pocket. What next?

After dropping off Nanette, who had started crying again and worrying about who might have seen us driving off together – Kym, for one – I drove around to Colin Mars Motors and got the bad news that the motor was wrecked and would have to be stripped. He told me that if I came back first thing in the morning and gave him a hand pulling the engine out, it would cut a fair bit off the final bill.

Back at the Railway Hotel, Kym was working the bar. She told me cheerfully that Nanette had left; she had come back from her drive with me and quit her job. Not only that, but she'd heard 'the whole story' from her friend and I needn't think she was going to sleep with me, just because Nanette had promised.

If Kym had expected me to be upset by this, she would have been disappointed.

'Good,' was all I said.

Down at the pool-room the next day, Old Bill was getting ready to go fishing. He invited me to come along and by early morning we were on the road to Kynuna in his taxi, with Bill following the stock route. Soon we came to a small waterhole in the middle of nowhere, no more than about fifteen feet in diameter. There were no trees for shade. Bill passed me a hand line, on it a float with a hook just under it.

'The bait's in the matchbox, Ken, just be careful you don't go and get bitten!' Bill warned, so I put the matchbox down and waited until he was ready to use it. I watched him open the box very slowly, until a hairy centipede started creeping out; when it was about an inch out of the matchbox, Bill shut the box gently, trapping the centipede. He threaded it onto the hook, then shut the matchbox fully, cutting off a piece of its body. This little trick worked well for Bill, but not for me. I was using exactly the same kind of bait, but mine must have had a sign on it warning the fish not to come near. Over the next two hours I didn't have a single bite, but Old Bill had five beauties. 'This lot'll feed us for a week,' he said with a chuckle. 'Lucky we're not counting on you, my friend.'

Things were looking bad for me back in town. No work and no car – it wouldn't be ready for a couple of weeks and then I owed Colin Mars for the repairs. As if that wasn't enough, the next car payment was due as well.

But sometimes, just when you start to wonder where your next meal will be coming from, something happens to turn it all around.

Art of the game

With my last £2 I walked into the billiard parlour and, using all the tricks Old Bill had taught me, made a killing. I left that place with well over £100 pounds burning a hole in my pocket. It was enough to pay more than half the bill for the motor and get the car payment out of the way; with the balance I bought myself two new shirts, pants and black shoes, and booked myself into the Gannon. I'd had more than enough of the Railway Hotel.

The Gannon was a real eye-opener. Maybe it was my new clothes that did it, but I found myself rubbing shoulders with bankers and their staff, and chatting with office workers from the woolbroking firm. Many of these men sat and drank at the same tables where they later ate their meals, rather than up at the bar. The room was large and airy, with some of the tables big enough to seat twenty, the chairs and tables French polished, the settings on them heavy silver. It was more of a dining room than a lounge bar, something I hadn't noticed on my first visit to the Gannon a year or more earlier, when I had been too sick to look around.

Just about every time I entered that room I was offered a job. Most of these were impossible for me to accept, because they would have involved reading and writing and given away my secret, but it was nice to be treated with respect for once in my life. Jobs that might have been suitable I knocked back; with money under my belt I was quite happy to wait for the droving trip to start.

'Excuse me, Ken, would you like to sit at our table tonight?' It was the teller from the bank. I took a seat and wondered what was coming next. It didn't take long. 'Look, I'm very sorry about the mistake that was made recently. I would like to apologise on behalf of the bank, and I'd like to say, that if you want to open a savings account with us, I'll be only too glad to do the paperwork.'

This was good news. 'Okay,' I said, 'I'll come round when you open and deposit that cheque.'

'No, no, Ken,' the teller whispered nervously. 'I told you, that cheque is no good. Get rid of it, please!'

Well – I was still stumped – what the hell was really wrong with the damn thing? Did they think I had stolen it or forged it or something? Or wasn't there any money in Alan's account to cover the cheque? Not being able to read what had been scribbled onto it at the bank, I was tempted to show it to somebody and ask what it said, but I wasn't willing to risk it. Nobody in this town was ever going to know that I was a dummy!

What Next You Bastard

I enjoyed the company of these men. They made me feel at ease. And if they started talking about things I knew nothing about, I either excused myself and left for a while, or nodded wisely and kept quiet. The amazing thing about being silent is that everybody around you assumes you know more than you really do, and more often than not, that you agree with them. It was during one of these times that I finally learnt the answer to my mystery cheque. Alan (or maybe his crooked nephew) had somehow 'found' himself a cheque book belonging to a customer whose account had been closed years before. No wonder the bank didn't want to touch it.

Ordering meals wasn't hard – whenever the person two down from me had ordered, I would pick up the menu, pretend to read it, then order the same as he had. I became a mimic. 'Specials of the Day' were always listed somewhere in the bar area, so I'd seat myself out of sight of the board, giving me a good excuse to ask what the special was, then say, 'Okay, that sounds pretty good.' Another trick I perfected was to pretend I couldn't make up my mind because everything on the menu looked so tempting. Without fail, someone would recommend a certain favourite meal and I would hesitate for a moment, then agree to try it for myself. I also trained myself to remember previous meals and ask for them without looking at the menu. If, now and again, the particular meal was not available that day, I would become thoughtful and ask whether they didn't have something similar. They usually did.

I never went hungry just because I couldn't read, and I never gave the game away.

Paying for meals in everyday pubs was usually no problem, because they would mention the amount and you just paid it. But in the better type of establishment, such as the Gannon's lounge, the bill was presented in writing and I had to rely on the total being correct. Reading numbers was still slightly easier for me than reading words, but I didn't always get it right. Luckily, as a guest of the hotel, all that was needed from me was my signature on the bottom of the bill, to be paid later. Each night I signed the bill and then slipped two shillings into the waiter's hand. And every night he said, 'Thank you, sir, anything you want, just ask.'

It was a great feeling and I think I could have kept on playing the gentleman forever, but Big Red finally came to town and it was time to think about doing some serious work again.

12. Big Red

Will Bright at the Railway Hotel led me to a red-haired giant at the bar. He was a mountain of a man, standing well over six and a half feet tall, and he must have weighed in at around fifteen stone. A bushy, fiery beard matched his flaming red hair exactly, and even if I hadn't already known his name, I would have recognised him anywhere.

'Big Red, I'd like you to meet Ken Hall, grandson of that famous bushranger, Ben Hall.'

I laughed at the introduction and shot out my hand. The meaty paw that took it was surprisingly lifeless, and limp as a dead fish. Touching it gave me the shivers and I couldn't stop myself wiping my hand on my pants when I took it back, as if trying to rid myself of something nasty.

'Ben Hall, hey?'

'No, not related at all,' I said.

'Two beers, Will,' he called, not taking his eyes off my face. 'How many trips you been on before, Ben?'

'Sorry – the name is Ken, not Ben. Just the one trip with Johnny Pens.'

'Thanks, Will. Drink up, Ben, you're hired. I pay top money for good men,' Big Red went on, taking no notice of what I'd said about my name. It was hard to tell whether he was a bit thick, or just taking the mickey out of me, but I decided to let it pass. 'This trip'll be over two hundred miles, so you'll be needing a good swag,' he said. My swag and my whip had been stolen but when I told him this he shrugged it off. 'Buy me a beer, boy, and I'll get you a new one. No, make that six beers.' After I had ordered the drinks to keep coming, Big Red said, 'Tomorrow, go to the store and ask for Sam Crawford, he'll fix you up; just tell him Big Red'll spring for it. Hey, lookee here! It's the rest of the boys.'

Five men, all over thirty, walked up to the bar. There were no handshakes this time, just a grunt from each as Big Red introduced them to me. They were a mean-looking bunch, making me wonder what it was going to be like working with them all. Funny thing – I noticed after a while that Big Red was knocking back the beer like there was no tomorrow, but whenever it came his turn to shout, he managed to con someone else into buying the round. Every time.

Early next morning my first stop was at Colin Mars' place to tell him to put the car repairs on hold. Next stop was getting myself a new sleeping bag, a simple thing, just a piece of canvas sewn up on three sides, with a small gap left to slide into, and a blanket stitched to the inside as a lining.

Julia Creek's one and only taxi, driven by Old Bill, must have looked like a tin of sardines as we left town, with seven men and one youth squeezed into a 1956 Holden! We couldn't even shut the boot, it was bulging so with all the gear we had crammed into it. Two and a half hours on dusty, rocky roads later, we arrived in the Channel Country, just outside McKinlay. This was where we expected to meet the cattle.

'They should be *here*, dammit! We couldn't miss *twelve hundred head*,' Big Red thundered, bashing his huge fist on the dash. 'Just drive slowly, they must be round the next corner.' A few more corners and a stream of foul language later, we came onto them so suddenly that Bill had to stand on the brakes, bringing the car to a skidding halt. I couldn't see a damn thing because my head was jammed between two large sets of shoulder blades, but by the time I was able to get out of the taxi, Big Red was already off and running, yelling and waving his huge hat at some riders in the distance. From where I was, he looked a lot like the kangaroo of the same name.

Station workers from Chatsworth had worked the stock for the past two days, but they weren't set up for droving. They were a good few days behind time with these Zebu cattle, which should have been in open country by now instead of wandering around in the brigalow.

Four riders appeared out of a creek bed. Dismounting, they handed their horses over to us and I ended up with one over sixteen hands high. 'Those bloody cows are yours from here on! We're goin' home,' one fellow said, marching straight to the taxi.

'But we need a count! You can't piss off yet!' screamed Big Red, still running around in angry circles.

'Forget it, mate – they're all yours! The boss from 'Stralian 'States will be out in the morning.'

There was nothing for it! The men were gone, whisked away by Old Bill, who looked pretty happy to have another big fare for the trip home. I was beginning to wish that I had gone back with them.

Big Red

'Where's the bloody packhorses? Shit, Ben, ride round and see if you can find the other horses. Frank – take Phil and Scotty and get this bloody herd together. Shit! This *really* pisses me off!' Big Red was throwing a tantrum and doing some kind of wild tapdance on his hat. Laughing at him would have been suicide.

Rounding up the herd and keeping it together was a nightmare. We had found about twenty horses, but the trouble was no one knew which ones were the packhorses and which ones the night-horses. There was no time for eating or sleeping on this first night. My mount certainly couldn't see in the dark, as I discovered the hard way. About a fifth of the cows had had calves taken off them only a few days before and all they wanted to do was go home; their udders were bursting with milk and, as they walked, it dripped and squirted onto the ground.

At sunrise Jack the cook provided some sandwiches he had put together, but it was nine o'clock before the head stockman and the manager from Australian Estates arrived. It took us most of the day to get a true count and finally Big Red, riding up front on the biggest horse, took off his hat, waved it in the air, and announced that we were ready to go. 'Move 'em out, boys!' he bellowed.

Two days of hard going finally brought us out of the Channel Country, with all its little crossings and streams, and we all relaxed a bit, glad to know that the way would be easier from now on. And, for a while, it was. I was 'riding tail' again, which meant bringing up the rear and keeping the herd moving forward. My skill with the whip was improving day by day and I had mastered it to the point where I could crack a fly sitting on the ear of any beast, without taking a hair from the ear. I was just starting to enjoy my job as a cattle drover, when all hell broke loose.

It happened in a way no one could have expected. The leading animals just turned around and headed back the way they had come, for no reason that we were ever able to figure out. One minute the beasts were plodding along in one direction, next minute the front ranks just turned tail and started trying to break through the herd. We had over twelve hundred head spread out over the stock route, with those in front colliding and merging with those following behind. Jack and Tom were a few miles further up the road preparing the next camp site, and didn't have any idea of what we other five riders were faced with.

What Next You Bastard

Whips cracked frantically, riders screamed at each other, horses pushed shoulder to shoulder with cattle becoming more angry and confused by the minute. We had to round them up in circles, trying to separate the rebels, who were growing in number as more and more joined them, from those who were still moving in the right direction. It was worse than a normal stampede because, rather than all running in one direction, we had bewildered animals bolting off every which way, bellowing and snorting.

Hours later we were still no better off. Our horses were so exhausted that they couldn't even break into a trot. The screaming voices had faded to hoarse whispers and our arms hung limply at our sides, worn out from swinging the whips over our heads. It had all been for nothing. We would just have to accept defeat.

'Fall back!' came the cry. It was Big Red, larger than life and with a face so flushed, it was hard to see where his beard ended and his skin began. 'Fall back, dammit!' So we formed a curved line well behind the crazed cattle and, to my amazement, they slowed down enough to still the panic; finding that they were cornered, they hung their heads low and moved forward once more. 'We've beaten the bastards!' Big Red laughed with relief. 'Now let's get going again!'

The third shift was mine that night, on a piebald gelding that had slightly better eyesight than my last one. The clouds shifted and, like a spotlight, the moon lit up the sleeping herd, showing me something that made me very nervous: the cows, which had camped with both legs under them in the Channel Country, were now lying with one foot out in front. I knew I would have to give them my full concentration or be faced with another rebellion.

To add to our troubles, we had to wait for any cows that were calving. Straight after they gave birth, we had to get them up on their feet with whips, and the horses would then start pushing them forward by leaning their shoulders against the beasts and forcing them to move along. The newborn calves would stand up on shaky little legs and try to follow their mothers, often managing a quarter of a mile or so before staggering and falling to the ground. It was sad to see them left behind, but with a herd this size there wasn't much you could do about it. Keep up, or die trying.

Calves that were born at night had the advantage of being fed by their mothers before heading out on the route, but even these usually lived for only a few days before their spindly legs gave out and they collapsed along the way, dying where they fell. At night some of the new mothers walked out of camp and tried to head back to find their offspring. We turned them back, but now and then we'd strike a cow that just couldn't be stopped. Too much disturbance while trying to head off one of these determined cows could easily start up a stampede and the risk just wasn't worth it, so the only way to deal with this situation was to wait and give the cow some time and distance before riding out after her and leading her back at the point of a whip.

Right then I was keeping my eye on one particular cow. She was black, with a full white face and a white line around her neck. She was of very small build, her belly nearly dragging on the ground. When I first noticed her, she was dawdling at the tail end of the herd, just a few paces in front of me. I rode up alongside her and let my horse give her a little nudge. The little cow stopped dead in her tracks, turned, looked straight at me and gave me a look that could only have meant, 'Come on – make me'. At this I raised the whip above my head and laid it lightly across her back. Before I could even think of doing it again, she had broken into a run, overtaking all the cattle in front of her until she was no longer in sight. This girl could move! And from that day on she always tried to be up front with the leaders.

But time was not on her side; the weight of her calf was slowing her down a bit more each day until she ended up near the rear once more, along with a couple of the old leaders who were also tiring from the endless pace. When she reached the back line, she knew that the whip was waiting for her and tried to keep just out of its reach, which is the main aim when driving a herd such as this.

My little lady was due to calve and one day I saw that her water had broken and two tiny feet and a bit of nose were protruding from her. Luckily we had just reached the place where we'd be camping for the night and I saw her walk off about fifty yards, where she laid herself down and gave birth to an all-black heifer. Although she had been a quiet cow until now, the moment her calf was born she developed an ear-piercing bellow that could be heard all around the camp. Within an hour, she had that calf up and walking beside her and doing everything that she wanted it to do.

By sunrise, cow and calf had positioned themselves in the middle of the herd, well away from the dreaded sting of the whip. And far from falling behind, the little calf seemed to grow stronger each day, until the two could be found amongst the front lines. The day even came when my black and white lady became the lead cow. Whenever I came near, she seemed to sense it, turning her head and looking over her back at me, then giving a strong bellow which I'm sure in her own special language told me to 'get stuffed'.

When Jack ran out of meat we were ordered to muster together the six steers that ran with the herd. We headed them towards a distant arabakka tree in which Big Red was waiting with his rifle. He was going to choose one and shoot it. When he had made his selection, a nice fat beast just to the left of where I waited on my horse, Big Red took aim and fired but missed. All six animals scattered in fright. Twenty minutes later he was ready to try again. This time he was successful, bringing the steer down with a single shot.

'Ben,' he said, 'you stay and help Jack with the butchering.'

'Hey, look! Your arm – it's bleeding pretty bad, Ben,' Jack pointed. Halfway along my right arm was a gash about three inches long, with blood pouring freely out of it. I hadn't even noticed! I was covered in blood. My saddle, my horse, everything had blood on it. 'You've been shot, m'boy, Red's first shot must've hit you.'

'Bullshit,' I replied, not wanting to believe it. I hadn't felt a thing, so how could I possibly have been shot?

'No, just have a look around,' Jack insisted, 'the only tree is that one where Red shot from, so it couldn't have been a branch. And the rest's all grass – there's no stones or anything sharp.'

My legs turned to jelly. I couldn't stand. 'A bullet! I could have a bullet in me!'

Jack grabbed me before I went down, holding onto my shirt. 'No, Ben, no bullet,' he chuckled, 'you were lucky, just a graze by the looks of it. But I bet you it was that first shot that done it to you. We better tear your shirt up for a bandage.'

We had packed most of the meat into the saddle-bag when I noticed Jack staring at something over in the long grass. 'Three of them – see there, Ben – three dingoes. Each night I see them just a short distance from the camp, one dog and two bitches. And the dog hasn't got a tail.' I asked Jack if he was going to catch them, but he shook his head. 'No, Ben, they been following us since the first night. Tonight they'll have a great feed, but, m'boy, tomorrow night they'll be at our camp site.'

'No way! They could live here for months like kings on this steer,' I argued, pointing at the carcass we were leaving behind us. 'Why would they bother coming to our camp?'

'I bet you, m'boy, tomorrow night, the same three will be just outside our camp. Been trapping them for years, boy, I know every move they'll make. You see, this kill is in the open and there's nowhere for them to hide in the daylight. Cattle bones are too big. They can't run and carry them through the tall grass, they'd have to drag them.'

'What about when they kill a kangaroo? They run with them in their mouth.'

'Oh yeah? You've seen them do that, have you?'

'Well,' I shrugged, 'not really, no.'

Jack nodded and narrowed his eyes. 'The only thing they can run with, m'boy, in their mouth, is a small bone or a dead cat.'

'What about their own pups?' I asked him.

'No Ben, not real far – they get too heavy, boy. Mum might drop it, then she has to pick it up again. But a cat has very small bones, when it's a fresh kill its body is very flexible, it kind of curls up real small and the dog can run without tripping over it.'

I told Jack about the cats at Tudor Downs and his eyes lit up. 'That's right, m'boy, anytime I want to set a trap for dingoes, I get cats from around the town. Works like a charm!'

Just halfway between Kynuna and Julia Creek a cattle buyer from the meatworks caught up with the herd. Earlier in the trip, some station owners had looked at the cattle and asked the price of a cow with calf. They had sent a man to make the deal.

While the buyer was inspecting the herd and making his selection, I was having lunch, but I met him when he came back to the camp. With a shock I realised that I knew this bloke. It was Kevin, the one I had driven to Brisbane with.

He recognised me at the same time. 'G'day, mate!' he grinned. 'What are you doing on this trip?'

'Droving,' I replied. 'What's it look like?'

'Shit, mate! I would have rather done the deal with you,' said Kevin.

'What deal is that?'

'Gee, mate, you could've bought the cows for thirty shillings each and then sold them to me for £12 a head. I just bought a hundred

What Next You Bastard

of them!' Kevin saw the look on my face as I struggled to figure out how much I could have made. 'See, what we do is split the difference and no one's to know. Sorry, mate, you missed out this time.'

Red and Kevin shared a bottle of rum to celebrate the profit they had just made: about £500 each. Lifting the bottle high into the air, Kevin called out as I returned to the herd, 'Next time, mate.'

One night the weather changed. Lying on the ground in my swag I could smell rain, but when I looked up at the sky there was not a cloud to be seen. I was out in the open on a slight rise, with my feet pointing downhill. Rolling over, I soon fell asleep.

I dreamed about swimming in the turkey's-nest and it seemed uncomfortably real. I woke up to find that my swag was half-full of water and rain was pouring down. Water was running down the slope and straight into my sleeping bag. Everything I owned was sopping wet, from the clothes I was wearing to the gear I always kept with me. There was nowhere I could go to escape the rain and I had no choice but to lie there in my watery bed.

I was still awake when it came my turn to do the night watch. When I climbed out of my sleeping bag I found that my boots were full of water. The rain had stopped now, but the ground had turned boggy and every step I took added another layer of thick heavy mud to my boots so that soon they were twice their normal size. Walking was impossible. My horse's reins were dragging in the mud and I managed to slip them over his head, but when I went to put my boot into the irons, it wouldn't fit because of all the mud. My hands were shaking from the cold as I fumbled in my pocket, looking for my penknife. When I finally managed to get it open, I scraped some of the mud off my boot. It helped. With a mighty heave I made it up into the saddle, only to feel the awful squelching of my waterlogged pants.

'Come on, horse, let's move it! Come on,' I urged, but my horse was having problems of his own, with the mud sucking at his hooves with every move. He took a step or two and then stopped and looked at me as if to say, 'Whose silly idea was this?' 'It's not my idea,' I told him, 'it's the bloody boss's. Now come on, the cows are walking, let's get you into a trot.'

We were getting the cows to turn back, but before we had finished the mud around my horse's feet brought him down nose first. I found myself sliding down and over his neck, then his head. My face was buried up to my ears in the thick claggy mud. I wasn't hurt, but pretty shaken up by the time I stood up again and the poor horse was back on his feet too, both of us covered in mud from ears to tail. With the saddle coated in grass and mud, climbing back on took all of my skill and most of my strength.

Half an hour before daylight and my mind was on nothing but getting clean, warm and dry. The time just before dawn always seems to be the coldest part of the night and this night was no exception. It was so cold out there in the open, with the temperature below freezing point, that my clothes were frozen stiff to my body. My bladder was full and though the ground was only four feet below me, I knew that if I climbed down now I would never make it back up again. When the sun came out after what felt like several hours but couldn't have been, there was not a cloud in sight. Riding into camp I saw that everyone had their clothes hanging on the one and only bush to dry out.

'Where's my clothes?' I asked.

'Over there where you left them,' yelled Tom, riding off.

'There's no water left to wash your gear, mate,' said Scotty, a man who reminded me of my father – always disgustingly clean, no matter what.

Sure enough, my sleeping bag and gear were still where I had left them, lying in a sodden heap. When I bent down to pick them up, I saw a slight movement in the swag. Slowly I lifted it, and two very large centipedes fell out. I had obviously not closed it properly. Then I put my hand inside and felt something warm, which gave me such a fright (What if it's a snake?) that I dropped the swag and jumped backwards. Something had touched my arm – and it was still there. Looking down I saw a field mouse sitting on my sleeve! My laugh of relief gave that poor little mouse all the reason it needed to do the best long-jump of its life.

Everything was soaked. I started to wring out my things but the boss stopped me. 'No time for that, Ben,' he growled, 'go get a feed. We're moving off in fifteen minutes.'

Tom suggested that I take old Bones, one of the spare horses, and hang my clothes off him while I rode. We must have looked a sight, the pair of us: I had draped my pants over his big bony rump, my shirt and towel across the length of his neck, and wore my underpants and singlet on my hat. Mum would have laughed her head off, saying that now she finally knew what a real clothes-horse looked like! It was slow going, but with the sun shining, all I could think about was enjoying the warmth. I was finding it hard to stay awake, and suddenly found myself landing on the ground with a painful thump. Bones was bucking and squealing at a small horse-stinger buzzing around his head. My pants had slipped off his rump and were being trampled under his hooves.

'Didn't they tell you?' laughed Red, riding past. 'He don't like stingers. If one comes anywhere near him he goes bananas.'

We were nearing the waterhole where Old Bill had taken me fishing – it was only a mile or so away – and the six of us, all but Scotty, stank to high heaven. 'Mr Clean' refused to be with the rest of us, preferring to take his meals and rest up wind. When he rode past, you could just about see a bed of roses riding into the sunset.

As we came close to the Tudor Downs turn-off, I had an idea.

'Red,' I said casually, 'I was just wondering – how much do you think I'll get in wages when we're finished?'

'Around a hundred quid if you stick with me to the end.'

'Can I buy some cows at thirty shillings?'

'Boy, you can buy as many as you like.'

'Look – I'd like to buy a hundred pounds' worth. I'm sure old Paul Wilkinson would let me run them on the back of his place, and ... '

'Forget it, kid! I can't sell them to you,' Big Red interrupted. When I asked why not, he said, 'Because it's my money you'd be using. And Paul Wilkinson, you said? No thank you. Now, piss off and get back to work.'

We were less than two hours from the waterhole where Jack and Tom had been sent to set up the night camp. Now a rider was coming our way. It was Tom.

'No water for the cattle, boss, the hole is boggy. Better to make camp here before the cows get a whiff of it.'

Twenty hours had passed since the last waterhole and it was a good three days' ride before the next one. Red's order went out: 'Right-o! We're camping here tonight and everyone's doing a double watch. If these bloody cows get so much as a sniff of water, they'll make a break for it!'

Everyone was disappointed when we passed the boggy patch that had once been a waterhole. I couldn't believe it. Only a few months earlier it had been filled with fresh water and jumping with fish. Even the cattle looked sad as they plodded past, kept in line by the watchful riders. My little black cow looked accusingly at me as she walked past, dropping her head as she nudged her calf along.

That night the herd was restless. As I sat beside the campfire eating, I heard a movement behind me. It was Jack, sneaking off into the dark, with a tin tray in his hands. I followed. 'What are you doing, Jack?'

'Doing what I do every night - leaving some scraps for the dogs, with a bit of tea.'

'Tea?' I said, thinking this fellow must have gone mad.

'They're thirsty, too,' he said.

'I never saw any dogs from that time you showed me them,' I told Jack.

'Well, m'boy, they've been with us from the start. And I can prove it, too.'

'Go on, then,' I challenged.

'Not now. But in the morning, when we move out, keep looking back at this camp site and you'll see them.'

Back at the camp, Jack was doing the washing up, with Scotty helping him. When they had finished, Jack used the dishwater to wash his face and hands, then Scotty took the basin, moved into the darkness, stripped and took a bath. Now I knew the secret of his cleanliness. But it didn't stop there. Scotty placed the basin on the ground and stood back while a small white head with a line on its neck sucked up the remaining water, mooed in thanks, and trotted off. Two riddles solved in one night! Now I knew how that little black cow had managed to keep up her strength all this time!

When we moved out the next morning, I remembered to turn around and look back at the campsite. Sure enough, three dingoes were scavenging around in the distance. Jack had been right on the ticket.

13. The mob

It was another two days before we saw water again, and learnt that we'd be camping here for two days. It felt like a holiday. Once the cattle had filled their bellies, the one lonely windmill and one long cattle-trough filled with water became bath, kitchen sink and washing machine. I stripped off all my clothes and lowered myself into the trough, the bitter bore-water slowly taking away the sting of my saddle rash. With a small bar of soap I washed my dirty clothes and noticed that I was sharing the water with my little black cow, who stood at the far end, watching me between sips.

As I washed between my legs I felt a strange lump. Kneeling up, I saw that a very fat tick had attached itself to my scrotum. I was so horrified that without stopping to think I grabbed it with my fingers, pinched hard, and ripped it out. It wasn't a clean job – the head of the tick was still buried in the blood vessel, but there wasn't much I could do about it.

After two days of pain, I finally used a thorn from a prickly acacia bush to dig out the head, but a few hours later on my horse, I felt a stickiness between my legs. I dismounted. Staring at me was a sight I wasn't ready for: my riding pants were soaked with blood. When I pulled them down, I could see why. The wound from my little operation was squirting blood. It took a good fifteen minutes of pressure before it stopped, and by then I was in no mood to get back in the saddle. Still, I had quite a bit of catching up to do, so I took a deep breath and rode after the others.

Julia Creek was only two miles away and we would be spending one night just outside the town before moving on. Big Red and Jack left early to get the yards set up, as the cattle had to be inoculated against redwater fever, and the stock that had been sold to Kevin had to be cut out from the rest of the herd.

Just on dusk, the taxi from town pulled up at the camp. Tom and Scotty were told that the boss wanted them in town. The rest of us were to hold the herd together until morning.

The mob

'It's not so bad, really,' I said, 'at least we have a fence on three sides of them.'

'Whaddya mean, not so bad?' yelled Frank. 'The bastard's there in the pub, getting drunk! Piss 'em! I'm riding into town.' Phil and I watched him go, knowing that it was now up to the two of us to watch the herd. Sleeping would be out of the question.

In the morning Frank and Tom returned in the taxi. 'We're to move them into the yards,' Tom told us.

'But what about our breakfast?' I asked, glad that the night was over.

'No time. Let's move them out.'

By nine that morning the cattle were in the yards, but there was still no boss, no cook, and no Scotty. The Department of Primary Industries men were ready, and the four of us worked well into the afternoon before we were finished.

'I still think that little black cow and calf should be in Kevin's count,' said one of the DPI hands.

'No! That cow's mine. She stays with the herd.' I had just given my first order and it felt good.

'Okay, mate, she's yours,' he shrugged.

An hour before sunset Big Red and the rest of the boys returned. They were rolling drunk. 'Move 'em out!' yelled Red.

'Don't be silly,' I argued, knowing that a herd was never moved at this time of day.

'Silly?' roared Big Red, his face like thunder. 'You call me silly? You little snot-faced bastard! Come here!' He lunged at me, but Phil stuck a foot out and Big Red took a big tumble, hitting the ground and staying there. He was out for the count.

'Ben and I are going into town for a feed,' Phil announced. 'Who's coming?'

'What about the mob?' I asked, half-starved from having no food for twenty-four hours.

'What about them? They can't go anywhere while they're in the yards, not unless that fool is drunk enough to try it. We've done our bit. Let's go.'

The sun was high in the sky before Big Red got to his feet next morning. 'I want that silly little bastard! Ben, where are you?'

'Over there, Boss,' answered Jack, pointing at the rails.

'Grab hold of him! I'm gonna teach him one lesson he'll never forget!'

'No, Red, you touch that boy and we all walk. Isn't that so, boys?'

'That's right! We're with you, Jack,' they nodded, standing with their arms crossed over their chests. It was the first time any fellow workers had ever stood up for me and I was as surprised as I was grateful. But I also knew, from the look of rage on Red's face, that it wasn't over yet. His own men were siding with me against him and he wasn't going to take that lying down.

That night the taxi arrived with rum and beer.

'Want a beer, Ben?' asked Jack.

'No! You're not wasting any of my beer on that scum,' growled Red.

That was it. I picked up my swag and walked away until I felt safe. By morning the grog would all be gone and, hopefully, things would get back to normal. My sleep was restless, marked with dreams of Big Red wearing a long kangaroo tail and ripping my guts out with his sharp claws.

It was almost time to get up, when I heard a voice from above me.

'Wake up, bastard!' I opened my eyes to see Big Red towering over me. 'This is from *me* to *you*!' he spat, driving his boot viciously into my back. 'I *said*, it's time to *move*!'

There had to be some way of bringing this big and powerful man down to size, and I spent every waking moment from then on, trying to think of a solution. One thing was for sure – it would have to wait until after I was paid.

Bones was walking with the cattle because the horse-stingers were in plague proportions, making the poor old horse unreliable for riding. He had been plodding along just in front of me when one of the pesky insects found him. He gave a squeal, reared on his hind legs and started biting at his skin. Then he bolted past me and threw himself onto the ground, rolling in the dust. Back on his feet again, he headed straight for me, stopping with his head only inches from mine. I found myself staring into two petrified eyes, rolling in their sockets with only the whites showing.

Then I saw what was causing the panic – the big black fly was now on the horse I was riding. I swung my hat and missed, sending the stinger around to the back of my mount. Bones spun around and kicked me on the leg, bolted a short distance, stopped and looked around, and with a loud squeal, came charging back at me. This time, I knew, he wouldn't be able to stop in time – I would

The mob

have to get out of the way. But it was too late. Bones' head was up high, his mouth attacking fresh air, his feet already on their way. His shoulder drove into my mount and it was all I could do just to hang on. The damn fly was now buzzing around on my saddle and I swatted it one more time. This time I hit home. Old Bones shook himself as if to say, 'Thank God for that,' and walked calmly back to the herd.

Working the tail was a dusty job and most times I couldn't even see the leaders. Something was going on up front though, because the cattle were all calling back and forth to each other, probably spreading the news that water was close by. A small ridge hid the view, but as we rode further I could see that we were back in timber country.

Two days later we were in the middle of Channel Country again, with the Flinders River only half a mile away. The sun had beaten us. We had planned to get to the river with plenty of daylight, as the cattle had had no water for a few days, but it wasn't to be.

'Damn! We're gonna have to hold the mob here tonight,' Big Red said with a frown. 'I want the campsite on the side there, between them and the river so's they won't try and make a break for the bloody water. I want the shift split into two – that means four of us with the herd all the time. And no sleep for Ben, he gets to do a double.' The boss was marching backwards and forwards as he gave his orders. 'Jack, get eight horses ready. Ben, you take the piebald, as you'll be riding all night. You'll get a cuppa later. Listen, everybody, we've got to keep on the alert the whole time, 'cos these cows were bred in this sort of country. They know what's what better'n we do. Ben – you ride over to the far side, so you'll be closer to the river. Got it? Then go!'

Darkness soon came; it was pitch black and the moon wouldn't be rising for another three hours yet. After a while Jack rode out to bring me a quart pot of some stew he'd made. As he handed it over, he looked worried. He had noticed, he told me, that the herd was stretched out across the whole stock route, and if I lost any I'd be in a heap of trouble with the boss.

He was right, too. They were spread out like Brown's cows. They had two legs out in front and every time I rode past they jumped to their feet. Most of the cows were trying all the tricks they knew to get past the riders to the water.

Dingoes were howling, the moon had risen and was full and round. It was such a clear night that you could see across the herd to the campsite. The rider who was supposed to meet me on his round was covering only a quarter of the distance, leaving me with a much bigger area to cover by myself. In the bright moonlight I recognised him as Phil. Before much longer, I found myself surrounded by the herd and tried desperately to push them back. Behind me, some of them were off and walking and I rounded them up just in time. From the moon I thought it must be around eleven-thirty, and there, with the silvery light shining off her horns, was my little black cow and her calf.

Some birds were calling from the river and the cattle knew the sound well. It was getting close to the second shift now and I was dying for a cuppa and a smoke, but decided to sing to the herd to calm them down instead. They were as restless as I'd ever seen them. 'Down in the *vall*-ey / The valley so *low* / Late in the *eve*-ning / Hear the train blow / Hear the train *bl* ...'

It was so quick. A loud roar came from way down deep in the river and the cattle jumped to their feet. My pony reared up in fright and the unexpected movement almost threw me out of the saddle. The ground was shaking from thundering hooves on the run.

Then I saw them – a thousand head of cattle coming straight at me.

All I could see was horns, rows and rows of horns, bearing down on me like a landslide. There was only one escape, and that was to ride my horse across the front of the herd. Not one to believe in prayer, I put all my might into my legs and sank my heels into the pony's ribs.

That pony seemed to grow wings. We were sailing across country filled with pot-holes, dead logs, low-hanging branches and small woody scrub all over the place. Looking to the right, my mind went into slow motion. I knew I was halfway across – I could see trees being flattened, beasts falling over and being trodden underfoot, while the noise just grew and grew. A low branch snatched my hat.

It was hard to believe, but I sensed that they were turning, that I had them. I kicked my pony harder and screamed, '*Turn*, you bastards, *turn!*' and I knew that I had done it. I had turned them around. The ground was still rumbling and a big tree was flattened by the stampede, but I felt great. 'There's the river, mate,' I told my pony, 'we're nearly home. Look – the moon's shining on it.'

The mob

(River? What's the river doing in front of me? Bloody hell! I'm going the wrong way ... I haven't turned the rotten cattle – they've turned me!)

Having realised this, I was now faced with riding across the front of the stampede again. I tried to stay about ten feet in front of it, because if the pony stumbled I would be history. When he did slip, just for a second, my heart was in my mouth, but he got his footing back and I found myself riding with head down and tail up, just like a jockey, as we raced along. I looked up once, only to see horns no more than a couple of feet away, shining as if they were polished steel.

Next time I looked I had to look again to be sure of what I was seeing. I had made it across safely, but there was no sign of the herd.

My piebald was tiring. He stumbled. There was also a strange noise coming from his nose – it sounded like an air whistle. I dismounted and checked him, sure that I had burnt the poor bugger out. Dropping the reins, I tried to lift his head, but the pony's body was shaking and his legs were bending with exhaustion. I tried to call for help.

'Coo-*ee*! Coo-*ee*!' I threw my arms around the piebald's neck, planted a big kiss on his forehead, but all I could do was watch him suffer. And I couldn't help remembering my father's last promise to me. Well, Dad, I got myself a piebald, but no thanks to you!

'Coo-*ee*!' I called again and again, until my throat was sore. Nobody answered.

I had to face the fact that we were lost.

It was quiet now. The night was as still as if my pony and I were the only ones left alive on the planet, with only the moon for company. 'What else have you got saved up for me?' I shouted, but the boss of the night sky glared silently down. So big and powerful, always watching, never helping. I raised my fist and shook it: 'What next you bastard!'

Tying the pony's reins to a tree, I pulled off the saddle and placed it on the ground next to a log. I used it for a pillow and curled myself up against the log, covering myself with the saddle blanket. It was a cold night and I was glad of the warmth the thin cloth provided as I drifted into sleep.

Daybreak. I woke up shivering. It was bloody freezing! I tried calling out a few more times, but there was still no answer, and no sign of life anywhere.

What Next You Bastard

The piebald seemed to have recovered enough to be led along with the saddle on his back, but it wasn't until I spotted some smoke in the distance that I had any idea of which direction to walk.

We found the campsite or, should I say, what was left of it. Everything had been flattened: blankets, pots and pans were scattered in the dirt, and the campfire had spread all over the place, starting small grassfires. 'Coo-*ee*!' Moving towards the river, I found two dead cows and a live one with her hind leg smashed. Then, of all things, a squashed kangaroo. Trees had all been snapped off at ground level and most of the grass had been trampled to dust.

Piebald let out a whinny – he had spotted movement ahead. It was the three dingoes that had been trailing us, standing over a dead calf. I yelled at them to get away and their heads shot up; they looked right at me, before trotting meekly off.

At last, the first sign of the herd – a few cows grazing at the edge of the river, up to their bellies in mud. Before I could look any further, I felt a wave of sickness hit me in the belly and, for the first time in hours, was reminded of how hungry and thirsty I was. Finding a spot along the muddy banks, I let Piebald have his fill. Then, with my quart-pot, I scooped up some of the water and stood ankle-deep in the mud to drink it.

Just a short distance upstream where the four cows were, a young heifer moved in beside them to take a drink. A moment later there was a splash. Then the heifer was flipped onto her back and was sailing into the middle of the river, with her legs kicking in the air. She was slowly pulled under. What the hell was that all about? I had never seen anything like it in my life. Then I saw something else I had never seen in real life before: two very large, long crocodiles.

I took off like a rocket, leaving Piebald behind in my panic. I heard another splash behind me, and kept on running, straight into the arms of Jack, the cook.

'It's you! You're still alive, m'boy!'

'What the hell happened, Jack?' I asked, glad to see him again.

'It was a bloody croc roaring last night that started the stampede,' he explained. I asked him where the others were and he said they were on their way.

A new count was done. Sixty cattle were dead or missing. Jack and Tom saved what they could from the camp and tried to put a

The mob

meal together. My hat had been found by one of the men, but my new swag was pretty much ruined.

And Big Red wasn't talking to me, which was a very bad sign.

The droving trip was finally over and despite everything that had happened along the way, I felt a bit sorry to see the stock go. The herd was to be given over to the manager of Devoncourt, and tears filled my eyes as the cattle made their way along the fence of their new home. Standing in front of me was the little black cow with her calf. She came back to the gate, gave me a 'Moo!' and a look that said 'See ya,' then walked away.

Town tonight! We were only hours away from sleeping in soft warm beds and the thought seemed to cheer us all up, until Big Red burst the bubble.

'Sorry boys, not tonight. Mr Hudson wants us to muster a paddock tomorrow before we go. Don't look so bloody blue, you'll get extra pay for it. Tonight we'll camp by the big lake. And one more thing, keep away from the Aboriginal camp. Those boys aren't too happy 'bout us being here, but I've been told they can't muster the paddock, so it's up to us. We'll start before daybreak.' With Mr Hudson standing right beside him, Big Red's language was pretty tame for once.

Mr Hudson asked if there were any questions, so I asked if there were any crocodiles in the lake we would be camping beside. His answer wasn't what I'd been hoping to hear. 'Not that I've seen lately, son,' he said, 'although there are some freshwater crocodiles that grow longer than six feet. But don't worry, they won't hurt you.'

That night I slept near the steps of the house. I wasn't taking any chances with the crocs.

Next morning I was the last to arrive at the yard where the Devoncourt horses were kept. The others were waiting for me to catch myself a mount; they were all ready to get started and I was holding things up.

'Hurry up, Ben!' Big Red said. 'Any horse'll do! Just catch one.' There was one with saddle marks on his shoulder and I thought he might be all right. I cut him out from the others and put him into a smaller yard, where I tried to saddle him up, but it was no good. No way would this horse stand still for me. 'Come on, move, it's time to go,' Red snarled, more annoyed than ever.

What Next You Bastard

The harder I tried, the more the boys sitting on the rail laughed.

'My boy,' yelled the station manager, 'get down on your hands and knees and crawl up to him, and touch him on his fetlock. That horse belongs to the Aboriginals!' I didn't know what the hell he was talking about, so he came over to me and said, 'Go get yourself a white man's horse, boy, that big bay will do you. A white man's horse you can walk straight up to. Here, the black man goes along the ground. We don't ride theirs and they don't ride ours.'

With a good ride under our belts we arrived at the paddock that held the cattle Mr Hudson wanted mustered. We were told that this paddock was called 'The Desert', on account of all the scrub and creepers looking the same. Big Red ordered me to take the fence, push whatever I got to Frank, who would push it to Phil, and so on. The plan seemed simple enough to follow, so I rode off.

They were right. The scenery behind and in front looked exactly the same. A few miles down the track I spotted some stock, but they saw me coming and disappeared from sight. Two cows came running out of the scrub, snorted and turned tail. I reached a gate which I was sure was the one I'd entered the paddock from, but after a good look, I realised it wasn't, and rode on. At three o'clock I spotted a small herd just off the fence, but once again they saw me and took off like a bullet. I tried to follow, chasing them into the scrub, but it was useless. I just couldn't get my bearings, with everything looking the same. Finding my own tracks, I headed back to the fence and finally managed to round up a few head. 'Frank, where are you?' I called, but he was nowhere to be found, and the cattle got away from me again. It was getting very late so I thought I'd better get a move on. Darkness fell and I was lost again. I couldn't even find the fence this time.

I followed a pad, a kind of narrow track made by the cattle, which led me to a windmill and trough, where I found myself a place to lie down and rest. Nothing more could be done before daylight anyway. Stars shone brightly above and the sky was beautifully clear.

A hot breeze on the side of my head woke me up during the night. I rolled over onto my back and tried to go back to sleep, but there it was again, a hot breath blowing right onto my face. Then I felt wet drops on my cheek. I opened my eyes to find the great head of a big bull with very long horns standing right over me. With eye to eye contact, I pulled in my stomach just as the bull made his move.

The mob

Luckily his horns only caught my shirt, ripping off a button, but the scream that came from the top of my lungs didn't sound like any voice I had ever heard before. It did the job, though. That bull took off with a hell of a fright. I couldn't get back to sleep after that – who could? – so I lay awake listening to the night sounds and trying to count the stars instead.

In the morning I found the gate and headed for the homestead. Just ahead of me were Red and Jack, also just finding their way home. I learnt that all of us had got lost that day, and Big Red was throwing in the towel. 'Forget it, Mr Hudson,' he said, shaking his beard from side to side. 'Soon as the taxi gets here, we're leaving for Julia.'

For once everyone agreed with him. Even me.

I asked Jack what would happen to the horses if we went home by taxi. 'They belong to Devoncourt now; they went with the cattle,' Jack told me. 'Forget about them, Ben. It's pay time and you can buy me a big long beer when we get to town. I'm too old for this sort of work anymore.'

'You know, Jack,' I said, remembering some of the things that had happened, 'I think I just did my last drive. It's too bloody dangerous.'

Sitting at the bar in Julia Creek's Railway Hotel, I felt relieved that it was all over. Tomorrow I would have money and a car again. Back to normal. In the meantime, I felt like letting my hair down.

'I'll have a beer, Kym, on the slate,' I said.

'Sorry. Can't do that. The boss wants cash up front.'

'Say that again?'

'No money, no service,' she told me smugly.

'Look, I've got money coming to me tomorrow,' I explained, but Kym just rolled her eyes and wiped the counter. One of the regulars sitting near me said he'd cover it for me, so I got my beer, but I was pretty stirred off by Kym's attitude.

Sitting on my other side was Bob, the old caretaker from Marland Station where James and I had eaten ourselves sick on eggs. He was rotten drunk. He stood up, pissed on the floor and announced that he was now going upstairs to shoot himself. Then he lowered himself onto all fours and crawled up the hotel stairs. All was quiet at the bar for a while until a single shot rang out.

Everybody flew up the stairs to find the old caretaker sitting on his bed with a .303 rifle positioned between his legs.

'Yeah, he missed. Leave him be,' came a voice from the crowd, so everyone returned to the serious business of drinking again.

Not much later another shot rang out. This time most of us stayed in our seats.

They found what was left of him in the hotel wardrobe. It was rumoured that by sitting in a wardrobe you couldn't miss, and Bob had proved the theory.

It was the sweat pouring off my forehead that woke me the next day. Most of us in the bar hadn't gone to bed before the sun came up, and it was now hot and quite late. My whole body was drenched, so were the sheets, and I stank of horse from the long drive. I decided that I'd take a shower and then go and get my pay.

I asked Will Bright if he'd seen Big Red and he said that he had. 'Left town early this morning,' he told me.

'What about my money?' I asked him.

'Don't look at me, I've not got it,' Mr Bright said.

Tracking Jack and Tom down was pretty easy and when I asked them if Red had left my pay with them, they shook their heads in pity. 'Nope. Ben, that man is broke. He spent it all last night. He told us he'd be away for six weeks on a job he had lined up.'

'Did he pay you?' I asked, feeling as if I had been kicked in the guts.

'Sure did,' Tom told me. 'We know that bastard. Got it before he started drinking. I can tell you now, you'll be bloody lucky ever to get your dough.'

14. Kilterry

Colin Mars listened to my story and wasn't impressed. If I couldn't pay for the repairs, I couldn't take my car – not unless I signed a paper stating that I wouldn't take it out of town. 'And if you do, I have a right to get the police to take it off you,' he warned.

Alex Kelly at Australian Estates lined up a job for me at a property just outside Nelia, a small town between Julia Creek and Maxwelton. He said they were looking for a cowboy and asked me if I knew how to milk. I was so desperate for work that I told him yes, which wasn't a total lie because I'd once had a go at it when I was small.

I would have driven straight over there, but Colin Mars refused to give me my car.

'Forget it, mate. You signed a paper. If you take that car out of town the police will pick you up as quick as look at you. If I were you, I'd leave the car with me.'

So I ended up getting a lift to Nelia that night with some people leaving town and next day the mail truck dropped me off at Kilterry Station just before lunch.

Kilterry was very different from the other properties I had worked on. Everything was beautifully kept and I got the feeling that Mr and Mrs Lord, the owners, really took pride in everything they did. There were buildings all over the place. Apart from the family homestead with its shady verandahs, there was a milking shed, a well-equipped butcher shop, a long shearing shed with its twelve-room shearing quarters beside it, horse stables, machinery sheds and garages. The lawns and gardens surrounding the homestead were manicured and in tip-top condition, and even the yards looked neat and tidy, with their white-painted posts and rails and gates. It was something special to see.

On my first day there I met my new boss. Mr Lord was a well-dressed, cleanshaven man in his thirties, who had the kind of eyes that seemed to measure up a person. His firm handshake made you feel like you had been friends with him for years.

What Next You Bastard

'Milk many cows before, Ken?' he asked, and it was a nice change to be called by my real name again, after all those weeks being Ben.

'One or two,' I said, crossing my fingers behind my back.

'Look, I have a good man away and I need someone to do his duties. So let's go into the kitchen and I'll get Mrs Alloway to put the kettle on for us.' In the kitchen he introduced me as 'our new man', which made me feel very grown up and important. We talked for a while about what sort of work I had done in the past and Mr Lord seemed very pleased. 'You'll do me,' he said. Then, to my surprise, he asked my advice. 'You've seen the land I've ploughed, haven't you, Ken? What do you reckon? Can I make a go of it?'

'I can't say, sir,' I told him truthfully. 'All I know is if you don't try, you won't find out.'

He nodded. 'Our neighbours around here believe I'm mad. Some of them are even betting on it. They say I'm wasting money. But I can tell you, I'm going to prove them wrong. There's a lot more to this land than just grazing. Well, Ken, I've got some office work to do now,' Mr Lord said, getting up from the table, 'so I'll leave you in the capable hands of Mrs Alloway.'

Mrs Alloway didn't waste any time giving her orders. She was a stout woman in her sixties, with a huge white apron tied around her waist and clearly the boss of the kitchen and all that went with it.

'Tea time, the bell will be rung around seven pm. Before you enter my kitchen you make sure you wipe your shoes, dress neatly and do your hair. In the morning you will find two milk buckets on this table. When you return I will be in the kitchen. You will find the cows in the paddock behind the milking shed – three cows with three calves. You bring them in around four in the afternoon, lock the calves in the holding yards and turn the cows back out – they won't go far without them. You can start on that today after seeing what Hugh wants done. He's the leading hand around here. Tomorrow I would like two sheep killed. I will see Hugh about having them in the yard for you. Well, Ken, as you can see, I'm baking a cake, so I'll see you at tea.'

That night I was late for my meal in the kitchen. Rounding up the cows had taken ages because they were at the far end of the hundred-acre paddock and played games with me when I tried to herd them in on foot. I apologised to Mrs Alloway, but she said it was all right, the first day was always the hardest.

After helping her with the washing up, I asked her what time she wanted the milk in the morning and nearly fell over when she said, 'Around five-thirty, please.' I even asked her to repeat it in case I hadn't heard her right.

It was still dark and very cold when I entered the kitchen at four o'clock the next morning. The buckets were on the table – not two, but three! Worst of all, under the buckets was a note. I did my best but just couldn't figure out what it said, so I dropped it onto the floor and hoped the message wasn't too important.

To my great relief, it didn't take me long to get the hang of milking. After a few false starts I soon had the milk pouring into the buckets until they were overflowing. If that's milking, I thought, I could do it all day long!

Mrs Alloway put a huge plate of chops covered with gravy in front of me; there was also some toast and two fried eggs, with piping hot tea to wash it all down. Then she wanted to know where the butterfat was that she'd asked for in the note. I told her that I hadn't seen any note, so she explained that the milk had to go through the separator so that she could have cream for making butter. It didn't sound too complicated, so I asked her to keep my breakfast hot, saying I'd be back soon.

Separating the milk looked as if it might be a bit tricky after all. It all looked pretty well set up, with something that might be the separator just sitting there waiting for me, but I had never seen it done and now it was up to me to figure it out. I lifted one of the buckets of milk and tipped the whole thing into the container, then started turning the handle. Nothing happened. The milk just ran through and came out the bottom, looking just the same as before, with no cream to be seen anywhere! I tried turning the handle the opposite way, maybe that was the problem. Nothing. In no time I had two buckets of milk again. 'Damn thing! It's got to work!' I thought of my breakfast getting cold in the kitchen and felt like kicking the wretched contraption. In a rage I filled the container again and grabbed the handle, spinning it wildly. And thick, beautiful, yellow cream started to fall into the cream bucket. Speed was obviously the secret.

Mrs Alloway smiled and shook her head when I handed over the buckets. 'Here, sit down and eat your breakfast now. You deserve it!' she said. 'I've never had so much milk or cream in my kitchen before. I must ask you, Ken – are you married?'

'No way! I'm only nineteen!' I burst out laughing, with a forkful of meat halfway up to my mouth. 'Why?'

'Oh, it's an old belief. It goes something like this: "Never hire a single man to milk a cow, as he hasn't had the practice." A married man is different,' she went on, blushing just a bit, 'he knows what he is doing.'

'I found it easy – the milk just poured out,' I told her.

'Well, my boy, there's more to the yarn. If any single man could milk, he was bait for any single woman. The story goes that when he marries, it's for life. He knows how to treat a woman.'

'Come off it! That's not me,' I said, finding it all a bit embarrassing.

Hugh Downey was the friendly young overseer, or leading hand, and one of the first things he did was invite me to play cards with him and his wife Vivien, and the cook's daughter Coral, who was the family's maid. We spent quite a few nights sitting around the Downeys' kitchen table, eating and drinking and playing hand after hand, while their little baby slept in her cot nearby.

I really loved this place. There was never any trouble here and everyone just went around doing his job.

'Take a seat, Ken,' said Mr Lord one morning, after asking me to come to his office. 'Next week we are shearing and I need a man who can help us muster, as well as kill two sheep for the shearers each day. We might also need a hand with the wool. Besides that, I have three horses I want broken in. That's a total of four separate jobs, and what I'd like to know is, would you like to do them on top of the one you already have? I'll pay you for each job – it means you'd be getting close to five wages a week. Before you answer, I want you to think about it.'

Five jobs! Five wages! I ran it all through my mind while Mr Lord sat and waited. I was already looking after the cows, milking them and supplying the mutton for the normal meals; slaughtering a few more sheep for the shearers shouldn't be too hard; mustering sheep was something I enjoyed because of the riding, so that would be fun; breaking in the horses should be pretty easy; and helping with the wool – why not? 'Yes, I think I could do it all,' I replied. 'It's just the horses that worry me.'

'You did tell me you know how to break in horses,' Mr Lord frowned.

Kilterry

'Yes, that's not the trouble,' I said. 'But I don't think there is enough light in the day to do it properly.'

'How about doing the horses on the weekends, and I'll pay you the breaking-in price,' he offered, so I told him he had a deal.

Shearing got put off for a fortnight, giving me time to start on the first horse. Mr Lord had three small children – two daughters and a son – and he told me that he wanted two of the horses for the girls, only I wasn't to tell a soul, or it would spoil the surprise. Three healthy-looking animals stood in the yard, a colt and two fillies. I was to break in one of them my own way, but the other two were to be done his way. Fair enough.

He wanted me to start with the colt, he said, and returned to the house.

The grey colt was a lovely horse with very fine bones, standing about fourteen and a half hands high. Slipping on leather gloves, I took hold of the lasso rope. First throw did the trick, falling right over the horse's head. I pulled the rope tight and suddenly the colt kicked out with his hind leg and hit the bottom rail of the fence. There was a loud cracking noise, the horse shot forward, and then went down.

I stared at his hind leg in horror. The fetlock was hanging just by a piece of skin, with the bone protruding from the upper part of the leg. The colt hauled himself back onto his feet, but his whole body was shaking. Every time he tried to put some weight on the leg he went down again, sweating and shivering and his eyes wide with fear and pain. I couldn't stand it. Slipping the rope off his neck, I made a dash for the office and told Mr Lord that we needed the rifle.

Not saying a word, the boss walked down to the yard, took one look at his colt, took aim and shot him. As the poor horse went down he gave one final kick. His whole fetlock tore away and with it came a piece of rusted fence wire. Somewhere, somehow, this horse must have stepped into a loop of wire, maybe in a paddock where a post had rotted away from a fence, and when he had stepped forward it had knotted itself tightly around his fetlock, bedding itself close to the bone. It must have happened quite some time before, because the skin and hair had regrown over the wire, making it impossible to see. I couldn't help imagining how painful it must have been for the colt, having his leg slowly ringbarked like that.

Mr Lord told me to get Hugh to tow the body away and start on one of the fillies. I wasn't to touch the other one – he wanted her broken in his way when he was ready.

The filly that I was to start on was a beautiful black with grey hairs in her undercoat, and fourteen hands high. I worked five days on her, spending as much time with her as I could to slowly gain her confidence. She was a dream! She did everything I wanted her to and was a very quick learner. Mr Lord was very pleased after test-riding her and agreed with me that she was 'child-proof'.

The shearing was put off again because the men had been delayed at another job and wouldn't be able to get here for a week or so, giving me time to break in the next horse. I expected it to be just as easy as the last one. I was wrong.

This one was slightly smaller than the black and heavily built. Mr Lord said he wanted to be there every time I worked with her, and his methods were totally different to mine. He gave the orders and I carried them out, which I wasn't too happy about. I still hated being told what to do, especially when it was something I knew I could do well.

I couldn't believe my ears when, early one morning, he told me to hobble all four of her legs: back to back, front to front, then side hobbles. His idea was that if she tried to move, she wouldn't be able to.

'Now stand back and make her go forward,' Mr Lord ordered.

'But she'll fall!' I cried.

'That's right,' he nodded, 'but she'll never do it again.' We watched as the filly tried to take a step, only to find that her feet couldn't move, and went crashing to the ground. 'Just leave her till she works out how to stand by herself,' he said, stopping me from rushing to her side.

Oh, it was terrible to watch. I was dead sure she was going to break a leg as she struggled with the chains and tried to balance her weight enough to stand up. It took more than an hour before she made it to her feet, shaking with fright and missing pieces of skin from where the cruel chains had bitten into the flesh.

Mr Lord was right about one thing, though. Once up, that filly never moved her legs an inch, and never fell down again. Next day she was hobbled again for several hours. I was told to walk all around her, pull her tail, yell out, even crack a whip. She didn't twitch an eyelid. Day three came and the bridle was put on very

Kilterry

tightly so it would make her mouth tender. The idea behind this, Mr Lord explained, was that she learnt from the very start to move her head in the direction that was wanted; resisting the pull of the reins would be too painful. At the same time I had to put the saddle on and off her back so many times that my arms ached. On the fourth day I got into the saddle, then out, then in again, over and over for hours without a break. I wasn't too happy about this part – what if she fell over and I got caught up in the hobbles?

On the fifth day Mr Lord wanted me to take off the hobbles and 'drive' her around the paddock with the long reins on the bridle, meaning that I should walk behind and 'steer' her. This was meant to teach the filly to respond to the signals and learn directions. Only trouble was, she didn't want to move. I couldn't blame her. She'd become too used to standing still no matter what. The only way to get her to move now was for Mr Lord to crack his whip onto the ground by her hooves, touching them lightly and spurring her into action.

To cut a long story short, despite Mr Lord's special way of breaking in horses, this particular one never really made a good horse for riding. After many more training sessions, she eventually learnt to trot quite well, but when it came time to canter, she'd drop her head and buck the rider off. Even the boss had to admit that it had been a waste of time. The only horse safe enough for his children to ride was the black filly I'd broken in by myself, patiently and gently. I decided right there that I would stick to my own methods in the future, come what may.

When the shearers finally turned up they were two men short. One wool-presser was missing and the roustabout never showed. The roustabout was the bloke who had to pick up the fleece from the floor and throw it onto the table, keep the floor clean, keep the pens full of sheep for the shearers, and have the tar handy in case of cuts. Wool-pressing was another job I picked up very quickly and though I would have liked to try my hand at shearing, there wasn't enough time to have a go.

Working with the shearers was great. They were all hard-working fellows and most of them had a good sense of humour to go with it. By the time I had done all my various jobs at Kilterry, I was too tired to play cards with the others, falling into bed at seven-thirty each night and going out like a light.

What Next You Bastard

I was sorry to see the shearers leave after only two weeks. Apart from the extra work, it had all been a lot of fun.

Now that my job was back to normal again and my days were less busy, I had time to stop and look back at my life so far. I knew that if only I could write, I'd have some good stories to tell one day. My only hope was to store them all up in my head until the time came that I would be able to put them down on paper. What the doctor in Brisbane had said about my memory worried me quite a lot. Just the idea of forgetting where I had been, what I had done, and the people and places I had known, filled me with dread. There was only one thing I could do in the meantime, and that was to test myself over and over again.

Lying in bed at night I would start at the very beginning of my life and force myself to remember everything about my childhood, the good as well as the bad. The days of hospitals and treatments and even the little schooling that I'd had; the holidays on the beach and the factory jobs; the food I had eaten and the films I'd seen all came flooding back just as clearly as if it had all been yesterday. I needn't have worried. All my memories were safely stashed away and I promised myself I'd remember every detail.

One good thing about not being able to read or write is that you develop a good memory. You have to rely on it. Sometimes your life depends on it. For a nineteen-year-old with practically no education, there was no other choice.

Three months passed too quickly. Even before they told me, I knew the Lords had no more work for me to do. The man I had replaced was back from wherever he'd been and it was time for me to move on.

Mr Lord gave me a cheque for the full amount he'd promised me, thanked me and said he might have some more work a few months down the line. I was truly sorry to leave Kilterry, where I'd worked hard, but everything had been fair and square.

On my way back to town I dared to dream that I might own a place like it myself one day.

Nothing much had changed at Julia Creek while I was away. With my big cheque in hand I strode into Colin Mars' place to collect my car, looking forward to having wheels of my own again. But Colin had other ideas. He took the whole cheque as 'part payment' and, though he let me take the car, refused to fill the almost-empty tank for me. He said that if he did, I would only shoot through on him. With no money for accommodation and no petrol to go anywhere, the best I could do was camp in my car.

Big Red was in town, staying at the Railway Hotel. As I made my way up the stairs to the bar I knew there would be trouble. My whole body was shaking like a leaf, but I reminded myself that the bastard owed me.

Red had his back to me and was talking to three men. I stood in the doorway and announced, 'Red, I want my pay.'

He slowly turned around. 'Shit, it's only you! I've got no money for you, but I owe you *this*! His hands moved so quickly that he had got me by the shirt and backhanded me before shoving me out the door with all his might. 'Go get that fucking car of yours! I want you to take me to Maxwelton in it. Then, *maybe*, I might give you some money!'

It was too much. Blind with rage, I cut loose, my right fist landing squarely in Big Red's gut. That brought him down a bit. But it was the left that got him down to my height, doubling him over and winding him more quickly and easily than I could ever have dreamed. In front of me now was a face I had learnt to hate. My arms moved like pistons, working in and out without waiting for directions from my brain.

The big red face split; blood was pouring from the cuts, from the nose, and one eye was already shut before someone tried to pull me off him. 'That's enough, boy! Leave him,' I heard, but I wasn't through yet. I wanted this man down at my feet where he belonged. Two more to the head gave me the pleasure of seeing this big coward collapse in a bloody heap on the floor. Standing back, I looked down at the mountain that had turned into a molehill without once having the guts to fight back, and wondered why I had always been so afraid of him. My knuckles were red with his blood, and they ached, but I felt damn good.

Red, who didn't look quite so 'Big' to me any more, was helped to his feet. His face was a mess, his swollen features bruised and dripping blood. Still, he managed to spit a few words out. 'Thirty poundth to *eddy-one* that belth thith *thit* up!' he spluttered. 'I'll give *thirty* to thee him in the dirt!' Then he was dragged away.

I was a king! Everybody wanted to touch me, slap me on the back. They called me 'Champ' and shouted me one beer after another. People I had never spoken to put money on the bar. 'We're paying, drink up, son!' It seemed that I had done what everyone else had been wanting to do for years: cut the big bully down to size.

Even Judy, the new barmaid I had never met before, came up to me and said, 'You, my boy, are sleeping with me tonight, so I can look after that bruise on your poor face.' My only other choice was to sleep in my car, so I accepted her offer.

The morning sun in my face woke me. Judy was gone. I went to get up, slipping my legs over the side of the bed and giving a push with my arms, but they were too weak to do the job. I collapsed back onto the mattress and after a moment, tried again. It was no use – my strength was gone and my head started to spin. Thinking it was just a hangover, I slept for a while, but when I tried again later, the same thing happened.

For two days and nights I lay there, nursed by Judy, before I had the strength to stand up. When I walked, I felt weak and dizzy, and a visit to the doctor brought the news that I had been dreading.

'It's your body, son,' he said. 'It's had enough. If I were you, I'd get back to the Big Smoke as soon as possible.'

What else could I do? In this sort of condition I wouldn't be able to work, and anyway, I had nowhere to live and no money for food. I would have to go home to Brisbane, even if just for a while.

The car was a problem. Colin Mars wouldn't let me take it, not until I had paid for the repairs in full. I told him I wasn't going to just leave it there, so he made me an offer to 'take it off my hands'.

'Tell you what,' he said, 'you sign it over to me and I'll pay out AGC for you and send you the balance.' I agreed because I didn't know what else to do, but when I asked Colin for just enough cash for my train fare, he refused. 'Nope. I'll buy your car to help you out, but it'll take a few weeks before the money comes through. When it's all settled, then I'll send it to you. That's it. Just sign your name there.'

I didn't want to sponge any money off my friends at the hotel so, feeling sick and tired, I made a reverse charge phone call to Mum in Brisbane, asking her to send me £5 for the train fare home. When it arrived I made my booking, then went down to the billiard hall to find Old Bill.

'I've come to say farewell, mate, I'm booked on the train to Brisbane tonight.'

Kilterry

Old Bill looked sad as he shook my hand. 'Ken, if you ever write your story, my name's Kumfer – Bill K-u-m-f-e-r,' he said, spelling it out for me carefully. 'Be careful, boy, I believe someone will try to earn that £30 of Red's before you leave.'

As I walked out the front door, I received a light punch in the midriff. Standing in front of me, and grinning from ear to ear, was Alex Rudd. 'I hear you're leaving town. By the way, do you mind if I claim that £30 I earned by hitting you just then?

'No mate,' I laughed, 'if you can, go and get it!'

Heading south to Brisbane. Goodbye bush. So long west. It was nice while it lasted. Maybe I'll be back again some day.

I came here with nothing and I was taking nothing home with me.

With not a penny to spend, it was going to be a l-o-n-g train ride.

15. The sander

The first thing I noticed about our house in Coorparoo was the big antenna perched on the roof. We had a television set! I couldn't wait to see what shows were on but Mum wanted to hear all my news first, so I had to leave it till later.

Being home again was strange. I had trouble getting used to it.

Mum was working at the South Brisbane Businessmen's Club as a cook-waitress and my brothers were working, so the house was empty all day. For the first time in ages I had no reason to get up and get busy. I made the most of it, staying in bed until early each afternoon, with faithful old Darkie snoring under my bed.

After three weeks of this Mum couldn't take any more. She could see that I didn't have any energy and it worried and annoyed her. She had been nagging me about seeing the doctor ever since I got home.

'I've just about had it with you, Ken!' she exploded one night after coming home from work and finding me lazing around in front of the box again. 'While you live under my roof, and not twenty-one yet, you'll do as I say. I've made an appointment for you to go to the new clinic. What I think is that you've been bitten by a tsetse fly.'

'Come off it, Mum, they live in Africa!' I laughed.

'Don't count on it, son! Today you can get anything in this great land of ours!'

To keep her happy I went along to the clinic anyway and had a thorough check-up. When I was dressed again, the doctor shuffled some papers around on his desk and cleared his throat noisily before saying, 'Well, I've got, er, good news for your mother. You haven't been bitten by a tsetse fly after all. But, er, it is serious, son, this lack of energy. We'll need some blood tests to, er, to prove it, but I'm fairly certain that you, er, that you have sugar diabetes. I want to see you again in, er, in one week.'

After sleeping away another week, I returned to hear the verdict.

'Well, my boy, it's, er, it's not sugar. I saw Dr James and we, er, we had a long talk about you.' He leafed through his notes for a while, then sat back and pursed his lips as if he was about to start

The sander

whistling. 'With all the facts we have, we, er, we both believe you are having a relapse of the old problems, and, er, at this time there is no, er, no medical help we can give you.'

It wasn't what I had been expecting to hear, not by a long shot. I didn't feel that bad. There had to be something – anything – that would help. 'If you were me, Doctor, what would you do?' I asked. Doctors were supposed to have all the answers; they weren't supposed to just give up on people, were they?

'Me,' he said, crossing his arms and dropping his chin onto his chest, then sighing loudly as if someone had let all the air out of his lungs at once. 'Well, I'd, er, I'd probably go home and, er, stay in bed until I felt strong enough, then I'd, er, I'd ...' He sighed again and when our eyes met, he shook his head and looked away. 'Damn it, Ken! I don't know what a young man like you would do,' he finished painfully.

So. That was it, then.

I stood up and thanked him, but as I turned to the door, he called me back.

'Hold it a minute! Please, er, sit down again,' the doctor said. He chewed at his bottom lip for a while, then seemed to make up his mind about something and leaned forward with both elbows on the desk. 'Sex, my boy. Have you, er, ever had it?'

His question took me by surprise. 'Yes,' I replied.

'I should be shot for this. As you know, I'm a very, er, strong Roman Catholic, and it goes against my beliefs ... However ... when you, er, have sex, how do you feel?'

'Good,' I said and couldn't help grinning.

'Well. I hope the girls aren't Catholic,' he said primly. 'Tell me, do you just, er, do you do it once in a night, or several times?'

'Oh, I don't know, a few times – it all depends on – the girl – you know?' I shrugged.

'Of course, er, I see. And when you've, er, done all this, can you get up and walk around?'

'Yeah, no trouble.' I was finding this all a bit embarrassing.

'No chest pains? No, er, tiredness?'

I just shook my head, wondering what he was leading up to.

He looked thoughtful. 'I believe I have it here somewhere,' he said, reaching across and pulling a heavy book down from a shelf behind him. 'Let's see ... yes, here it is, that's it. I'll, er, I'll be with you in a moment.' The doctor searched through the pages until he found what he was looking for. 'Yes, it might just, er, work. Sex, my boy. They say in this paper that it's rather good for the heart. Gets the blood, er, circulating. I think you should go out and, er, get as much as ... as you can.'

What? I couldn't believe my ears! This man, this Roman Catholic doctor, was actually telling me – no, encouraging me – to sleep around? To do the thing that was supposed to be taboo for young people, a part of life you 'earned' when you got married? And here he was, prescribing it like a tonic or tablet, a treatment for me to take as often as possible – without even having to feel guilty!

As I left the surgery I tried to picture Mum's face when she heard about my new 'medicine', and laughed out loud. I decided on the spot that she wouldn't be hearing about it from me.

When I got home, Mum very casually mentioned that she had registered me for National Service. I nearly hit the roof, not because I didn't want to join the army, but because she was trying to run my life for me again. Some papers had arrived for me while I was out west, she told me, and she had filled them in and sent them back. But now that I was home, she had thought it proper to inform the authorities of the change.

'That's it, Mum, sign my life away without even asking me,' I said sourly.

'Don't get all shirty, love, they won't take you anyway. Not with your medical history.'

Day by day my strength slowly returned. Neighbours and friends were surprised to see me walking around with Darkie at my heels. They called out things like, 'George, come quick! It's Kenny Hall, he's walking!' and, 'Your mother is so worried about your health, Ken. Please don't go back out west again!' Most of them were under the impression that I was dying this time for sure.

One of the first things I did was catch up with my old mate Brian. He'd heard that I was back and had tried to see me, but my mother had set a strict no visitors rule, so he'd been turned away. Good onya, Mum! The two of us soon got into the habit of cruising around at night in Brian's 1946 Austin A40, which was blue and sleek and powered by a four-cylinder engine; top speed downhill was 60 miles an hour. As Brian so often said, 'What a gas!'

The sander

Brian had a routine: 'Let's grab a dozen coldies, then up to The Mater (hospital) and see if we can get us a coupla nurses for the night.'

I could only grin and say, 'Just what the, er, doctor ordered!'

More often than not we got what we wanted: the nurses were willing, and the secluded parking spot on top of White's Hill was put to good use, even though the terrific view was wasted on the likes of us.

Only Myrtle Hall wasn't happy. 'Where in the hell have you been, Ken?' she screamed at me as I crept into the house carrying my shoes just before dawn one morning. I nearly jumped out of my skin when she appeared out of the shadows, her face tight with anger. 'I've been worried sick!'

I told her that I was old enough to look after myself, thanks very much, and that anyway it was all the doctor's idea. Oops! Before she could put her hands on her hips and demand to know what that was supposed to mean, I told her to forget it and stormed off to bed, leaving her standing in the doorway with her mouth hanging open.

'That's right, leave me in the dark, like you always do,' she yelled after me. 'Oh, and by the way, mister, if you're well enough to play up all night, you're well enough to do an honest day's work. So I got a job for you! Did you hear that Ken? Next Monday you start working for Payne & Butler,' she announced, sounding very pleased with herself. I was too angry to answer, so I slammed my bedroom door instead. When the hell was my mother ever going to stop interfering in my life?

Payne & Butler was a flooring company in South Brisbane. After spending half the weekend tossing up whether I would take the job or not, I had finally admitted to myself that I was getting pretty bored just sitting around at home so I decided to give it a go. I didn't know anything about the company except that they laid fancy flooring called 'park-a-tree' or something like that. What my job was going to be I had no idea.

When I got to the address Mum had given me I found nothing but a shop. Thinking that the shopkeepers might know where Payne & Butler's factory was, I went inside to ask.

A woman in her forties with pearls around her neck ruled the counter. 'May I help you, sir?' she asked.

'Sorry to bother you,' I said politely, 'I'm looking for Payne & Butler'.

'You have found it, sir. How may I help?' she smiled.

'Where are the owners? I'm here to start work as a labourer.'

'A labourer!' If looks could kill, I'd have been flat on my back on those fancy wooden floor tiles before you could say 'sir' a second time. In a voice of steel she said, 'If you would only look, there's a big sign outside pointing to the back! Can't you read? This shop is the retail part!'

She bristled like a guard dog defending its master's property and her eyes flashed angrily. I was pretty stirred off myself, let me tell you, and when I didn't move she came around the counter and started pushing me towards the door. If two men hadn't come in at just that moment, I might have done something unthinkable.

'Can we help you?' one of them asked.

'Yes,' I said, glad of the interruption. 'My mother, Myrtle Hall, sent me for an interview about a job. My name is Ken Hall.'

'Interview?' one of them said. 'No way! Look, you're Myrtle's boy, you don't need an interview, you can start right now. I'm Mr Butler and this is Mr Payne. Come on through.' When we entered the shed I was introduced to four other men. 'This is only a third of our staff, the rest work in the suburbs. Here we are,' he said, speaking slowly and clearly. 'Now, this job is very simple. First you take a box, then you place it under this chute. When you have fifty of these bundles stacked, you close the lid and start again.' Mr Butler smiled. 'Sorry, I should have asked if you can count to fifty.'

'Yes, sir,' I said, my face hot with shame. I wondered what my mother had been telling them.

'Good,' he continued. 'I believe you have quite a serious problem, and I want you to know that while you work for us, we will keep it nice and easy for you.'

That night I had it out with Mum. I really did my block, asking her who the hell she was, telling everyone that I was a dummy. 'Every bloody job, you open your mouth!' I screamed. When she tried to deny it I only got angrier. It was up to me, I shouted, up to me to tell them if I wanted them to know. It was my business, not hers, that I couldn't read or write.

There was more to my frustration: Mum was treating me as a brainless child again. I had spent the past couple of years out west

The sander

as an adult, an equal, working hard and doing responsible work. No one had ever had any reason to suspect that I was handicapped in any way. I had almost forgotten about it myself. And now, back in Brisbane, it was all coming back at me again. Same old story. Was I ever going to get my chance at a normal life in this city?

Mr Payne and Mr Butler never gambled on horses. What they did was invest a regular amount of money in the Golden Casket Lottery. Not just single tickets – they bought whole books of tickets at a time. And every time the Casket was drawn they got their money back. Over the years they had won the major prize three times, and with the winnings they had built up their business: floor-sanding and polishing, laying tiles, and parquetry. When I heard about this I couldn't help wondering what my father had spent his Casket winnings on, though it wasn't too hard to guess. He probably threw most of it at the horses and drank the rest.

My first few weeks were spent doing the kind of work that I'd been doing in factories before going west: packing, cleaning, sweeping and taking the lunch orders. My old system of using a code for the orders came in handy again, but I was careful to keep the notepad in my pocket and away from prying eyes.

After many weeks of factory work, they sent me to my first on-site job: an old Queenslander-style house in Spring Hill that was to have its wooden floorboards sanded. The grumpy old man in charge of the job expected me to unload the heavy machinery from his truck each morning, then sit back and do nothing but watch him for the next eight hours of each day before loading it up again. He did his best to ignore me for a whole week. I was itching to have a go at working the floor sander, but it wasn't until Mr Butler had a talk with him that I got my wish.

His name was Davis, he told me on the following Monday, and he apologised for the way he had treated me for the past week – his partner had died less than a fortnight before and he was still trying to get over it.

Davis explained what had to be done and introduced me to the sander. I learnt how to fit the coarse gritty sandpaper that was needed for the first cut onto the bottom plates, and then he strapped me into the machine.

'Okay, Ken, let's see what you learnt from watching me last week.'

The sanding drum was one foot deep and ten inches in diameter;

it was driven by a one and a half horsepower electric motor, and a four-inch leather belt ran across my back and was fastened securely to the machine. The switch was positioned halfway down the post, meaning that one hand had to be lifted off the handle grips to turn the power on or off.

With a flick of the switch, the sander roared into life before I could even grasp the handle properly; my feet went out from under me and I was dragged down the long narrow hallway like someone chained to a runaway train. Over the noise of the sander I heard Davis yelling out, 'Lay back! Dig your feet in!' Easier said than done, mate. When I finally got a foothold on the dusty floor, the machine came to a stop, but the sanding drum was still turning, and cutting a large groove into the pine boards. I didn't dare take my hand off the bar to press the switch. I needed them both to steady the damn thing.

Davis made a dive for the power point on the wall and pulled the plug. Silence. I braced myself for the lecture I was surely going to get for spoiling his floor, but Davis was surprisingly understanding, and spent a good amount of time teaching me how to tame and control this roaring monster. Just a few hours later I had mastered it well enough to be of some real help.

The dustbag was full and I was sent outside to empty it. The lady of the house had a suggestion: she had a fire burning in the backyard, she told me, and I might as well tip the sawdust into it. When I got there the flames were small, but there was quite a bit of heat coming from the twigs and leaves that were smouldering on the ground. I unzipped the side of the bag and shook the freshly ground dust onto the fire.

Without warning, a great fireball erupted right in front of me. Particles of dust still clinging to the bag burst into flame as the fire reached up with greedy fingers, snatching even the bag itself. I let go of it, throwing myself backward. My clothes were on fire, and I rolled on the ground to smother the flames. The bag! I grabbed a stick and hooked the burning dustbag out of the fire, jumping on it till the flames went out.

Black with soot and ashes, and coughing up smoke, I returned to the house and on the way noticed a strange smell like singed chicken feathers. Looking down, I saw that all the hairs on my arms and legs were gone. What about my face? I found a mirror and saw that my eyebrows had disappeared, giving me a very surprised look, and a lot

The sander

of my hair was burnt. Davis and the lady of the house were enjoying a quiet cuppa when I appeared at the doorway looking like a chimneysweep. They shook their heads in wonder when I explained about the fireball, both saying that they'd done that kind of thing many times before and nothing like it had ever happened.

Later, as we ate our sandwiches, Davis remarked, 'That wife of mine sure spoils me – chicken again.'

'But … I thought you said you lost your partner, Davis,' I said.

'No, no, not my wife. My partner, Ted. We worked together for thirty years. You, my boy, are here to take his place. But I'm sorry to say that, once you get the hang of it, I have plans to retire. I've had enough.'

We finished that job and worked together on several others. Davis had been a good teacher and now we were ready to start the floors in the new Chermside Hospital building. I arrived early and made a good start by myself, but when eleven o'clock came around and still no Davis I became worried.

Then a phone call came for me. It was Mr Butler. 'Ken, I'm sorry,' he told me. 'Old Davis passed away this morning. Can you get back here, pick up the truck, and drive yourself back to the job site?'

Poor Davis. Retirement can come very unexpectedly.

'Letter for you, Ken,' my mother said one night when I came home from work. As she passed it across the table, I saw that it had been opened.

'Dammit, Mum! It's my mail, you shouldn't have read it!' But after a while I had to eat my words because I couldn't make sense out of all those neatly typed letters. 'So what's it say?'

'It's from Her Majesty's Service. You have to go for a medical next Thursday evening. Waste of time, if you ask me.'

Looking around the hall, I found two faces from my school days – Tom Sherwood and Ricky Ryan. While we stood and waited, we overheard some of the others planning to beat the system; they were willing to do anything they could to get out of National Service. One had swallowed pieces of silver paper to foil the X-ray; another had brought along a big bottle of urine that belonged to a friend with a rare disease, and was trying to sell small quantities for five shillings a pop.

During all this a man in his late twenties approached us. 'I believe I can keep you lads out of the army for a small price if you're interested,' he said, speaking out of the corner of his mouth and looking over his shoulder at the same time.

'No, mate, sorry,' I told him. 'They won't be taking me anyway.'

'What about you?' he asked, turning to Ricky, who shook his head. When Tom said that he might be interested, the man removed a matchbox from his pocket. 'In this box is a drug you add to the urine test. Never fails.' Seeing the curiosity in Tom's eyes, he said, 'One pound, gentlemen, just one pound.' And Tom bought some.

Double doors swung open to reveal a long room with some chairs and tables at the far end. We were ordered to strip down to our underpants and line up in alphabetical order. I had heard all about this routine from others who had been through it – turning the head to the left and coughing once, turning to the right and coughing again, while bored-looking white-coated men sat on low stools in front of us and cupped our genitals. They pronounced me 'fine' and then supervised me while I filled a container with my water.

'Tom,' I called on my way out, 'how did you get on with the dope?'

'Bastards! They were ready. I got sprung.'

My big brother Steven and his wife had bought a half-finished house at Mt Gravatt. They were hoping to get the roof on in two weeks and move out of the caravan they had been living in. When I looked it over, Steven asked me if I'd like the job of sanding the floor – it had been exposed to the weather for ten months and was splintery and warped. I had hoped that the firm would let me hire the sanding equipment for a reasonable price, but was pleasantly surprised when they allowed me to borrow it over the weekend for free. By the time I was finished with it, that floor was better than brand new.

But the best thing of all was that it led to my having a car again. I really missed my Townsville taxi and had finally faced the fact that 'good old' Colin Mars wasn't ever going to send the money he had promised me for it. So when Steven offered me his Whippet utility for only £50, I snapped it up. It ran like a dream, but trying to stop was a major problem. The brakes were mechanical and you could never tell which wheel was going to lock.

The sander

One afternoon, driving along Cavendish Road with my foot flat to the boards at thirty-five miles an hour, I came up behind a woman in a Morris. She was indicating to make a left turn, so I pulled to the right and went to pass her. But she suddenly changed her mind, wanting to turn right instead, and the Morris swerved sharply, cutting across my path. I stood on my brakes; the right-hand wheel locked; the steering-wheel was wrenched out of my hands and went onto full lock. The ute almost rolled over – and the bitumen was looming towards me.

I couldn't hold on. My body slipped towards the road and my foot came off the pedal. With a sickening thump the ute righted itself with all four tyres on the road again, but now heading back the way I had come. It was lucky for me that no other cars were behind, and lucky for the missus in the Morris that she didn't stick around long enough to hear what I thought of her.

It had been a narrow escape, and though I ended up spending a fortune on the brakes, the problem was never fixed.

A second letter arrived for me from Her Majesty's Service and this time I didn't even bother trying to read it. Mum's face told me that she already knew what was in it, and she didn't waste any time letting me know the contents. I had been drafted. Mum ranted and raved about how there must be some mistake, because they couldn't possibly want a boy who was as sick as I was. She threatened to go and 'get this silly business straightened out tomorrow'.

'No, Mum, for once in your life, stay out of it!' I shouted. 'It's up to me! Anyway, I might like being in the army.'

Mr Payne was disappointed at my news. He told me it was a great pity, because my work had been very satisfactory. But Mr Butler took a different attitude, and just a few days later he was waiting for me at the job site.

He must have been looking for any excuse to get rid of me before I did my stint in the army. I'd heard from a mate of mine that if you were called up for 'Nasho' while you were employed, the boss had to guarantee that your job would be waiting for you when you returned, whether this was convenient or not. Mr Butler was obviously the type who found it damned inconvenient to do without a trained worker for three months, preferring to get rid of me now and hire a new guy in my place.

What Next You Bastard

Anyway, there was some half-baked complaint by one of the foremen about my belt leaving a mark along the wall every time I backed into it, and now Mr Butler was throwing his arms all over the place.

'See that line?' he screamed at me. 'And now we have to pay to get it repainted. You're fired!'

16. Nasho

Youths from the Brisbane area were gathered outside the city headquarters of the Australian Army, saying their goodbyes to parents, wives and girlfriends. At the side of the road, coaches stood ready to ship us off to the Wacol Army Barracks, our home for the next three months.

There was a forty-five minute delay before boarding, so I spent the time thinking it all through. If I wanted to, Steven had told me, I could choose to join up with the regular army troops while I was doing my Nasho – no exam, no paperwork. Only one little hitch, though: I might be sent to South Korea and be killed in the fighting. 'But it would be full-time employment, and that's worth thinking about, isn't it, Ken?' he had said before dropping me off.

A loud voice boomed, 'Let's go, gentlemen! Take your bag with you, and give your name as you get on the bus.'

When we arrived at the barracks less than an hour later, I still hadn't made up my mind. Outside the gates of Wacol Barracks were the families of the boys from country areas, and after the last farewells they joined up with the city recruits. We were all herded like livestock into a building. Inside were rows of desks with a doctor in a white coat standing beside each one. Above his head hung a letter of the alphabet and I headed for the queue lining up under H. If there was one thing I knew how to spell, it was my own name. (The only useful thing my father ever gave me was a short surname.)

'Hall, Kenneth William, would you please come forward.' I was being called to the desk for a second time. There were two doctors now – something must be up. They got me to remove my shirt again and listened once more to my chest.

'Mr Hall, you don't have to stay – we have the power to send you home. It's up to you: Army, or home?'

'Army.'

'Harris, Andrew John, please,' came the next name.

I stepped back and couldn't believe that I had just chosen to stay. And now that the decision was made there was no turning back. I walked out of the building and lined up with the other recruits, but suddenly my mind was on home. I thought about all the things I would be missing during the next three months, so I didn't hear my name being called out at first.

'*Hall!* For chrissakes, *answer* me, *Hall!*'

'Here mate,' I said, coming back to the present. A wiry little man in army uniform was standing in front of me, the brim of his hat touching my forehead. The beady eyes staring up at mine did not look friendly at all.

'*What* is your name?'

'Ken Hall,' I said, thinking he must be a bit thick. Hadn't he just called out my name a moment ago?

It obviously wasn't the right answer, going by the angry face, but it was the only name I had – unless he wanted the middle one too. I was just about to give this when the man's voice rose to a high-pitched scream that nearly made me laugh. '*Ken Hall*, see these three stripes on my arm? It means you call me *Sergeant* Gilbert! I want you to call out your name and say, *Sergeant*! Come on, I'm *waiting*!'

'Ken Hall, Sergeant,' I said politely.

Still not good enough. 'I'm sorry, I can't *hear* you,' he said, cupping a hand behind one ear. 'I want *everyone* to hear, so *scream* it out!'

'KEN! HALL! SERGEANT!!!'

'*That's* better. From now on your name will be on the *top* of my list. Fall in with the other nice gentlemen, Hall. Come on, get in line. Okay, *gentlemen*, let's make three rows. Make sure you have your pack with you, that's it. R-i-g-h-t turn, quick *march*!'

Watching each other's feet we pretended to be soldiers, and we must have looked a pretty sorry bunch as he led us towards the back of the camp.

'Halt, l-e-f-t turn! You squirts are now in the army – *my* army,' the Sergeant said with a smirk on his face. 'Back there at the fence we couldn't really raise our voices at you whole damn lot of little squirts, because the *newspapers* and some *mummies and daddies* were there to see their *little boys* off. But now I have you, so get this: *from here on in you belong to us, and we will do with you whatever we like!* Right turn, q-u-i-c-k *march*!'

'When you enter this room you will receive your uniforms.' The room was crammed full with army-issue clothing. In front of us was a long counter, behind which stood young soldiers in uniform.

Nasho

'Tell these men your size. Okay! Get with it! *Hall*! I'm *watching* you!' bellowed the Sergeant. Before long I was balancing a stack of items from my waist to my chin: there were underpants, singlets, long pants and shorts; shirts, boots and shoes; pyjamas, webbing, hat and beret, and one long coat, with all but the footwear tightly folded.

Now we were standing in front of a long timber building with a door at each end and narrow windows sandwiched between steel-framed beds. 'These are your quarters for the next three months. And don't *anyone* think this is home!' No chance of that, I told myself, looking around for a TV set that wasn't there. The building was just off the main road and on the other side was the Migration Centre. My bed was the third on the right and I had just dropped the gear onto it when the voice I was quickly learning to hate blared again.

'Fall *out*! Come on, get a move on, out, out, *out*!' As we stepped outside he added, 'You are going for your bed linen now. At the same time we will show you the toilets and showers, and the mess.'

Back at our quarters again after the guided tour – this man didn't believe in wasting time – we were ordered to put our uniforms on and to stow our civvies out of sight.

There were about twenty of us to each platoon and as each person stood up and shouted his name, he was given his individual serial number in return. I was now officially Private Kenneth William Hall of the Wacol 1959 11th National Service Battalion, Fourteen Platoon Dog Company, Light Ack-Ack. (Somebody explained to us that the 'ack-ack' was short for Anti-Aircraft, or 'AA'.)

Entering the mess that night, I noticed a couple of younger men in army uniform, but with a slight difference: they wore a white band around the upper arm. One I recognised from my neighbourhood in Coorparoo, and I knew that he couldn't have been eighteen yet. When I asked him what he was doing here, he told me that he'd been caught stealing a car and the judge had given him the choice of spending three months in jail, or three months in the army. 'So I took this,' he said with a grin. 'It's better than jail.' But when I wanted to find out more, he waved me away. 'Can't talk – they can send us to jail just for talking.'

Later, in our quarters, we were ordered to polish our brass and clean our webbing. 'Boots and shoes! Lieutenant Prior wants to see his *face* in them in the morning!' We polished and cleaned for hours, but that mirror-like shine he wanted just wasn't there.

'Get *up*! It's time to *move*!' Sergeant Gilbert roared, whipping the blankets off our beds as he walked up the aisle on our very first morning. It was still dark outside.

'*Hall*, I can't *s-e-e* you!' he sang.

'Here, Sergeant,' I yelled, leaping out of bed – but I slipped and went crashing to the floor. Everybody laughed and someone even clapped.

'*When* you've finished the show, *Halley*,' he smiled dangerously, 'just remember you've only got half an hour to shower and dress.'

The sun was just breaking over the horizon when we reached the shower block, a long narrow building with rows and rows of shower heads. Trying to avoid the needle-sharp sting of the icy water was pointless as there was nowhere to hide; the establishment stood by and made sure that everyone got a thorough drenching.

Fully dressed again, but still shivering with cold, we lined up for our first inspection.

'Stand at ease. I will tell you my name for the last time: it is Sergeant Gilbert, and that is Corporal Daley. And now, Lieutenant Prior has a few words for you men.' (I thought it was interesting that he only ever called us 'men' in front of his superiors.)

'Over the next three months,' began the Lieutenant (and a buzz went through the ranks – 'Jeez, a bloody Pom!'), 'you will do what Sergeant Gilbert and his staff tell you. I will be watching him carefully. Any trouble, I will take it out of his hide and, *believe me*, he will take it out on you. This is my first time here. I come from England and simply *won't* settle for second-best. I only have *the* best. On my shoulder I have a crown. I have worked very hard for it, and when I'm finished with you I'll have more. Thank you, Sergeant.'

'*Attention!*' Sergeant Gilbert walked to the end of the line and started his inspection. 'You! After breakfast, go get your hair cut. And you, you too,' he said, picking out one after another. Then he came to me. 'Well, lookee *here*, it's Private Hall. *Haircut*! And tell the barber *short*!'

Army barbers don't ask you what you want, they just do the job: same for everyone. And there are no mirrors. I closed my eyes and felt the clippers make the journey from forehead to neck about eight times. 'Next!' called the barber.

Nasho

When I finally saw my reflection I got a hell of a shock. My ears stuck out like saucers and seemed to flap in the cold breeze like wings at take-off. The hair on top of my head was no more than a sixteenth of an inch long and felt like a door-mat. This man could have a good future as a shearer, I thought.

Four days later we were still no closer to getting a mirror shine on our shoes. Each night we worked at it, polishing till the lights went out. One bloke shook his head and said, 'Bloody marvellous, this is! You know, I went to a Catholic school for eight years – any sign of polish on our shoes and we got a clout across the ear, 'cos the nuns reckoned we could use them to see up the girls' dresses.'

By the sixth night we were done in, too exhausted from spending the past three days marching around the bull-ring. No one had the energy to polish leather.

'*Attention!*' In came the Sergeant. 'I've been told that none of you are polishing your shoes tonight.'

'Come off it, Sergeant, we're rooted!' somebody said.

'*Rooted*, Private Jones? I do not believe the word *rooted* is in the army dictionary. But I do know that the word *polish* is! And I can tell you *this*, if you don't polish your shoes tonight, you will *all* spend two extra hours practising your marching in the bull-ring.' Then he must have noticed our tired faces, because he added something that showed us for the first time that these two slave-drivers might be human after all. 'Before I leave, Corporal Daley and myself will show you how it's done.'

He picked up a tin of shoe polish and held it up for all to see. 'First you place some Nugget on the soft cloth, then you spit on the shoe, and work it in with little round circles. This, gentlemen, is where the expression "spit and polish" comes from.'

It worked well. In no time at all our boots and shoes were so shiny that the Catholic bloke began to see what the nuns had been worried about. 'Pity there's no girls around, hey?' he said with a wicked grin.

There is a saying that the army marches to everything. Well, for the next six weeks we did exactly that. We marched to lectures and to sports sessions; we marched to meals, to the toilets and even to bed. Not surprisingly, I marched in my sleep, my dreams filled with rows of mirrors, where a hundred reflected soldiers looked like a thousand, and all of them marching: left, right, left, right, left …

What Next You Bastard

Sport was a big deal in the army. The officers in charge of each platoon took great pride in having their men outdo those in the other platoons – it reflected on their own abilities and qualities. Competition was important. Winning was everything.

Sergeant Gilbert had a tug-o'-war team and it was said that his team had never once won the event, usually having to take second place. And Sergeant Gilbert, as we all knew only too well by now, did not take kindly to losing. In this respect he was a lot like the Lieutenant. The Sergeant also knew that this would be his last chance to win, because our lot had been the last intake for National Service. For some reason it was going to be abolished from now on. We were the 'lucky' last!

I had heard a rumour that the Sergeant wanted me on his tug-o'-war team, for no reason that I could possibly think of. But in the meantime I was told to report to Sergeant Garth at the boxing stables, because he also had picked me to be on his team. What the heck was going on here? This had to be some sort of con, I told myself, I wasn't a fighter. Maybe Gilbert had set this up to force me into joining his tug-o'-war game.

'Hall, get onto those scales,' Sergeant Garth ordered. 'Nine stone. Hmm, yes, I could do with a lightweight. So, you reckon you can punch, do you?'

'No, not me, Sergeant,' I said, putting him straight.

'Well that's not the story I got,' Garth frowned. When I asked which story he was talking about, he said, 'The one you tell about Julia Creek, I believe.' (Oh hell! Me and my big mouth! Serves me right for bragging about the time I put Big Red's lights out.) 'We start training in two weeks, Hall.'

But I had other ideas. If we could choose any sport, the shooting competition was definitely the one for me. Entering should be easy, from what I'd heard – every time we went to the rifle range, our scores would be totalled, and the man with the top score would receive a badge with crossed rifles on it. Those with the badges were obviously the best shots and would be asked to enter the competition.

It was a beautiful morning for a lecture and all of us from Fourteen Dog Platoon were sitting on the freshly mown grass some distance from the barracks. The speaker, who had just returned from South Korea and was an explosives expert, had us in the palm of his hand. Every eye was on him; every word he spoke got our full attention.

Nasho

BOOM!!! BOOM!!! The world was suddenly exploding around us.

My heart was gone, it left me, I was trying to stand, to run ... but my knees buckled and, weak with fright, I couldn't do more than throw my arms up to cover my head. Dirt and grass was showering down all around us. When it stopped, I opened my eyes.

'There's one over here, sir,' called a soldier from somewhere behind us. He was bending over some bloke who had run straight into the butt of a large tree in his panic.

When the dust had settled and the casualty had been rushed away by ambulance, the speaker calmly continued his lecture. 'As you men just witnessed, *fright* can kill more than the explosion itself.' It certainly made an impression on the rest of us.

Our platoon was made up of youths ranging in age from eighteen to twenty and from all levels of society. But there was one thing we had in common – a 'friend' who went everywhere we went.

It was our .303 rifle with bayonet.

'*Rifle*, not *gun*!' was drilled into us over and over again. Those careless enough to forget the difference were taught the hard way – by humiliation. Each time one of us called it a gun, he would be made to stand up in front of his mates and raise the rifle above his head with one hand while pointing at his penis with the other and shouting at the top of his voice: '*This* is my *rifle*! This is my *gun*! This one's for *fighting*! This one's for *fun*!'

The rifle became part of our family. We had to clean it, oil it, kiss it, take it to bed – and never, never go out without it, unless ordered.

And now the time had come for me to prove that I could shoot.

We marched from the camp to the rifle range at Redbank. Two clips were handed to each person for the first shoot. Our instructions were to stand and fire four shots, then lie down and fire four more, leaving two in the magazine. Simple enough, I thought, and gave it my best.

But when I looked at the pointer behind my target I just couldn't believe it: I had missed a target the size of a house! The rifle sights were so crooked that all I could think was, Thank God this isn't real combat, with my life on the line!

'Give me that rifle, Halley,' the Sergeant barked, 'we need some fine-tuning here.' He took a steel hammer and gave the front sight two good whacks. 'Try that.' My mouth dropped open in amaze-

What Next You Bastard

ment. *Fine*-tuning? 'You have two shots in the magazine. On the command, I want you to walk. When I give the order, fire one, then put on the safety and start walking again. On my next command you will fire again. Now, start walking.'

On my left was Spiro the Greek, who stood about five foot two and weighed around fifteen stone. He had the sort of body that was easier to jump over than walk around, and he did wrestling for a living.

'Fire!' roared the Sergeant.

Off came the safety, up went the rifle. I fired. Then my eye caught the Greek – his rifle was pointing straight at me. Moving was no good. The rifle in his hands swung around and followed me. It all seemed like slow motion – the barrel pointing at me, and Spiro trying to pull the trigger while working on the safety catch at the same time.

'My rifle won't work!' he yelled angrily, too busy looking down his sights and fiddling with the catch to notice me.

'Hit the ground, Hall!' I heard the sergeant's order but couldn't move. My body froze.

'Hit the *ground*, Hall! That means *you*! Hit the ground *now*!'

As if in a dream, the words finally got through to me. I dropped to the ground but somehow knew that the rifle was still pointing at me.

Corporal Daley ran out and stood right in front of Spiro, who still didn't seem to notice the trouble he was causing. The Sergeant came up behind him, swung a clenched fist into the back of his neck, and Spiro went down. Taking the rifle, Daley gave it a good look before pointing it at the target and squeezing the trigger. Bang!

Looking at me, he shook his head and held up two fingers just half an inch apart. 'Hall – *that's* how close you got to being shot.'

They dragged the unconscious Spiro off the range and it was time for my second shot. I decided to aim at the bank below the target. I fired, but the bullet was still a good two feet to the right. The hammer was brought out again, some more fine-tuning was done, and my results improved slightly, but not enough to make an impression or win me a badge.

Back at the camp I had a go at fixing the rifle myself. I placed it between two chairs, removed the bolt and pointed it out the rear door of our quarters. Looking down the barrel, I lined up a mark on a tree, then moved the front sight till it pointed at that spot. Next time on the range I ranked among the best, but after scoring no points on the first day I was out of the race. No shooting competition for me, after all.

It was time for action. We had the rifles more or less sorted out and now we were ready for the big stuff. In front of us were three light anti-aircraft guns. In groups of six to each gun, we were going to learn yet another way of defending our country during war. My job was to stand on a platform, find the target and give the order to fire.

'As you men stand there, you must picture a clock-face in front of you at all times. Hall – when you see your target, you will yell out where on that clock-face it is. If you see a plane at two o'clock, you will yell out, "Target, two o'clock!" With this, the two men sitting can swing onto the target. Let's try it.'

One thing puzzled me. The five on the ground each learnt the others' jobs, yet I wasn't expected to. 'Corporal,' I asked, 'why don't I have to learn all of it?'

'Easy. As the look-out, your life expectancy is short, very short. Under attack you're the first to cop it. That's why the other five have learnt each job; when a man is shot, they grab him and pull him away, and take over.'

Some days the guns would be towed around. Imaginary aircraft would come in to attack. With a stopwatch on us, we practised and practised. When an aircraft was spotted, we had to unhook the gun from the truck and have it up, ready to shoot.

And every single time we were taken out by the enemy.

17. Tug-o'-war

One Friday orders came through that all weekend passes were cancelled. We were moving out, and 'full kit' was the command.

'You are on your way to Amberley Aerodrome to get some practice. Your targets will be the planes flying around Amberley.' Amberley was where the Air Force was located. Somehow the idea of gunning down our own aircraft seemed ridiculous to us, even though we all knew it was only a drill.

Someone spread the word that there was going to be a party the next night – if the privates brought the beer. It sounded like fun. Boarding the trucks, we made the hotel in Oxley our first stop after leaving the barracks. My contribution to the party was a bottle of sweet sherry and a dozen big bottles of beer. Our next stop was a small shop where we purchased the skyrockets that were also on the list. These would be used for night fighting: by placing the stick of a rocket down the barrel of a rifle, taking aim and then lighting the fuse, the rocket would shoot out in the right direction. We all looked forward to trying it.

Two miles from the far end of the aerodrome we set up camp. It wasn't much more than a few rows of two-man tents and a mobile kitchen. Just before sundown we heard a rumour: instead of staying till Sunday, we would be heading back to Wacol in the morning. By nine that night it was official: after breakfast, we'd be leaving. A groan ran through the camp.

'But what about the party, sir?' I asked, saying out loud what most of the others were probably thinking.

'There will *be* no party,' said the Sergeant sternly. 'And all the grog is to be left here together with the skyrockets. Anyone caught trying to slip grog into their quarters will be charged. Do I make myself clear?'

Damn! What a disappointment.

It was close to one in the morning and I still couldn't get to sleep. If we couldn't have a party and we weren't allowed to take the grog back to the barracks, what the hell were we supposed to do with it all? No way was I going to hand over my beer or my skyrockets to

Tug-o'-war

those bastards who'd conned us. Officers! Who the hell did they think they were?

Carrying one of my skyrockets, I slipped out of my tent. I spotted two guards on watch but getting past them in the dark was easy as pie. I headed for the bush and got ready. Feeding the long thin stick of the skyrocket into the barrel only took a moment. Then I pointed my rifle into the air and lit the fuse. What a beautiful sight! The rocket shot upwards with a whoosh – but hit a tree branch and ricocheted towards the camp, where it exploded with a white flash and showered sparks all over the tents. I held my breath, waiting for the camp to come to life. I would be in heaps of strife, that was for sure, but I wasn't a bit sorry I had done it.

Minutes passed and nothing happened. The guards were still talking to each other and no one in the tents had run out screaming. I shook my head in amazement. What easy targets we would have made for an enemy.

Before going back to bed, I carefully wrapped my bottles in clothing and stowed them in my kit bag. They would be coming back to the barracks with me, no matter what.

'Before you men get on this truck,' Sergeant Gilbert roared, 'we want to make quite sure that the grog you brought will be left here!' He positioned himself beside Corporal Daley at the back of the truck and told us to line up. 'As your name is called, throw your kit bag onto the truck, then get up yourself. Hall, Kenneth!'

Taking a deep breath, I swung my kit onto the truck, where it landed on the steel floor with a clank and a rattle. I climbed up after it, expecting a hand on my shoulder to stop me at any moment. But no, 'Bates, Thomas!' was all I heard, and the next bag landed by my feet.

How I got away with it, I'll never know. Any fool could have heard that racket!

Pulling up at the barracks, we were put through the same procedure. 'When we call out your name, throw your kit out first!' When I hesitated, the Sergeant yelled, 'Come on, Hall, throw it!'

This time it sounded like glass breaking for sure, but once again not a word was said. Looking back I noticed the sly grins on the officers' faces as their little game continued.

When I unpacked my bag on my bunk, I did it very carefully, not wanting to cut myself on the broken bottles. You can imagine my surprise when not just one or two but all twelve beer bottles, and even the bottle of sweet sherry, emerged from the clothes I had wrapped them in, completely undamaged.

We had to wait until lights out, of course, and it had to be kept very quiet, but we had our little party after all. I wasn't the only one who had broken the rules and smuggled grog back. Our quarters smelled like a brewery, what with all the beer that had seeped into the kit bags from broken bottles, but what remained was more than enough for a good drinking session.

Now only my bottle of sweet sherry was left. It stood all alone on the floor of our hut and nobody wanted to help me drink it. 'That's for little old ladies, mate,' they scoffed.

Someone in the background yelled, 'Bet you ten shillings – no, make it a pound, Halley – you can't drink that bottle down in one minute!'

'You're on, mate,' I nodded, picking up the bottle and pouring it down my throat.

Winning the bet was easy.

And then the room started spinning, spinning, and I stumbled into a chair, knocking it over with a noisy crash. 'I *think* ... I'm *drunk*. Hey! How about a *sing-song*? C'mon, join in with me ... *Blue M-o-o-n* ...'

'Halley, shut up and get to bed. If they catch you, you'll be gone!' yelled Doc.

'Cassh me ... *Blue M-o-o-n* ... Hey! Who turned the lights on?'

'Attention!' At the door stood the Sergeant with his friend the Corporal. 'I had a report that I could find *beer* in this building!'

'No, Sergeant,' answered Len Hornick. 'No beer here.'

You missed out, mate, I felt like saying, bad luck, it's a-l-l gone!

'Hall! Stand still!'

'I am, Shar-shant.' But why was he dancing in circles around the room? One of us was going to get dizzy. 'No-one wantsa sing wi' me ... *Blue M-o-o-n* ...'

'Private Hornick, put that man to bed and shut him up! And make sure all the bottles are out of here by roll-call!' Sergeant Gilbert slammed the door on his way out.

'Put to bed? No way! 's time for talkin'.' No one was going to tell *me* when to go to bed.

'Get in that bed, Halley,' Len Hornick ordered, and I could tell he was annoyed with me for stirring up trouble with the Sergeant. 'If we hear *one* more word, we'll put you outside for the night.'

'I'm your mate,' I assured him.

Len had had enough. 'Right, that's it! You're going outside!'

'*Bed* – I'm goin' to bed, don' worry.'

In the morning I felt fine. No headache, no sign of a hangover. I felt on top of the world, except for a slight dryness around the mouth. I found a tap and drank water until I couldn't hold any more.

As I walked to roll-call my legs felt strangely light. Just as I went to line up with the others, I stumbled and fell to the ground. There were a few snickers, but nobody had the guts to laugh out loud. The problem was obvious: I was still drunk. Dragging myself to my feet, I stood and waited for my name to be called. It didn't take long.

'Private Hall!'

I opened my mouth to respond, but nothing came out.

'Private Hall, Kenneth!'

This time I managed a small squeak.

Corporal Daley came and stood right in front of me. He wrinkled his nose and narrowed his eyes. 'Private Hall, I believe, is not well. Could be under the influence of alcohol, Sarge.'

'*Sick*, is he? Right. Well, after breakfast I want to see him – *on the parade ground with all the others*!' bellowed Gilbert.

'All of you, your marching is *shocking*! You will be marched over to the bull-ring to practise the marching-out parade, and you won't be coming back *till it's bloody perfect*!'

Four hours later we were still at it. My stomach was churning and my head was full of cottonwool.

'We will try again – any mistake will add on one hour. Q-u-i-c-k march!'

We were coming into the home turn, with only one last right turn to go, when the Sergeant pounced. 'Stop! Hall, step out!'

'You *did* it, Hall! I *knew* you would! You were *out of step*! For that, you and your mates will stay out here for one more hour.' He smiled from ear to ear.

My rifle came up all by itself. I was ready to drop the Sergeant.

'Swing that rifle, Halley, and I'll drop you.' It was the Corporal; he'd been standing right behind me and I hadn't even noticed.

'Halley, I want you in my tug-o'-war,' Gilbert was saying. 'Join, or I'll keep you *and all your mates* out here for another hour, and then I will ask you again. If you still say no, then we will do *another* hour.

What Next You Bastard

Get the picture?' When I nodded, he smiled again. 'Now, fall in, and q-u-i-c-k march!'

That afternoon when I arrived for practice Sergeant Gilbert called me over. 'You did *exactly* what I wanted you to do, Halley.'

'What was that, sir?'

'You broke under pressure, and I got you. Now you will help me to win my first tug-o'-war.'

Sunday dinner was salad with mashed potato. One of the boys noticed a lettuce leaf moving on his plate. When he turned it over he found slugs crawling on the underside. A quick inspection of our plates turned up a population of six altogether. We arranged them on a tray in the middle of the table and watched them squirm while we ate.

At one point Cory left the table to get some more bread and a quick look passed between the rest of us. We were all thinking the same thing: this was an opportunity too good to miss.

Cory returned to his seat and resumed eating. He never noticed the empty tray in the middle of the table. He never noticed the way his salad was doing a slow walkabout either. He dug his fork into the lettuce and smeared it with mashed potato. We were sure he was just pretending, and would at the last moment flick the forkful onto someone else's plate or lap. So when Cory placed the food into his mouth, closed his lips and started chewing, we sat and watched with horror and fascination. It wasn't until he had actually swallowed that two of the boys leapt up and dived from the table, dry-retching.

Doc couldn't stand it when Cory scooped up another lot. 'You're eating the slugs, mate.' But Cory just smiled and nodded, smacked his lips together and kept eating.

To this day, I'm convinced he didn't believe us.

Our platoon was on Special Duty. Today we were going to blow up a bridge. A bus took us to the forest at Greenbank and from there we marched for three miles through the trees, lugging a heavy box between us. The old wooden bridge, when we finally found it, was in very bad shape – most of the planks on the top were missing, twelve weak-looking piers acting as supports looked as though they would topple over with the next breeze that came along. We needed explosives for this?

Tug-o'-war

The case we had carried was full of dynamite, but we were told we wouldn't be using it after all. We were shown how to rig up the plastic explosives and now were ordered to stand clear – she was ready to blow.

Watching from a safe distance as one pier after another was taken out on a time relay, the demo didn't take too long. What a letdown. The show was over, and what had been a rickety old bridge now lay in an untidy heap in the gully. Even the wolf in the fairytale could have done the job with a huff and a puff!

Marching back to the bus with the heavy box in tow, we came across a grey-headed major standing beside a small waterhole.

'Bring that case of dynamite over here,' he instructed. The hole was about four feet in length, two feet wide and ten inches deep. 'No use dragging that box back to camp. Place it in this hole, give it a two-minute fuse. You men will stand here,' he said, pointing to a patch of ground close by. 'When you see the fuse lit, we will all turn and *walk* slowly away – but *don't run*! When it explodes, turn and have a look.'

This promised to be exciting.

The Major lit the fuse and we all started walking. It seemed like hours before the explosion came. First the ground shook under my feet, then a strong gust of wind hit me. When I turned, all I could see was dust. Looking up I noticed very small items flying upwards. Some were falling – and the closer they got, the bigger they got, till they were the size of dinner plates.

'*Run*!' yelled one of the officers. 'And don't stop till you reach the bus!'

We lined up and a head count was done. Luckily no one had gone 'missing in action'. We were ordered back to the hole to inspect the results. As we got closer we could see that trees had been stripped bare of branches and leaves. Stones and rocks covered the area that had been clear earlier, and what had been a small hole only a short while ago was now a bloody big one.

All the officers got together for a little meeting before the Major addressed the platoon. 'You men, gather round. Today will be a day I won't forget. The demo we planned for you went a bit wrong. I hope when we return to barracks I will hear nothing on this matter. That's all. Please return to the bus.'

Somehow or other, though, everyone seemed to know all about 'the bomb' even before our bus reached the camp.

It was time to shoot the Owen and the Bren machineguns. Once again we marched towards the rifle range where we learnt that the Owen would be fired, but no targets would be used. Receiving three full clips, we would shoot from the hip position, first on single-shot, and then on fully automatic.

With the Bren things were different. For these, targets were used. Soldiers from one of the other platoons were on target duty, meaning that they had to crouch behind a small hill, or mound, and hold up the long pole or stay which had the target on its top end.

The first few rounds I aimed at the target. It wasn't hard to hit, but it was boring. Before long some of us realised that we'd have more fun aiming at the top of the mound and trying to cut the stay that held the target aloft.

'*Cease fire!* You men are not firing at the target! Let me tell you, next week you will find yourselves *behind* that mound, working!'

My eyes caught a creek to our left. It was full of water. When the order came to 'Fire at your own time!', I still had fifty rounds left and that water was looking good. Looking around, I noticed that the officers were busy talking. So, swinging the barrel around, I fired at the creek and its flat surface was cut by a perfect row of bullets, throwing the water into a swirl.

That afternoon one of the Owen machineguns found its way into our hut. I don't know who managed to smuggle it in, but at some point during the night it was shipped out. And some farmer got himself a real bargain.

'The Bull' was over six foot tall and built like a wall. He was a soldier with an attitude problem, a grudge against the whole world. He was a very fair man, though, because he treated everyone the same: like dirt.

Dog Platoon was due for its third round of injections. We had already received two needles earlier and were now walking up the steps of the building where the doctors waited. My path was blocked by the Bull. He was standing by the door and I thought I heard him talking ... no, mumbling.

'What's that, Bull?' I asked.

Looking down at me was a very white face. The Bull's eyes were glazed and his lips moved slightly. He was muttering something I couldn't understand.

Tug-o'-war

'Get a *move* on, Hall!' called the Sergeant from behind me.

'Come on, Bull, move out the way,' I said.

Reluctantly, the Bull inched his way through the doors, but as soon as he set foot inside the building his head went back and his huge body went limp. Before he had even hit the ground, two men grabbed him. The doctor held his arm, scratched the skin and applied the serum, then they placed him on a mattress.

Whispers were going around that the Bull had fainted. When he came to, which was pretty quickly, he caught up with me at the exit and leaned right up close to me. 'You, Halley! Not a word about what you saw inside, *got it?*' warned the Bull.

Later it was time to see who needed the tuberculosis injection. I was first in line.

'No needle for this one,' said the doctor.

'Private Hall, you will stand here and help us when we need it,' said the Corps Officer.

Spiro the Greek appeared in the doorway, took two steps inside, turned white and went down.

A few others came and went without incident. Then the Bull entered the room. He had trouble seeing where he was headed and almost crashed into a table. No wonder – he had covered his eyes with a towel.

'Where are you, Doctor?' he mumbled.

'Over here,' smiled the doctor. The second he touched the Bull's arm, the big man hit the floor. The doctor shook his head at the ceiling as if to say, 'Why me?' He was just remarking to the Corps Officer that it was always the big tough-looking ones who were the most trouble, when he had to eat his words.

'One left, Doctor,' someone said.

'Well, bring him in and let's get it over with.'

Bring him in! They were *dragging* a skinny youth of about five foot five. He was kicking and screaming, tears pouring down his cheeks and his eyes rolled up in their sockets.

'Throw him on the floor!' ordered the doctor. 'Hold him down. Get over here, Private, and help us.'

It took four of us to hold him down and one to push the needle in.

'Get him up,' the doctor said, sounding disgusted. The youth was back on his feet. He looked at us, turned around and skipped out of there as if nothing had happened.

The Sergeant was furious that so many of his men had let him down. 'You *boys* can return to your barracks the *long way* – with a run across country,' he snapped.

I was jogging along with ease – until I came to the creek that ran through the middle of the camp. A huge spotted gum had been felled to bridge the creek and my legs just went on strike all by themselves. I sat down on the bank and watched the others walk across it. The Bull ran across.

But there was just no way that I could do it.

'You okay, Halley?' someone yelled as they crossed to the other side.

'Yeah,' I lied, 'I just got a stone in my boot.'

When the last person had crossed, I had no choice but to give it a try. I stood on the end of the trunk with both arms stretched out at my sides, feeling like an apprentice tightrope-walker in a circus and probably feeling just as nervous. I took a few tiny steps. Then I had a better idea – after all, no one was around to see me. So I sat down and wrapped my legs around the log as if it were a horse. Using my hands as levers, I pulled myself all the way across and brushed the dirt off my seat when I got there.

There, among the trees, was the Bull, of all people!

'You okay, Halley?'

'Yeah, I'm just no good at heights,' I admitted.

'Like me,' the Bull said sympathetically. 'One tiny needle and I flake out.'

18. An angel on her way to heaven

Film nights were something we always looked forward to, but tonight we were in for a special treat. We had been promised a sex film as a reward for all our hard work. A thousand voices carried our excitement as we sat in long rows and waited impatiently for the lights to go down. For most of us it would be the first time we had ever seen a 'blue movie' and we laughed and joked noisily.

'Attention!' came a voice from the loudspeakers. 'We want you to shut your mouths and behave like gentlemen, as we do have a few ladies here with us tonight.' I looked around and didn't see any ladies, but then the lights went out and the film began.

For the next thirty minutes we sat quietly, but when the lights came on and it was all over, the buzz of excitement had gone. There had been no plot, no romance, and no lovemaking. It was a film from the 1940s, a documentary on sexually transmitted diseases. We'd been had.

On Friday afternoons the usual weekend passes were handed out. For those on the list it meant freedom until ten o'clock Sunday night. The uniform we hated so much in the camp became our best asset as soon as we set foot outside it. It seemed to have magical powers over the opposite sex. Even the shortest soldier felt ten feet tall in his army gear.

Four of us ended up in Stones Corner just after seven o'clock one Friday night. People filled the streets. Some were heading for the picture theatre, others were just window-shopping. One of my mates mentioned that he felt like a woman tonight, making the rest of us hoot and giggle and agree that he looked a bit like one too! When we had finished clowning around, we decided it would be great to find some girls and have some fun. Except for one thing: the film on diseases we had just seen had us a bit worried. None of us had any protection. French letters, or condoms, were something we had only heard about, but never seen.

Drawing straws always sounds like such a fair way to decide on who gets to do the job that no one wants to do – until you're the one who ends up holding the shortest one. Yes, it was me.

My mates pushed me in the direction of the nearest chemist shop, where I hesitated on the doorstep and took a deep breath. After two steps inside I stopped. No way! The grey-haired woman behind the counter looked like a poodle and was in her fifties at least. Turning quickly, I headed back to the door and ...

'May I help you?'

I was caught. Biting my lip, I asked, 'Is the male chemist in, please?'

'No, I'm sorry, it's his night off. Look, can I help you?'

(Just my luck!) 'Yes, I believe so. Could I have a couple of ... no, a box of ... French letters?'

The woman's face changed. Now she looked like a bulldog. Her bosom rose and fell and she had trouble speaking. 'You ... filthy human being! How dare you come into this shop and ask for something as low as that!'

Before she had finished I was back-pedalling out the door and she was following closely, her voice rising to a shriek and her eyes blazing. 'You can't be a Roman Catholic! You're ... you're one of those heathens sent by the Devil!!!' A crowd had gathered on the footpath to see the show and they were really getting their money's worth. 'Look at him! Take a good long look at him! He has dirt on his mind!'

Fleeing the scene, I could feel every eye in Stones Corner on me. Even my good mates had done a disappearing act. I walked a few blocks to cool down and then I walked some more. About an hour later I found myself in the Valley, where a couple of shops were still open. One of them was a chemist's. I told myself that I'd probably get the same reaction here, but then I noticed a white-haired man by the till, so I decided to give it one last try.

By the time I got up the nerve to step inside, he wasn't there any more.

A girl's head rose from behind the counter where she had been rearranging stock on the bottom shelf. She had her back to me. As I watched, she slowly emerged like a mermaid rising out of the sea. Then she turned around and I found myself staring at one of the prettiest faces I had ever seen.

'May I help you, sir?'

She was done up like a peach. Long black hair hung straight down over her shoulders and shimmered in the lights. Her lips were painted bright red and matched the extra-long fingernails that she was using to smooth down the folds of her uniform, a white uniform that went in and out in all the right places and showed off the deep tan of her arms and legs.

'Can I help you?' she said a second time and I could have drowned in her soft brown eyes.

'Yes – can I see the boss, please?'

'Sorry, sir, he just stepped out, he won't be back for about fifteen minutes.' She offered to help me herself, but I just thanked her and said I would come back later. 'Sir – would you be after something you feel you can't talk to me about?' Her smile nearly knocked me over. 'Please ... I'm here to help.'

It couldn't have been easier. This girl acted as if I was only buying shoelaces or toothpaste or something ordinary like that – even asking me what kind I wanted. Were there different kinds? I said that any kind would be fine, thanks, and after she'd wrapped the box and I had paid her, she asked me something I never would have expected in a million years.

She asked if I would like any help using them!

I swung around in a full circle to see if anyone else was in the shop. There wasn't. I didn't know what to say, so I said nothing, but I must have looked pale because she asked me if I was all right. Holy smoke! The girl told me that she would be finishing work at eleven and, unless I had someone else lined up, she'd love to meet me at the phone box on the corner.

I still wasn't sure she was actually talking to me, so I looked around again.

Outside the shop I threw my arms up into the air and did a little jig. Boy, you just never know what will happen next, I told myself.

Cheryl Cupitt was her name. She lived in a small flat that was decorated in brown and white. All the walls were white and the furniture brown; even the bathroom was tiled in brown and white. When Cheryl finished undressing me and asked me to undress her, her underwear was crisp and snowy white against her tanned skin. Under a chocolate-coloured bedspread were immaculate white sheets. It wasn't till I knew her better that I found out why she loved these two colours so much.

She had already slipped between the sheets and was waiting for me to join her, when I suddenly remembered the package in my coat pocket. I went to get it, but Cheryl just smiled and told me not to bother.

Breakfast was ready when Cheryl woke me. I thought I was still dreaming when I opened my eyes to see her standing there wearing nothing but a small white apron. She hated wearing clothes, she said, and when I asked her about her even suntan she pointed up to the ceiling, where six ray-lamps hung above the bed.

Over two steaks, a couple of eggs and a bottle of wine (definitely my favourite kind of breakfast!) I learnt that Cheryl had been born in Noosa on the Sunshine Coast, but had moved here two years earlier.

'What made you do that?'

'A small thing called a tumour.'

'What in the hell is that?'

'It's a growth in my head.'

I sat there and tried to understand what this meant, while Cheryl poured me some more wine. 'This thing you call a tumour ... will it hurt you?' I asked.

'Yes,' she nodded, 'one day it will kill me.'

I tried to say something to this, but what was there to say? I just sat there like a stunned mullet, so Cheryl explained it.

Two years earlier she'd had a bad headache which, after tests and X-rays, the doctors had decided was caused by a small growth beside her brain. There was no operation which could be done to remove it. Two months ago some more tests found that the tumour had grown and Cheryl would have only a short time left to live. This was why she had moved to Brisbane, to be close to her doctor and the hospital. She was almost twenty-one.

I still couldn't speak. My throat had closed up and my eyes were stinging. Leaving my seat, I took Cheryl into my arms and held her tight. We cried together.

My weekend with Cheryl stayed in my mind over the next few days. By Wednesday morning I couldn't stand it any more, so I got myself a special leave pass for that night by pretending that my mother was sick.

Hitch-hiking most of the way, I arrived at the chemist shop to find that Cheryl had gone out on a delivery, though she was due back soon. The chemist was very friendly. He said that all he'd heard about since the doors opened on Monday morning was this soldier called Ken. He even shook my hand.

Cheryl's boss allowed her to knock off work early and she took me home, telling me on the way that her parents would be waiting for her at her place and, if I didn't mind, she would love for them to meet me.

'This is him, Mum,' she said as we walked in the door. 'Ken, this is my mother and father.'

Mrs Cupitt put her arms around me and kissed my cheek. Mr Cupitt did his best to shake my arm out of its socket and they both treated me like a long-lost son. The simple meal that had been prepared for three was quickly stretched into a feast for four and by the time we had finished eating, three empty wine bottles stood on the table. We talked about everything, like one big happy family, and I wanted it to last forever.

'Gosh, look at that, it's eight o'clock already!' Cheryl's mother said. 'We'd better go home and leave you two lovebirds alone.' We all stood up and then she asked me if she could have a minute alone with me. While Cheryl and her father walked to the car, Mrs Cupitt said, 'Cheryl told us what went on last weekend, Ken. I want you to know you have our blessing. Our family is strictly Roman Catholic, but time is running out for our daughter – so please treat Cheryl very special.' Her voice was shaking as she spoke, and her eyes begged me not to let her daughter down.

Every weekend pass after that brought me to Cheryl's flat. We shared candle-lit dinners and champagne, swapped life stories, laughed and cried and made love. Knowing our time together was limited, we made the most of every hour and every day.

Cheryl had just been telling me all about her childhood in Noosa. 'I had my whole life ahead of me. And then' (*thump!* her fist crashed down onto the table, making the glasses rattle) 'just from nowhere, I got this pain in my head. It was so bad, Ken, it made me sick. Only lasted about ten seconds each time, but it was terrible.' Cheryl dropped her head and dipped her finger into one of the puddles of spilt wine, drawing patterns on the table top. 'So I just sort of ... pushed it aside, but then it started coming back more and more often. Everyone said it would go away, it was just growing pains or something. Except for this one priest, who believed my mind was being torn between the Church and evil.' She looked up and smiled at this part, but it was a sad smile, the kind where you know the person is hurting inside.

One day, she explained, she had just collapsed while out shopping; the next thing she knew she was waking up in a hospital bed. That was when they did the tests and learnt the bad news. Cheryl and her parents had decided to keep it a secret that only the three of them would share. Over the next three months they went from one doctor to another, hoping to find a cure, but nothing they tried ever worked. She even went to church every day to pray, but God wasn't listening.

'Why me?' Cheryl sobbed, and I squeezed her hand but didn't know the answer. 'I haven't done anything wrong. That was two and a half years ago, when they gave me two years to live, so I suppose I've had at least six months more than I should've.'

She had made friends with a girl in hospital who was older than her, and had the same problem. She had told Cheryl a secret: she could do anything she wanted with her life, because she knew when and how she was going to die. This friend had lived her life to the fullest, with parties every night and a new boyfriend each week. Then, just a few weeks ago, it was all over for her.

I asked Cheryl if she had followed her friend's example and she said that since she had learnt her fate she hadn't wanted a boyfriend. Her parents and doctors had urged her to live it up, let her hair down and do whatever she felt like. 'The Lord will forgive, they told me, but I didn't see any point in it. Then you walked into my life,' she smiled. 'All I want from you is love and friendship, Ken. Can you give me that?'

I only nodded. I knew that if I tried to speak now I would break down. Cheryl was much braver than me.

Another weekend I asked her about the brown and white colour scheme. She had a very simple explanation.

'They're my favourites. They feel like they're free of germs. Living at the coast, everyone always looked so healthy with their nice brown tans, and the white sand always looked so clean. So, to me, those two colours stand for health and cleanliness, and that's the sort of world I want to live in.'

It all made sense and I looked around the flat with new eyes.

'Ken,' Cheryl said late one night, 'do you think there's an afterlife?' She looked so fragile and tired that I didn't have the heart to tell her, no, I didn't believe in all that. So I lied to her and said I thought there must be, and then I sat beside her on the edge of the bed and held her hand until she had cried herself to sleep. After a while I stood up, opened a bottle of wine and set about getting quietly drunk.

An angel on her way to heaven

National Service was coming to an end. During our last week we had our Sports Day. Sergeant Gilbert gathered his tug-o'-war team together for a final pep talk – which was more threatening than encouraging – and Fourteen Dog Platoon was ready to win the trophy he wanted so badly. In the first round we made short work of Charlie Company. It was the first time I had ever been part of a winning team and as we lined up for the finals I was determined to give it everything I had. Winners were grinners, but losers – no one wanted to know them.

Gilbert had placed me right in front for this one. He leaned right over me and breathed in my ear, 'I've got just *one* thing to say to you, Ken Hall. *Do – or die.*'

We were ready, but the umpire was not. He wanted that knot dead centre. Our team gave him some slack and so were taken by surprise when he yelled, 'Ready, Go!' without any warning. Those first seconds nearly cost us the game. We were pulled off balance and headed towards the opposite team. Sergeant Gilbert was yelling, 'Pull! Pull!'

Somehow we managed to hold on to that two-inch rope and keep Easy Company from dragging us over the line. With only half an inch to spare, we dug our heels in, gritted our teeth and leaned our weight against the rope.

Then we moved. It was only a little bit, but we did move backwards. Next it was an inch, followed by another inch. We had the enemy on the move – we were slowly breaking them. Gilbert was jumping up and down. If he'd had a whip he would have used it on us, that was for sure. 'Pull, you bastards, *pull*!'

But now the pendulum was swinging back. Easy Company had somehow found themselves a new lease on life and were dragging our team forward again. I could see the umpire with his hand up in the air, ready to drop the flag. His hand came down halfway, but then it went up again, then down, then up, like a conductor who wasn't sure of the music. And Sergeant Gilbert was roaring like a wounded bull, calling us every name under the sun.

Just when it seemed that all was lost we gave it our last drop of energy and hauled the Easy boys towards the line. Gilbert was out of control. 'You *have* them! Don't stop, you flaming bastards! Pull, *pull*, PULL!!!' The umpire raised his hand – and sliced the air. It was over.

'*We won! We bloody won!*' screamed Gilbert, jumping up and down with both arms high above his head. We gathered around him, grinning like schoolboys, and raised him up onto our shoulders. It was a very special feeling – one that only a winning team can ever experience – and it felt so good that my whole attitude towards the army changed in that moment.

Later Sergeant Gilbert stood in front of me. He was smiling, but it was a genuine smile, not one of his dangerous barracuda brand. 'The day I first laid eyes on you, if anyone had said to me that I would *ever* be thanking you for something, I would have called them a fool. Thanks, son,' he said, and held out his hand.

Later that week we had another event. This was the Big One, the passing-out parade. We were soldiers and very proud of it. As we marched past our families, our chests were puffed out and our heads held high. Mum and Ian had come to watch and, like all the others, I felt like a hero.

After the parade we still had two days left before leaving the barracks and in our huts we passed our pyjama tops around to be signed by all our mates. They had all become good friends and I hoped that we would meet again some time.

On my last day as a soldier I was feeling so happy with myself that I joined the queue at the Administration hut.

The government was in trouble because ours had been the last intake for National Service and from now on they would have to rely on volunteers. They were looking for young men to enlist in the army on a permanent basis and I decided that it would be a great career for me – regular work, steady pay and lots of action. They needed soldiers to send to Korea, but that was fine with me, too. I would serve my country happily and proudly, even die for it, if it ever came to that.

Earlier we had been given forms to fill in. 'I hope you know that your parents must sign these before you can sign your lives over to us,' one of the officers had warned.

There was a civilian by the name of Mr Simons seated at the table when my turn to apply came around. He waved me to a chair and looked over my papers. Simons had the foulest breath I had ever come across – when he opened his mouth, I expected flies to rush into it. Mr Simons frowned at me once or twice, then threw my papers across the table. 'Why are you wasting my time, Private Hall?'

'What do you mean, sir?' I asked.

An angel on her way to heaven

'Don't call *me* sir, this is *shit*!' he exploded. 'We don't want you, Private. It's easy to see you can't read or spell. Then there's your health – bad heart, tuberculosis. How in the *world* did you ever get in? And how dare you waste the government's and my time! You can leave by that door!'

Job searching was hard. School passes were a must wherever I went. The only job I managed to get was in the storeroom of a chemicals factory, where on my first day I was told, 'Your job is to make sure the women don't do any heavy lifting. As you can't read, I must ask you not to touch anything. This place is full of poison.'

For some reason Cheryl didn't want me to contact her and though it was hard to stay away I had to go along with her wishes.

I had been out of the army for two whole months when she called me one night at home. She told me that she hadn't wanted anyone to see her for a while because she had been too sick, but now she needed to talk to me. She would be going into hospital the next day and I could visit her there in Ward 2A, if I still wanted to. I did.

As the phone went dead I found myself remembering that other hospital ward where I had spent much of my youth – Ward 1A. A shiver ran through me as I replaced the receiver.

Cheryl was sitting up in bed when I found her. She looked so small in the big hospital bed and held out her arms to me. I moved into them. 'I love you,' she said, making my heart miss a beat. We held each other tightly and our tears flowed together.

'I'm so sorry, Ken,' she whispered. 'I fell in love with you and I never knew it. I didn't mean to – it just happened. From the start, I thought we could just be friends and … you know, just lovers … but then I saw you that day at the parade …'

'At the parade? But I didn't know you were there! I didn't see you.'

'I know, I didn't want you to. But I saw you there with a lady and a man …'

'My mother and brother.'

'… yes, I thought they must be. And I was so proud of you and then I realised that I'd fallen in love with you.' Cheryl covered her face with her hands. 'But it's all for nothing, isn't it? It's too late now,' she sobbed.

'Ssh, no, it's not.' I rocked her against my chest and told her that I loved her too and that of course it wasn't too late. This was the beginning for us, not the end. Then her parents came in to visit and I promised I'd come back again later. As I walked out of the ward I recognised the smell around me. It was a place of death.

I visited Cheryl whenever I had a free moment. One morning a few weeks later the sister in charge of Cheryl's ward phoned me, saying that Cheryl would like me to visit that night, and that she would be alone.

To my surprise, she was waiting for me outside the ward when I arrived, talking to the ward sister and dressed in her normal clothes, not in a hospital gown. She looked wonderful. She had a glow on her face and my first thought was that she had been miraculously cured and was allowed to go home.

Taking my hand, Cheryl said, 'Come with me.' She led me out of the hospital and down the driveway that ran past the maternity wing. After a few more twists and turns we arrived at a small wooden building that looked deserted. 'This must be it,' she said, explaining that the sister had been very understanding and had told her where to find a quiet place for the two of us to be together. A long corridor had rooms on both sides of it, most of which were locked. At the last room the door stood open. Inside was a small table, a couple of chairs and a bed.

We spent two hours together without speaking. There was no need to. Our hands and lips and bodies did all the talking and said more than words could ever have expressed. Only one thing troubled me: a feeling inside me that this would be our last time together.

When we were dressed again, Cheryl stood up and looked at me for a long time.

Then she kissed her fingertip and gently touched it to my lips. 'Please ... not one word,' she whispered. 'I'll leave by myself. You wait for a while and then go straight home. And don't ... please swear to me ... you won't try to see me again.'

When I bent my head to hide my tears, she said, 'Ken, promise me!'

They were the two hardest words I had ever had to say. 'I promise.'

'One day we'll meet again. I just know it.'

I only nodded. When I looked up again she was already walking down that long and lonely corridor. As I watched, she reached the end and opened the door that led onto the street. One of the street lights pierced the darkness and caught her in its rays, briefly lighting up her white dress. At this moment she turned and waved, then the door closed and she was gone. I had just seen an angel on her way to heaven.

Cheryl died in her sleep two days later.

19. Janice

It was 1960 and work was getting me down. The factory made hand cleaner, disinfectant and hair shampoo. There were two kinds of shampoo – at least I thought there were at first, until I noticed that the bottles were identical and only the labels were different. Half of them had just a few words written on them, the others had about twenty words more and looked prettier. Words sure were expensive, I told myself, because they put the price up by a whole £6 a box. Somewhere along the line I heard that the bottles with the fancy labels were sold to posh customers who thought they deserved a better quality shampoo, and didn't mind paying for the privilege.

There was no challenge in the work I was doing, no sense of achievement. Lifting boxes day after day was making me feel like a robot. If I'd had somewhere better to go, I would have walked out without once looking back.

Mum reluctantly guaranteed another loan for me. My old Whippet utility was not built for a young man with a future ahead of him, so I sold it for £20 and went looking for a replacement. What I needed was a later model car and I was lucky enough to find one right away. It was a black Wolseley 450 and I just had to have it. The rego was NJR 300 so I nicknamed it Naughty Junior. Driving around town was a breeze, but on longer trips, anything over two hours, there was always trouble.

We had heard that a couple with the same kind of problem had received a brand new car from the Wolseley factory for their trouble, so I got Mum to write to Sir Nutfield in England to complain. We never got a reply, though.

While working on the motor one Saturday afternoon, I had a bit of an accident. I had removed the bonnet and placed it on the driveway in front of the car. A jack was holding up the car on the right hand side. I was in the middle of adjusting the front brakes. I finished with the spanner and laid it on top of the mudguard. From there it rolled down into the engine and made contact with the starter motor.

My car roared into life, shot forward and ran over the bonnet.

Janice

The jack had caught itself under the cross-arm and as it went past it bashed into my right wrist, sending a pain shooting up my arm. The driver's door was open and it caught me, knocking me down and dragging me towards the house. As the Wolseley hit the brick wall, the door crumpled and the car came to a stop. My arm was pinned from wrist to shoulder between the car door and the house and I had to fight to keep myself from passing out with the pain.

I yelled for help but nobody turned up. A bit later I heard an ambulance and thought, hooray, someone must have heard me after all – but instead of stopping it kept on going down the street.

Pins and needles were setting in. Lying on my back, I worked with the jack and my good arm to free myself. Blood rushed back into my fingers at a hundred miles an hour, making my whole arm throb.

I was still sitting there, nursing my arm, when I heard the ambulance again, this time coming back the other way. By the time I picked myself up and made it down the driveway to flag it down, it had already gone past.

That night I heard that one of my neighbours had been pinned beneath his car when the jack slipped, bringing the full weight of the car down on top of him, crushing several ribs and killing him. I was a lot luckier – but still, my arm was swollen up like a balloon and I could hardly move it.

This was bad news. I was pretty sure it was broken, but if I went to the doctor now I would be put off work without pay, and I needed the money.

On Monday morning the pain was worse and so was the swelling. My arm was twice its normal size. I put on a long-sleeved shirt and went to work. During the morning I was told to move some heavy crates from the loading bay. Here was my chance. I made a half-hearted attempt to shift one off the top of the stack, and with only one good arm to balance it, the damn thing came crashing down on top of me.

Factories can be very dangerous places!

They told me that my arm was fractured in two places, a plaster cast was put on, and I was off work for four weeks – with pay. Looking back, it was a pretty lousy thing to do.

When some months had passed and I was still stuck with a job I hated, I started going to interviews on Saturday mornings. Over and

What Next You Bastard

over, it was the same old story: 'Sorry, we need a younger person – an apprenticeship goes with the job.' Too old at twenty?

Mum was up to her tricks again. One way or another she always managed to find jobs for me. 'Remember Craig Brown?' she said in the middle of ironing one Friday night. Of course I remembered him. Mum had gone to school in Nambour with Craig's mother, and my brother Steven and Craig had done their apprenticeships together. 'Well, he's started his own business and he'd like to see you tomorrow around ten.'

Craig Brown's carpentry workshop was in Capalaba, which was a fair way out. Driving along the dirt track with tea-tree bushes and grass-trees brushing the sides of my car, I felt as if I was out in the bush again. Water from a swamp crossed the 'road' and ran through the Browns' property. A Land Rover would be useful here, I thought as I bounced along. I was just starting to wonder where the blazes this factory was when the track ended. There in front of me was nothing but a small cottage. No factory to be seen. This was it?

The cottage was a partly built house standing on seven-foot stumps. There were no front steps and the front door was just a sheet of iron nailed over the doorway. Some of the windows were the same. A blue Vanguard utility was parked under the house, beside it leaned a motor bike, and next to the house sat a Ford coupe.

Ada, Craig's wife, was hanging out the washing and had a mouthful of pegs. When she saw me, she pointed towards a small shed that I hadn't seen behind the house and kept pinning up sheets. The sounds of a drill told me that this was the factory – or work shed. I walked along the short end and when I turned the corner I saw that it had no front – the whole width was wide open.

I saw a docking saw on the right, a six-planer in the middle and, just behind that, a surfacer. It was a very small shed, but behind it an extension was being built. And there, fitting doors onto a wardrobe, was the man himself.

Shaking Craig's hand was like putting your fingers into a steel vice and waiting for the bones to crunch.

'Your Mum told me you like working with wood and you want a job,' he said, by way of greeting.

I tried to say yes, but his grip had taken my breath away.

'Ever worked a docking saw?'

'Many times,' I answered, finding my voice again. 'I've worked all the machines you have here.' And it was true. At Frank Snowdon's

Janice

place I had been doing really well until Mr Trusty-Stopwatch from the UK came to town with his fancy ideas.

'Okay, start Monday at seven. Pay will be the award wage for your age. See you then.'

I was happy to be working with wood again. It was something I understood, and I enjoyed being able to use my hands for something more than just lifting.

First thing on Monday morning Craig said, 'See that pile of wood next to the docking saw? Well, we need that cut into one foot six lengths. Can you do that?'

I nodded. Certainly I could. It would be a pleasure.

About an hour later Craig came up to me and said, 'I've got to go out and measure up a job. While I'm gone, I want you to do this for me.' Bloody hell, he was holding up a board with words and numbers all over it! 'It's all written down, you should be all right.'

When he had left, I took a deep breath and looked at the board. Craig hadn't even asked me if I'd be able to handle the job – whatever it was – just trusted me to do it. I didn't want to let him down. I was also afraid that not being able to read was once again going to cost me a job I really liked.

My instructions turned out to be mainly a list of numbers, all the familiar-looking figures that were normally used in carpentry work. These were the only kinds of numbers that I had ever been able to understand. What a relief! I guessed that all he wanted was for me to cut the different lengths for him, so I crossed my fingers and made a start.

When Craig returned he ran the tape over my finished work while I chewed on my knuckles. Then he stood up, slapped me on the back and said, 'Okay, it's time for dinner. Come on, we eat upstairs.'

This was a first for me, eating with the boss in his own house!

We climbed up the back way, where some sort of structure had been rigged up until proper steps could be made, and Ada had dinner (lunch in my language) ready for us when we entered the kitchen. Inside the house were no doors or floor coverings and as I looked around I got the impression that Craig's home was always last on the list to be worked on.

From that day onwards I always ate my midday meal with them, and Ada was a wonderful cook. She was forever bending over the stove, preparing something tasty. For afters there were always freshly baked Anzac biscuits or sponge cakes that stood six inches high and weighed nothing. Smoko was always in the shed, though.

More and more I found myself working alone. Craig spent a lot of his time away from the workshop, quoting on jobs. Most of our work was for the State Government where tenders were called for. I reached a stage where I could pick up any plan, take a plain piece of timber and turn it into the article that someone had ordered. Many of the plans came to our factory directly from the State Government office and more than once I came across some error in the plans. I learnt to check each plan carefully before wasting timber by cutting a length that the draftsman had written down wrongly. Then I would find what was needed, machine the timber, put it all together, polish it and pack it. Seeing it loaded onto the truck was always the highlight for me.

My love-life was full of ups and downs. Getting over Cheryl took me a fair while, and most of the girls I met after her were either too good or too bad to interest me. One or two tried to trick me into marriage, but I was only twenty and settling down was the last thing on my mind. So I ran a mile. There were some very strange girls out there!

But then I met Janice and everything changed.

My car had died yet again. It was in bits and pieces and needed a new motor. Getting to work was a problem. Sometimes I borrowed Mark's motorcycle, sometimes Ian's Holden, and now and then I hitch-hiked some of the way and walked the rest – shanks's pony, as Mum called it. So when my mate Clive Bowen turned up in his trusty two-door Anglia with the canvas top and announced that he was going 'on the prowl', I joined him.

We were cruising along Cleveland Road towards Camp Hill when we noticed two girls standing in a phone box. They were wearing tennis outfits and when we passed them one of them waved.

Clive backed the Anglia up and, wouldn't you know it, they pretended they hadn't seen us. We sat in the car and waited for a while. Beyond the phone box were the lights of a tennis court which was obviously where the girls had come from.

Finally one of them poked her head out of the booth. 'Are you wanting to use the phone?' she asked.

Janice

'No,' I said, feeling cheeky, 'we're looking for two girls to go out with us.'

'We can't,' she replied. 'We're playing tennis.'

Clive and I did our best to talk them into coming to the drive-in with us, but the girls resisted. They giggled a lot and chatted with us for a while, but nothing seemed to work. Right at the last minute, just before they went back to the tennis courts, they gave us hope that they might be willing to see us the following week at the same time.

The tall one (we still didn't know their names) asked, 'Would you bring us back before eleven?' She seemed fairly keen when we nodded, but the other one looked worried. They had a little conference and then the tall one stepped forward. 'Okay, then, we'll meet you here next week.'

Clive and I turned up early the following Tuesday night, half expecting to be stood up. When we saw the girls walking towards us from the tennis courts we were over the moon.

'You *promise* you'll bring us back in time?' the tall one asked.

'Yes. Come on – jump in.'

She moved towards the car and took a good look inside. I opened the door, stepped out and climbed into the back seat. 'Okay,' she said to her friend, 'you get in the back and I'll get in the front.'

The friend didn't look too happy about this, making me wonder if she was just shy, or if she would rather have been with Clive in the front.

I looked at this quiet girl beside me. She was very pretty, with long auburn hair tied up in a ponytail. I guessed her to be about eighteen years old. She wasn't as tall as her friend, but looked to be about five foot five or six and built like Sabrina, the film star. Mum had an expression that had something to do with an hourglass and for the first time I understood what it meant.

'What drive-in are you taking us to?' were her first words to me.

'How about the Capalaba one?'

Miss Tall turned in her seat and said, 'That's fine by us, but we *must* be back by eleven so we can get a lift home.'

'We can take you home,' Clive offered.

'No way! You promised to take us back to the phone box. That way our parents will think we went to tennis.'

'My name is Ken. What's yours?' I asked when the film started.

'Janice,' she replied, her eyes glued to the big screen.

'Do you live around here?'

'Don't tell them,' said the girl in the front, so I didn't get an answer.

After a while I put my arm around Janice's shoulder and at one point I even stole a kiss from her, but whenever I tried to get any information, both girls just played dumb.

Clive and his girl were too hot to watch. Sitting right in front of us, they seemed to be getting along like a house on fire. But each time I tried to get fresh with Janice, my hands were pushed firmly away.

'I'm here to see the show!' she hissed.

Just as we promised, we dropped the girls off at their phone box near the courts before they turned into pumpkins, but not before we had arranged another date for the following week.

Over the next few weeks we met the girls regularly at the same spot. Each time I learnt a little bit more about them. They came from Mitchelton on the other side of town. Clive's girl, Sally, worked in the office of a well-known solicitor in the city and Janice worked as a switch operator but wouldn't tell me where. I really liked her and got quite a shock when I found out that she was five years younger than me – only fifteen and a half! But there was something very special about this girl and I just couldn't stop thinking about her.

Sooner or later it had to happen; the girls' parents found out about us.

Sally's parents said that Clive and I were bad, and warned Janice's parents. Our outings came to a dead stop and we lost contact.

My car was still out of action and I was saving to buy an old Wolseley for spares. So that I could get to work and back, Craig lent me £50 to buy the old Dodge that his next-door neighbour was selling. It was better than nothing.

Work had built up. We were now working on weekends to try and get ahead of the orders. On one of these weekends, Craig's brother Tony came to visit and brought his wife with him. I couldn't believe my eyes: it was Nurse Cavendish, the one I used to call 'Bananas', from the Children's Ward! What a small world. She seemed surprised but pleased to find me still alive and kicking.

Janice

It was finished. The Wolseley was back on the road. I was ready to paint it black and bought the dearest paint I could find. Nothing but the best for this little beauty!

The whole time I'd been working on the car I kept thinking about Janice. I couldn't get her out of my mind. Months of trying to find her had led to nothing. She never went to the phone box any more, she had never told me her last name, and I had no address for her.

And then one afternoon, just as I was about to spray the last coat of black onto the car, something happened that gave me a clue. The radio was blaring as usual and all at once I heard an advertisement that said 'Morton's will be open all this weekend'.

That's it, I realised, that's the name of the lawyer where Janice's friend Sally works! At long last I had some place to start.

At first Sally refused to help me. She said Janice's parents would kill her. But I begged and pleaded and swore that I would never reveal who told me, so she finally gave in and I got Janice's phone number at work. 'And please stay away from me!' Sally added. She needn't have worried. It was her friend I was after, not her.

Monday morning. The phone was ringing and my heart was thumping.

'Good morning, Wolfe & Sons.' It was Janice!

'Hi – it's me, Ken Hall. Would you like to go out Saturday night?'

'No.'

'Why not?'

'Please hold on,' she said, taking another call. It seemed like ages before she was back on the line. 'Sorry about that – the switch is busy. No, I can't go out with you.'

'Come on – I'll pick you up from your place.' I couldn't stand the thought of losing her again after all this.

'No way. You live too far away,' she said.

'No, I don't, *please* come out with me?'

The line went very quiet and I didn't dare speak in case I said something to make her hang up. 'All right then,' she sighed, and told me her address.

'I'll pick you up around seven,' I said calmly, but I was dancing a jig in my head.

'My mother and father will have to meet you first,' she warned, but nothing like that was going to stop me, so I said that would be fine.

What Next You Bastard

Saturday seemed like a lifetime away. Several times a day I recited her address until it was burned into my memory. I didn't trust myself to write it down, knowing that I would never be able to read what I had written anyway – but the idea that somehow or other I might forget Janice's address kept me awake at night.

When the big day finally came around, I spent the whole morning polishing the car and working out the best way to get to her house. With its new paint job the Wolseley looked very expensive. Good. I wanted to make the best impression I could on Janice's parents.

By six-fifteen I was on my way, driving through South Brisbane and smiling behind the wheel – until a utility shot out of a side-street and ran smack into me. He had only hit the front mudguard, but by the time we both managed to stop our cars, one whole side of my shiny black Wolseley was flattened. I felt like doing the same to the driver of the ute.

He was standing in front of his own vehicle – well, swaying might be a better word – and he was having trouble staying on his feet. I rushed over to him, worried that he might be hurt, but then realised the truth. Bloody hell! The bastard's drunk and crying like a baby!

'Please, no police, I'm too far gone; they'll put me in jail,' he whimpered. He was pitiful. 'Look, here's my licence; take the number and call me tomorrow. My insurance will pay for the job.' He fished his wallet out of his pocket and started leafing through it.

There was nothing to write on, and before I could even look for a pencil, people started pouring out of their houses. A woman shouted, 'I'll call the police!'

The drunk pushed me aside, climbed back into his ute, which only had a small dent in it, and quickly drove off. Oh well, I thought, at least I got a good look at his rego number. I made a mental note of it and hopped back into my car. It could wait. Right now, though, there was something much more important on my mind. I couldn't afford to be late for my first official date with Janice.

She was waiting on the front verandah when I pulled up. My hands were shaking as I opened the front gate and by the time I had climbed the steps to where she stood, my whole body was trembling.

Janice was looking more beautiful than I had ever seen her and I realised that it had been almost a year since our last date. She stood by the door, smiling shyly as I walked towards her. Her long ponytail was shining like a polished copper penny under the porch light, and that sprinkling of freckles across her nose and cheeks gave her a bit of a saucy look. Her dress fitted like a glove and now that she wasn't wearing her tennis outfit I could tell I had been right about one thing: she did have a perfect hourglass figure. I wanted to scoop her up and make a quick getaway, but her parents were waiting for me inside.

The lounge room was poorly lit so it took my eyes a minute or two to adjust. Janice introduced me to her parents, Mr and Mrs Greer, and then to a tribe of six children, one of them crawling on the floor by my feet. To hide my nerves, I bent down and picked it up.

'Where are you taking Janice tonight?' asked her father.

'The local picture show, if that's all right,' I managed to answer.

To Janice he said, 'Make sure you're in by eleven. Have a good time.' And with that it was over. Whew!

After the film we sat in the car and talked. Janice asked me to call her Jan, as she didn't like the name Janice. I said I knew the feeling, because my proper name was Kenneth, which I loathed. Jan and Ken, Ken and Jan. It had a nice ring to it.

Jan loved tennis; she had played fixtures that day and won.

On our next date a week later, Jan confessed that she had a boyfriend called Arthur and they had been going together for three months. Her parents had told her that she could only have one boyfriend at a time, because it wasn't fair on either of us. So she had given it a lot of thought, and chosen me!

Just when I needed a reliable car most, it was out of action. The drunk driver had been uninsured, wouldn't you know it, and skipped to New Zealand. Now I had to pay for the repairs myself, leaving me without a car for six weeks. But this boy was in love, and nothing was going to stand in my way.

Mitchelton and Coorparoo are at opposite ends of Brisbane. Using a combination of buses, trams and trains, I made my way across the city to see Jan whenever I could. Sometimes we stayed out a bit too late and I missed the last transport and had to walk all the way home – but it was always worth it. On one of these nights, just down the road from my place, I came across a small Morris Eight that looked abandoned. When I dropped by the next day I learnt that it was unregistered and it stank from sitting out in the rain, but the motor purred like a kitten. I offered the owner £10 to take it off his hands and he seemed glad to be rid of it.

There wasn't as much cleaning up to do as I had expected and before long I had a useful little car to run around in.

When I finally got the Wolseley back, there were three cars with my name on them sitting in front of the house, and my brothers each had cars as well. Mum was starting to object to her front garden looking like a wrecker's yard.

When Craig Brown closed his factory for the Christmas holidays, my first thought was that I would be able to see Jan every day. But it wasn't to be. Mum wanted us all to go up to Hervey Bay to stay with her father who lived there, and when I asked Jan's parents if she could come along with us, they said no. Besides, she had already made plans to go to Bribie Island for the holidays. Seeing that Jan wasn't going to be in town anyway, I decided to go to the north coast with my family.

Boy, was I going to miss that girl!

20. Hervey Bay

Seven hours in a car can be pretty dull, but Mum had her own special way of keeping us entertained. While I drove, she used the time to fill us in on the local histories of towns we passed, as well as telling us countless stories about her relatives.

'Take my Uncle Fred Wilson,' she began, settling herself more comfortably in her seat. 'Now when he fell in love, he travelled *miles*. As a young man he lived around Dubbo in New South Wales. He found work as a cane-cutter. Strong lad, he was. Then, one day, just by chance, he met a traveller from Kingaroy in Queensland. This traveller told Uncle Fred about land being opened up around Coolabunia, which means "land of the sleeping bears" – you know, koalas. So young Fred gets himself a swag and a billy, hops on his pushbike, and sets out to ride all the way up there. Took him ages. Coolabunia's inland, between Kingaroy and Nanango, just so's you know.

'Anyway, sometime after his arrival, he met my Aunt Caroline – not that she was my aunty then, she was only a young girl – and they fell in love. Fred didn't believe in writing, so he rode right back to Dubbo to tell his parents he was getting married. Course, then he had to ride his damn bike all the way back up to Coolabunia again, to be with his girl.' Mum broke off here and smiled. 'I can remember him telling us how he rode down those steep ranges on the dirt tracks. You see, he had no brakes, so he would cut a large shrub and tie it behind his bike, and then set off down the range. That was his braking system. He did the trip three times.'

I asked Mum where Uncle Fred would have got an idea like that.

'In those days, love, if you had a dray and you had a range to go down, a tree would be felled, then tied behind the dray to slow you down. Your great-grandfather lost his dray and two horses going down a mountain once. The chain that was tied to the log broke, the dray picked up speed and bowled over the poor horses, and the whole sorry lot ended up over the side. My grandfather somehow jumped off in the nick of time, but he lost everything.'

She made some clicking noises with her tongue and shook her head at the terrible memory.

Six hours into our journey we came to Maryborough, which Mum called Pushbike City. The town was settled in the late 1800s, she told us. And now, with the boom of the 1950s, Walkers Limited alone employed 650 men of all ages at their top building yards. Their ship-building yard employed another 400 or so. Of these, at least ninety per cent rode a bike to work.

'When the hooter sounds at the end of the working day, the Five-Ways, Kent Street, March Street and Bowen Road all get taken over by about a thousand riders going home. They cover the roads from footpath to footpath, I kid you not, boys. Wall-to-wall wheels! Ha! They *whoosh* down the streets, and people driving cars have to pull over and make way for them all. All those men and women from thirteen to sixty-five pedalling past them – what a sight! Glad we're passing through early, that's for sure. This is one town where bike riders *always* have the right-of-way.

'But it's not only the workers that ride the bikes,' she said, leaning out the window for a better look. 'Little kids here learn to pedal before they can hardly walk. Even old folks – in their late eighties, some of them – they go sailing around on their bicycles. Nobody walks or drives a car unless they have to, or they're visiting from someplace else, like us.' And each time she noticed someone on a bike after that, she made sure we saw them too, just to prove that she wasn't making it up.

We were all glad to put Pushbike City behind us.

It was another hour or so to Hervey Bay. 'Funny, isn't it,' said Mum, 'because you spell it with an e but you pronounce it *Harvey*.' We had all been to visit our grandfather, George Wittmann, before, but we were small children then and you see things differently when you're closer to the ground.

'Hervey Bay is the home of the large aquatic herbivorous mammal called the dugong, or sea cow,' Mum pointed out, making the most of her captive audience. She reminded us that in the winter months humpback whales and the southern right whale roamed the waters around the bay and that the mainland was the home of platypus. Sugar cane, timber, dairy farms and small crops kept the area going all year round.

Hervey Bay

Hervey Bay, a sleepy hideaway, was declared a settled area under the 1868 Lands Act. By December of 1960, almost a hundred years down the track, its population had reached 3,500. Eighty-five per cent were retirees from surrounding areas such as Coolabunia, Nanango, Kingaroy, Goomeri and Bundaberg, among others. Blocks of land on The Esplanade could be bought for £35. Swamp grass grew to a height of seven feet at the end of Mary Street. If you wanted a block at Shelley Beach, all you needed was ten shillings an acre.

'From 1874 onwards the dugong meat from Hervey Bay was sold for human consumption, you know,' Mum continued, sounding more and more as if she had swallowed a guidebook of the area. 'So was the oil from it; that was used as a cure for all sorts of ailments. They used to place the fat in the sun till the oil melted off it – used to get about seven gallons from each one. The largest dugong they ever caught came in at about eleven feet ten inches long and, if I remember rightly, it was eight foot five inches across the middle – picture that! It must have been a real roly-poly!' Mum laughed. 'After that, they killed hundreds of them every year, and I suppose they ran out eventually, because now they're a lot harder to find.

'The coffee they grew right here at Dundowran was absolutely the best coffee you could get – even won second prize at the Franco-British Exhibition in ... 1908, I think it was. Anyway, it was the Mecca brand of coffee, and for forty years they were doing great business, but then there were some new laws about not having children in the workforce, and that made it too expensive to grow. And also there was some problem to do with clearing away a lot of the dense jungle that was growing along the coast. Probably because people planted sugar cane instead and that took away the protection from the sea winds and killed off the coffee bushes. So that's what put an end to coffee-growing up here. It's a crying shame if you ask me, because they were some of the best coffee plantations in the world.' Mum sighed loudly, as if she would never again drink a decent cup of coffee. 'See, I told you boys, everything changes.'

Mum was silent for a while, probably brooding on her favourite topic of how everything was better in the Good Old Days, so I let my mind drift back to that earlier visit when I was a little boy.

I remembered a day when the water had been like crystal, not a wave to be seen. Birds were everywhere, but nothing else seemed to move. Two rowboats sitting out on the water looked as if they were perched on top of a sheet of glass. The tide was out, and when I walked down the beach and put my feet in, the water was hot. I had to take another ten steps before my ankles were even wet, and thirty more until the sea just covered my knees. Then suddenly the sand was gone and I was stepping onto coral. I had walked all the way out to a reef!

Grandad had taken us fishing one morning and we had filled a sugar sack with whiting. We smoked them and placed them on wire racks under the house, keeping only a few aside to be cooked fresh. Most of the neighbours were related to the Wittmanns – the Carl, Wilson, Jorgensen and Hart families. And each family seemed to have its own special way of smoking the fish – some used cypress pine, others used silky oak or tea-tree – each with its own distinct flavour.

There had been long walks on the beach, from Point Vernon to Urangan Pier, which in those days was a busy place. Wharfies would be unloading the trains that were shunted by the railway men onto the pier, then loading ships from as far away as France. At the end of the pier many good-sized holes had been cut into the deck. These were used to feed the giant grouper, enormous fish that lived under the pier.

On one of Grandad George's fishing trips, Mum and I had gone along in his small rowboat. Just off the sandbar we fished for whiting. There was a strong tide and a breeze coming from the north and the boat rocked so badly that my belly had started to heave. Grandad's remedy for seasickness was two junket tablets taken without water, and though this might have worked for him, for me they did exactly the opposite. My last three meals were sent over the side of the boat and I was trying to hold onto my fourth, when Grandad got a horse mackerel on his heavy line. Mum pleaded with him to take pity on me and go ashore, but her father wasn't listening. 'No way, Myrtle, the fish comes before the boy,' he grumbled. 'Besides, I owe Fraser a good fish.' With the anchor on board, Grandad tied a line to a large wooden peg that was fitted to the nose of the boat. Soon the mackerel was dragging the boat, and all of us in it, towards Point Vernon. Then it turned and swam back towards the pier, again taking us along for the ride. This went on for quite some time, with Mum calling her father all the names under the sun, and me dry-retching in the bottom of the boat. 'I can see him!' he

Hervey Bay

yelled, 'won't be long now!' Another half hour, and the huge horse mackerel, with blood pouring from the deep gash in his neck, lay beside me on the splintery boards. I don't know which of us felt more miserable.

When we reached the shore I was too weak and dizzy to stand up and Grandad ordered Mum to leave me lying on the sand. He said he was sure that I would come home later when I felt better, and would she just hurry up and give him a hand carrying his catch back to the house.

I was too sick to care. Dressed only in a pair of shorts, I lay on my back and slept for two hours in the sun. Grandad laughed his head off when I finally dragged myself up the stairs of the house. 'Look, Myrtle, I have an Indian for a grandson!' The bathroom mirror showed me what he meant. From head to toe I was a painful shade of red.

My other memory of Hervey Bay was of meeting our new grandmother, his strange second wife, who took her daily instructions word for word from an old German Bible and had us all scared to death. Grandad had married her after his first wife, Mum's mother, died, when he left his building business in Brisbane and returned to Hervey Bay. Some said she might have been an old girlfriend of his, because they had known each other since he was a boy of eighteen. In my wildest imagination there was just no way that I could picture this woman as anyone's girlfriend, ever!

Our new grandmother was called Min. She was a large woman who dressed in long dark frocks that almost covered the holey slippers she always wore inside the house. Her dull grey hair was twisted into tight braids and curled into a small nest at the back of her head. We boys were sure she bred spiders and snakes in there.

Once Mark took some coins out of a tin in Min's room, and we traded them one by one for ice-creams at the local shop. When we were caught out, Mum had begged the shopkeeper to give them back, but he refused. Min was furious with us. 'Dese vere *velliable* old coins and *verrry* rare,' she screamed. She beat us with a broom handle until our backsides were black and blue, then finished the job by sitting us on the back steps for hours while she punished us with gloomy passages from the German Bible and shook her finger at us. 'Hell-fire and Dam-*na*-shon! The Devil vill be vaiting for you *vicket* boys in e-*tairn*-ity,' she warned.

But now it was only Grandad George who waited for us. He didn't seem to be doing too badly without Min, who had taken ill and died one night. None of us knew the details, but we Hall brothers liked to imagine that she had frightened herself to death with her own Bible. And wouldn't it be funny if she ended up in the dreadful place she had told us so much about? Oh boy, was the Devil going to be in for a hard time!

Grandad was a bit of a beanpole, standing over six feet tall and thin as a stick. He wore his shaggy mane and silvery moustache a bit longer these days, but one thing hadn't changed: his love for scruffy, rumpled clothes. He always wore long-sleeved flannel shirts and baggy trousers – gentlemen didn't wear shorts in those days. His clothes were rolled up to the elbows or knees at times, and usually looked as if they could stand up by themselves. Grandad didn't see much point in washing something that was only going to get dirty again five minutes later. At seventy-eight he was proud of his good health and seemed to take satisfaction from knowing that he had outlived two wives.

There was one difference though. Grandad had taken up talking about his youth. Whenever he had one of his grandsons in his boat, he dredged up stories from the old times – which was pretty strange, seeing that he had always been so quiet about it before. Maybe now that Min was gone he didn't have to be a saint anymore.

'Koala bears, those furry little creatures,' he started one afternoon. 'Shot thousands of them for their skins. Coolabunia and Kingaroy were lousy with them, and roo – kept me in money for years. After that I got into the fight game. I took boys from town to town, you know, like the Jimmy Sharman Show.'

'You took boxers around? Come off it, Grandad.'

'No, it's true, boy. Your mother will tell you I had a great stable. My Aboriginals were clean fighters and, gee, could they punch!'

'Slow down, Grandad, I want to remember all this,' I said, seeing a new side to the old man.

'Yessir,' he said, baiting a hook while I watched and listened. 'Those boys put me on my feet. Without them I could never have built the first peanut silo in Kingaroy.' He stared up at the sky, checking for clouds, I supposed. 'That was in '32, if I remember rightly. Got the contract to build it and never looked back since. Kingaroy was the town, yes it was! I was so close to being the champion axeman that year. My oldest and closest friend, Bob Otto, just shaved it from me. He went on and won the Australian Open standing-block event and became the Australasian Champion. For years we did exhibition woodchopping at the Brisbane Show.'

'Your parents, Grandad, tell me about them.'

'Let's see now. My mother – there will never be another woman like her – was Kate Pohlmann. She was born in 1850 in Holstein, Germany. Couldn't read or write, but she made up for it with all the love she had for everyone. My father was very hard, though. Born in 1846 in Germany in a place called Dörzbach, Württemberg. Arrived in Australia at the age of nineteen, spoke seven languages. His name was Johann, that's the German for John.

'He told us a story, and he passed it on to his grandchild, your mother, so now it's my turn to pass it on to you. Said he was a cousin of the Kaiser, the king of Germany. When he arrived here he kept a very low profile, worked at the lunatic asylum at Woogaroo in Ipswich as a wardsman or some such thing. And then he was the interpreter for the Australian Government all through the First World War. Yessir, Ken, that man had a few connections, I'm telling you. That's probably why none of us had to go to the holding camp down at Beenleigh, where all the other Germans were rounded up and kept for the duration of the war.'

Grandad hauled in a couple of fish before he continued. 'And he was forever mixing with the politicians, campaigning for changes and all that kind of thing. He pushed for them to get the railway to Kingaroy. Good thing that was, too. The old man was funny about one thing, though. Never believed that we should have a good education. He always said he could read and write for his children, so we needn't bother. That bastard,' Grandad said fondly and winked at me. And neither of us could keep from smiling.

We moved on to talking about how my great-grandfather had lost his dray coming down the range and Grandad smiled. 'Oh yeah, and then there was the sale-of-the-horse story. Nearly forgot about that. The old man had a horse that jibbed on hills whenever he had to pull the cart. It just hated those hills! Anyhow, he decided to sell it. Well, he found a buyer for it all right, but the trouble was, just outside of our home was a hill that this horse always jibbed on. So on the day of the sale, my father got me and my brother Jack to hide in the bushes. When they arrived, we had to run out and push that cart up the hill while he kept the buyer's eyes straight ahead.'

What Next You Bastard

'Come off it, Grandad, no way!' I just couldn't believe this part.

'Strike me dead if I'm telling a lie,' he swore. 'Yes! That old rascal sold the horse the very same day.'

Wednesday 4 January, 1961, came and went, but other than wishing me Happy Birthday, nobody made much of a fuss. Normally this wouldn't have upset me. After all, it wasn't the first time my birthday had gone uncelebrated, but this time it was special. It was my twenty-first.

For much of the day I felt sorry for myself, but during the afternoon I started to suspect that maybe they were all planning a surprise party for me that evening, so I kept my excitement to myself until dinner time. My two older brothers had both had pretty good parties for their twenty-firsts, so I was really looking forward to mine.

I shouldn't have bothered. There wasn't one.

After a very ordinary meal, I swallowed my disappointment and left the house. Nobody tried to stop me. The sun was just setting as I walked down to the beach and sat on the sand with seagulls for company. Ever since I was a small boy I had been looking forward to this day, and many times I had been told I would never see it. But here I was, a real adult at last, only without the special key to prove it.

It was the first time I had ever really thought about what the future might bring, and I found myself thinking of Janice. What would it be like to marry such a wonderful girl and raise four children of our own? One thing was for sure, I promised myself, when they had birthdays, especially important ones like twenty-firsts, there was no way in the world that I'd forget them.

Early next morning I said goodbye to the family and headed home to Janice. Mum had driven up with Mark and me in my Wolseley, but Ian and Steven had followed later in their own cars, so I wouldn't be stranding anyone by leaving a week early. I just didn't want to be away from the girl I loved a single day longer.

21. Narrow escapes

Janice was still away when I called in to her place, so I decided to kill some time by painting our kitchen cupboards. It would make a nice homecoming surprise for Mum, I thought. The corner store only had a few very small tins of paint left, so I brought them home and got busy.

When the job was finished I stood back and admired my work. The doors and drawers were glossy and smooth, so smooth you'd think I had sprayed the paint on. Ian was the first to see the surprise and his reaction puzzled me: 'Oh no, bloody hell! Wait till Mum sees *this*!'

Mum appeared at the kitchen door and nearly dropped the bags she was carrying. Her mouth opened and closed like a fish in a glass bowl. It was hard to tell if she was going to laugh or cry. 'Oh my Lord, Ken, what *have* you done?'

'Don't you like it?' I asked, feeling a bit hurt.

'No, I ... yes, I ... it's a good job, thank you,' she managed to say, but held back her laughter till she got to the toilet. I just couldn't understand that woman sometimes.

Jan came back from holidays a few days later and Mum invited her over for tea. I was in my bedroom, sprucing myself up for her, when I heard voices coming from the kitchen. 'What on earth happened? Oh, it's horrible, Mrs Hall, I've never *seen* colours like that! Purple, and bright red ... and that green would turn *anyone* off ...' When I came into the room she rounded on me angrily. 'How could you, Ken? Your mother's kitchen is a joke!'

Mum did her best to defend me. 'He can't help it, love. He's colour-blind – always has been. Anyway, not to worry, Ian's bought some paint and he's going to repaint the whole kitchen for me this weekend.'

Colour-blind? Mum had mentioned it once or twice before, but I didn't really know what it meant. After all, I could tell the difference between most things of different colours. I knew that grass is green and the sky is blue, that it changes to a red or pink when the sun goes down; people with freckles all over their faces have red hair, pale eyes are usually blue. But I guess I just didn't see these colours the same way most other people did.

By Easter the whole thing was forgotten. Mum's kitchen had been repainted. Privately I thought it was a waste of time; to me it didn't look that much different after Ian had 'fixed it up'. Everyone else was happier, though.

For these holidays we were going fishing to Yamba and this time Jan was allowed to come with us. Mum went with Ian and Mark, but I waited for Jan, who couldn't get away from work for two more days.

It was dark when we reached the New South Wales border on a road we had never travelled before. A low mist was covering the ground in the gullies, so when the road started to climb upwards we felt more comfortable. There was no moon and it was so black that in some places we couldn't even see the edge of the road. Taking it very slowly, we rounded a bend. Heading straight towards us was a car with its lights on high beam, blinding me for a second or two. I swerved to the left and hit the brakes. The wheels locked as they hit the gravel and we skidded to a stop. I got out of the car for a moment to steady my nerves, and Jan did the same.

'*Help, help me, Ken!*' came a scream.

I ducked back into the car, because her voice seemed to be coming from there, but from the front seat I couldn't see her. 'Where are you, love?'

'Here! *Quick*, grab me!' Her voice was coming from the direction of the floor.

It was pitch black and as I leaned over I could just make out some lights that seemed to be miles below us. Then I saw the top of Jan's head and realised that she was clinging to the open car door, with her feet dangling in space! We had stopped on the side of a very high mountain and on Jan's side was a sheer drop. I grabbed her under the arms and pulled her back into the car, both of us shaking with fright. If she hadn't been able to hold on the way she did, I could have lost her that night.

We camped in the caravan park at Yamba and had the time of our lives over the next four days, fishing from morning till night and filling our bellies with some of the largest bream we had ever caught. It was heaven.

It was a good year. I was busier than ever at work, with Craig Brown spending more and more time away, quoting on jobs.

Narrow escapes

One afternoon I was working on a piece of maple with a slight bend in it. Using the surfacer, I was taking the piece of wood over it one last time when suddenly the wood snapped. My hand felt tingly and warm and when I looked down I saw blood; my whole hand was covered with it. Then I saw that my middle finger was missing its nail, as well as most of the tip. What surprised me was that I felt no pain, nothing at all.

Ada was busy sewing when I walked into the kitchen and told her I might have another job for her.

'What in the world have you done?' she gasped.

'Dropped my finger into the surfacer.'

She grabbed my hand and pulled me over to the sink. 'You get blood on my sewing and I'll kill you,' she warned. 'Let's get this hand clean. Are you all right?'

'Yes,' I said, but then my legs turned to jelly. 'I ... I feel a bit strange.'

Ada quickly reached out. 'Hang on there, you'd better sit down. And don't worry about the sewing.'

'I've never done this before,' I said, feeling really stupid. 'Blood's never worried me.'

'But this time it's *yours*.' Ada had gentle hands and once the wound was covered up, it didn't seem so bad any more. 'There, I've put a light bandage on; you should be right to drive to the doctor.'

The surgery's waiting-room was crowded when I got there and now the pain was setting in. My hand started throbbing. I had to wait an hour and a half before the doctor was free and by then the bandage was stained a deep red. Quite a few stitches were needed to close up the top of my finger and I was told not to work for a month.

Though the pain was awful, and the bandage made me clumsy, I still went to work each day. This was one job I just didn't want to lose. I was pretty slow, though, and when work got behind, Craig hired a lad to help me.

When Guy Fawkes night came around in September, there was a sour note in the air. This was going to be the last one in Queensland. Politicians had passed a new law that fireworks could only be used by licensed operators from now on. Most of the children and parents had promised themselves that if this was going to be the last, then it was also going to be the biggest and the best. They bought double the usual amount of everything for the great night.

What Next You Bastard

It was a celebration. It was exciting. It was war!

We gathered together in the Greers' backyard. Of Jan's tribe of brothers and sisters, all those old enough to join in the fun were there. Landing a big bunger right beside someone was nearly as thrilling as dodging the ones that were thrown back. We were always careful with our aim, though, because accidents sometimes happened.

Jan's young brothers had saved their money for months and were very proud of themselves. They had a whole shoebox full of fireworks, and had built a bunker next to the dunny in the backyard.

My sixpenny bunger was going to be next. I lit it and drew back my arm, putting my army training to good use, then threw it into the air as hard as I could. It didn't go straight up, though – it went sailing towards the bunker instead. Even before it exploded, the boys came charging out, running for their lives. I was about to go and investigate, when the bunker began to hiss and glow. Next thing, there were sparklers burning where they lay, skyrockets trying to fly, Tom Thumbs jumping all over the place, penny bungers exploding together and Roman candles lighting up the backyard. My sixpenny bunger had landed in an arsenal: right in the boys' shoebox!

And that was it. The whole evening's entertainment over in less than two minutes.

A piece of army wisdom came to mind that night: 'Fright can kill more than the explosion!' Well, nobody dropped dead from fright, and luckily no one was hurt, but it was weeks before those little boys forgave me and spoke to me again.

It must have been the season for accidents. On a sunny day in December, Jan and I were fooling around, laughing and joking and chasing each other around a tent. I had almost caught her when she grabbed the corner rope and spun around, accidentally knocking me in the groin with her leg. I collapsed to the ground, the pain sucking every bit of energy from my body. Jan was running on the spot, embarrassed and upset, but not knowing what to do.

'Help me to my feet,' I gasped, and she took my arm and tried to steady me. It was quite some time before the pain faded.

For the next few weeks I was fine, but one morning in January I woke up at one-thirty with the worst pain I had ever known. Sweat was pouring off my body and my testicles were on fire. The weight of the sheet was suddenly unbearable and I pushed it away, but even my pyjama pants felt like a ton of lead bearing down on me. I had no idea what could be wrong. Opening the flap to investigate wasn't possible, because I hated the way pyjamas pants gaped at the front and always got Mum to sew them up, something I regretted right now. Trying to pull my pyjamas down wasn't any good either, as it was too painful to move. So, very carefully I picked at the stitches that held the flap closed. It took me ages.

Placing my hands underneath my crown jewels eased the pain slightly, so I wedged a pillow between my legs and cushioned them for a while. I was starting to feel sick from the constant pain and for the next few hours I drifted in and out of consciousness.

It was turning into the longest night of my life.

When the room began to take shape around me I knew it was nearly morning and that Mum would soon be waking up. I waited till I couldn't stand it any longer, filling my mind with all sorts of nonsense just to keep me going a while longer. This was the very same bed, I reminded myself, that I had spent so much time in when I was a boy and they had all expected me to die. Well, maybe now my time had come. I made up my mind there and then that if I came through this alive I would never sleep in this bed again.

The sound of Mum's alarm clock was one of the sweetest noises I had ever heard. Thank God she was an early riser! Quickly I pulled the sheet up to cover myself. At last her door opened and I called out to her.

'Mum, I need help! A doctor ... please get a doctor!'

Like all mothers, she panicked. Flicking on the light, she rushed into my room and bumped straight into the edge of my bed – oh, the agony! I couldn't help myself and a high-pitched scream came from way down deep inside of me. It woke Mark and Ian and they flew into my room. Now I had three frightened faces staring down at me.

'I'm hurting down below, Mum,' I whispered with the only breath I had left. 'Please – get the doctor!'

'What do you mean, hurting?' asked Doctor Mum, who liked to know all the facts, even when her son lay dying right in front of her. 'Let me see.'

'No, Mum! You can't!' I cried, horrified at the idea. After all, I was a grown man now, no matter what she thought.

She rolled her eyes and clucked her tongue. 'Oh, lovey – I've seen a lot more than that little bit you have.' She reached out a hand.

'Mum, *please*!' I wailed. 'It really hurts! Don't even touch the sheet.' And for once Myrtle Hall gave in.

The doctor was a very young man. He poked and prodded and questioned me. It was like one of those movies where they torture the spies for information about the enemy. I was ready to confess to anything, whether I had done it or not, just to make him stop. He wanted to know all about my sex life and I said there hadn't *been* one for more than a year – which was in honour of Janice. Then he asked me if I remembered anything happening to me down below, such as a fall, or a knock, and I told him about what had happened with the tent. The doctor nodded thoughtfully.

From his medical bag he produced a syringe and said that he was going to give me an injection now, and that he'd be back again the next day. In the meantime I was to stay in bed and rest. As if I could have done anything else.

Jan came over as soon as she heard the news. She was very upset and blamed herself. 'It's all my fault. I might have ruined you for life.' This was something I hadn't even thought of. Could it really mean the end of my sex life? I was barely twenty-two!

Next day the pain was just as bad and I received another injection. The doctor was just leaving my room when I heard Mum ask him how I was. He closed the door before he answered, but I heard his words all the same: 'Not too good, I'm sorry to say. If he's not better when I arrive tomorrow, we may have to operate and remove them.' There was a muffled gasp which must have been from Mum. 'But please, Mrs Hall,' he finished, 'not a word to the boy.'

Remove them? No bloody fear! He wasn't going to make a woolly wether out of me. No way, mate. Four kids, I want, and Janice is going to be their mother.

Night came and the pain still hadn't let up. I was fighting sleep because I didn't want tomorrow to come around too quickly, bringing the doctor with it. But eventually I gave in and slept until mid-morning.

When I opened my eyes, there stood the man who was planning to use the Big Knife on me. I didn't want to see him so I turned away and faced the wall, curling my knees up to my chest.

And then I turned back again, because I suddenly realised what I had just done. Moved my whole body, and felt no pain!

'Could you do that again?' asked the doctor, looking as surprised as I felt. 'I don't believe it. I was so sure we'd have to operate that I had the theatre booked for you.'

'What was it, Doc?' I asked after he had examined me one last time.

'I really don't know for certain,' he said, shaking his head. 'All I can say is that you've been very lucky. And don't go chasing pretty girls around tent ropes anymore.'

On our very next date I proposed to Jan. We had been sitting in the car and I was holding her tightly in my arms. When she tilted her head back and looked into my eyes, I nearly drowned in them. I kissed her slowly and when we parted, said, 'Marry me?'

'Yes,' was all she said. And it was all I needed to hear before I kissed her again. I was the happiest man on earth!

After work the next day I stopped at a jeweller's shop and bought a ring. The Greers had invited me to tea that night and after the meal, while Jan was helping to clear the table, I called out, 'Catch!' and tossed the small jeweller's box to her. Her face lit up with pleasure, and slowly she opened it.

Words failed her. She just sat and stared at the ring. Her parents looked shocked and disapproving and their faces told me that I had done the wrong thing. One of Jan's sisters yelled, 'It's an engagement ring!'

'No, no way,' I said quickly. 'It's only a dress ring; please, it's only a gift!'

Everyone relaxed after that, but I realised that sometime soon I would have to pluck up the courage to ask Jan's parents for permission to marry their eldest daughter.

Craig's factory was getting too many orders to handle. We had just finished a job for the new Tax Office and work was still flooding in. More staff had to be hired. I now had two lads working under me, and a new cabinet-maker called Michael joined us as well. Trouble was, the shed was much too small for so many people and so much work.

So Craig bought a block of land in Redland Bay Road, which was still in Capalaba, but much further out. The locals were laughing. Who would be silly enough to build a factory out here? No living person with a brain in his head would want to live or work this far from the city! But Craig Brown had ideas of his own and no local yokel was going to stand in his way. After a long search, he found a steel igloo that had been used as a plane hangar in the war. It was the sort of thing that could be stripped and reassembled without too much trouble, so he hauled it to his new site and set about rebuilding it.

A huge electric roller had been hired to bend the long iron sheets for the roof into shape. It stood out in the open, just beside the shed where I was working. Craig was by himself, finishing the last of the sheets.

There was a loud scream.

Dropping my tools, I ran outside and saw Craig struggling to keep himself from being dragged backwards into the roller. He had dug his heels into the ground and was straining forwards, his head down, using his arms to brace himself against the machine. The tail of his shirt had been caught between the two giant drums and was slowly being fed into the roller. To slip his arms out of the sleeves would have meant letting go of the monster, which would have swallowed him whole in an instant. It was a brand new army shirt, made of very strong cloth and just about impossible to tear, but Craig stood his ground as it was wrenched from his body.

I had seen all this in only a second or two and was already running back to the shed to pull the power plug. By the time I got back to Craig his whole shirt had disappeared into the machine. Luckily Craig was a strong man. But his skin was marked where he had strained against the tearing cloth, and he carried those bruises for weeks afterwards.

There was another lucky escape for my boss a couple of months later.

It was July and most of the machines had arrived at the new factory. Craig was busy fixing the switch on the planer. He was in bare feet, kneeling on the concrete, and poking a screwdriver around inside the switch. Suddenly he flew into the air and was hurled bodily backwards. Sparks were still flying when he stood up and shook himself. He was okay, but the screwdriver – we searched for hours and never saw it again.

The day had come for me to speak to Mr Greer about marriage. Jan and I had planned the whole thing very carefully so that we would catch him in a good mood. She was due to play tennis that evening and it was up to me to invite her father to watch the match with me. The idea was that I would have him to myself for a few hours to

Narrow escapes

have a chat, make a good impression, and finally ask him for Jan's hand. It had sounded perfect when we cooked it up, but now that the time had come I was nervous as hell.

We arrived at the courts at two o'clock and watched Jan play an excellent game of tennis. She looked so lovely with her white skirt twirling and her ponytail bouncing that for quite a while neither of us said a word.

Every now and again Jan looked at me expectantly, waiting for the signal we had agreed on, which meant I had asked her father. She had to wait a long time, poor girl.

I finally got Mr Greer talking and we covered just about every topic under the sun, bar one. The afternoon wore on and, in my head, I practised asking The Question over and over again. Why was it so easy to say in my head, yet so hard to say out loud? Each time I opened my mouth to say the words something else came out, like: 'Fishing should be good on the Gold Coast this year'. Damn!

Four o'clock rolled around and Jan walked onto the court for her last set. Her expression told me to hurry up. Now the players were at the net, her team had won the game and were shaking hands. Mine were shaking too. It's easy, you idiot, I told myself. Just ask the man. Do it now!

'Mr Greer, I would like your permission to marry Janice.' There! I had done it! And Jan was already coming over to the car. I held my breath.

'Yes, Ken,' he said. 'I'd be very proud to have you as a son.' With that he shook my hand.

This time I was buying a proper engagement ring. Jan and I made a trip into the city to one of the leading jewellers. They had a special room for newly engaged couples.

The saleslady was all over us like a rash. She called me 'sir' and flattered Jan, insisting that my beautiful fiancee deserved a ring that would complement her smile. Tray after glittering tray was offered to us for inspection. Most of the rings had large diamonds in them and when I learnt that they were priced at £300 or £400 I nearly fell over. How I wished that I could buy her one of those, but my budget didn't stretch quite that far.

The last tray contained rings of gold and silver and some of them had stones, but they were so tiny that you would have needed a magnifying glass to be sure. The saleslady had lost the plum in her mouth after taking away the £100 tray and now she looked bored. Jan and I settled on a pretty gold ring with a single tiny diamond for the princely sum of £25.

We walked out of the jeweller's with Jan's face glowing as brightly as if I had just bought her the most expensive engagement ring in the world. How I loved that girl!

In August her parents gave us an engagement party. We knew we would have quite a wait before we could be married, because they were still deep in debt from their eldest son's wedding. It didn't matter to us. We had plenty of time.

Jan was given a promotion, which meant working at the main branch of her firm as a junior office girl. Here she made friends with the senior office girl, Pat. Pat and her boyfriend Greg often came out with Jan with me, making it a foursome and lots of fun. One Sunday we drove to the Albert River for a picnic and a swim, but it was a day that nearly ended in tragedy.

Jan couldn't swim and I talked her into letting me teach her. It took a lot of doing, but finally she decided to trust me. I had to promise that I wouldn't let go of her, and that I wouldn't go in any deeper than chest high. Jan was just learning how to float on her back and was even starting to enjoy the lesson, when I suddenly went under.

What the hell? One moment I had been slowly side-stepping with my hands supporting Jan and now my head was about two feet under water. Jan had slipped out of my hands and was desperately trying to wrap her legs around my neck. Then her fingers were grabbing my hair. The more I tried to push her off, the tighter she held on, her weight keeping us both down. I tried to step back onto the ledge, but only slipped further into the muddy water. And I knew that I wouldn't be able to hold my breath much longer.

If I opened my mouth the water would rush in and fill my lungs. What could I do? Panic was setting in. Jan let go of me and I was free, but I was so sure she had drowned that I almost wanted to sink to the bottom and join her. But my feet kicked all by themselves and I felt myself slowly rising to the top. Before I could even break the surface, a strong pair of arms grabbed me and dragged me towards the bank. My throat was raw, and burned as the air rushed back into my lungs.

And there was Jan, also being dragged to shore. She had made it!

Narrow escapes

We had been very lucky. Most people had thought that Jan was just playing around, but Pat and Greg knew that she couldn't swim. When I disappeared under the water they had rushed in to help us. Two other couples, only a few feet away, hadn't taken any notice of Jan's cry for help.

'That's the last time I'm going for a swim,' she said, and I didn't blame her one bit.

We spent the rest of the day lazing around, eating, drinking and talking.

Pat was wearing a new swimsuit and that raised the topic of money. She earned only a little more than Jan did, and neither of us could understand how she could always afford luxuries. Pat explained that she paid just as much board as Jan did, but saved every penny that was left so that she could buy what she liked.

'How come she can save, buy new clothes and still have money to burn when you and I can't?' I asked Jan on the way home.

'I don't know. I've tried, but I never have anything left.'

In 1963 more personnel were hired for Craig's workshop. We now had a grand total of five. Ada came by while the kids were at school to help in the office. We saw more of her than we did of the boss, who was out most of the time giving quotes. Sometimes quite a few days went by without my seeing him. As the worker who had been there the longest, it was usually up to me to take phone calls and deal with customers, but I was starting to get in too deep. This kind of thing wasn't for me. I only wanted to work with my hands, not my head. Some of the details needed to be written down, as Craig wasn't there to handle them. I was sick with worry that my secret would come out. What then?

One of the cabinet-makers was starting to get suspicious. He had his eye on me every time I turned around and it was only a matter of time before he set a trap and I fell straight into it.

The day soon came when he wrote down an order for me to cut. I checked the figures, ignored the rest of the writing, and got busy.

When I had finished, the cabinet-maker marched up to me, hands on his hips. Sounding disgusted, he said, 'Shit, mate! You can't even read! See that sheet? On the bottom I wrote: "If you can read, you won't cut this order." So I want your job as supervisor.'

From day on I let him answer the phone and talk to the customers. I didn't miss it one bit, but I was getting worried about my position there. Would it always come to this? Each time I was making progress somewhere, would my handicap steal it away from me?

When Craig hired a new machinist, our staff grew to six. The new bloke was very friendly and told me all about the place where he used to work until he came to us: Stradbroke Island. I had never been there, but I knew it wasn't far, just a short boat trip across the bay. His tales about the work and the lifestyle soon got to me.

Maybe it was time for a change.

22. The island

Through the blue haze that hung over the calm water of the bay, I could just make out the white sands of Stradbroke Island. I was standing at the end of the Cleveland jetty, wondering if I was doing the right thing. Oh well, I might as well see what it's about, I decided. This was why I had taken a day off in the middle of the week.

The wharf was made of heavy planks with a railway line running along it. A wooden trolley sat on the tracks, loaded to the top with boxes and crates.

'You!' came a shout. 'Are you going to the island?' A weather-beaten man was hurrying towards me. 'Can you help me push this trolley to the boat? Name's Negus, Neil Negus, captain of this craft.'

The craft he was talking about turned out to be the ferry. It had a timber hull, the captain informed me, it was powered by a diesel motor and had seating for fifty. She lugged all types of goods from the mainland to the island and back again. Strapped to the hull were 44-gallon drums of fuel.

'Only the two of us today,' he puffed. 'Let's get this gear aboard and get on our way. Stand by the ropes – when you hear the whistle, let the ropes go forward.' The boat was soon slicing its way through the crystal waters of Moreton Bay. 'If you're coming back with me, lad, I be leaving at two. Sorry, but this trip will be a bit longer than usual. Have to look around Peel Island for a missing dinghy.'

As we got close to Peel, I could make out some kind of settlement on the land. 'Who lives here?' I asked.

'No one, my boy. That's the old quarters for the lepers.'

'Leopards!' I said in wonder. 'What sort of leopards?'

'The human type,' he grinned. 'The government closed it in '56 and now the whole island is out of bounds.'

We circled the island but if there was a dinghy we didn't see it. The captain took us back on course and pointed out Bird Island and Goat Island on the way. North Stradbroke was now taking shape in front of us. It was like standing at the base of a mountain, looking up. On one side was a peak, blackish in colour, and as we drew closer it glinted like gold in the sun.

'What in the world is that, Neil?'

'That's just sand from the mine; it has no value.'

Dunwich glided into view. This was where the ferry landed. It looked so clean with its neat little houses and shops. Cows wandered around, providing a free lawnmowing and fertilising service. The treatment factory for the mine was on a slight slope up to the right.

'Okay, lad, get ready with the ropes up forward,' the captain ordered, and once we had tied up I stepped onto the jetty.

Only one man was fishing from the side, dangling his legs over the edge. 'Hold it there,' he said. 'I'm the local policeman. What's your name and what's your business here?' I explained that I had come over to see about working on the island and that I was only here for the day. 'Right,' he nodded, 'but when Neil leaves, you be with him. By the way, if you do get a job on this island, stay at the camp, not here in town. I want no trouble.'

The mining office was easy to find; it was also very small. My interview was short and sweet. It consisted of three questions rolled into one: 'Your name, your age, and can you start Monday?'

I answered, 'Ken Hall, twenty-three, and yes.'

'Bus leaves here for the camp at six on Monday morning. Be on it.'

It never occurred to me to ask what job I would be doing, or what I would be paid for doing it.

That night I would be seeing Jan. I was very anxious about how she would take my news about switching jobs. How could she possibly understand my reasons for doing it? Unless I went into great detail about my handicap, which I wasn't willing to do in case it scared her off, it was going to be very hard to explain. We were seeing each other most nights now, but with the new job we would only be able to get together on weekends.

Jan surprised me. 'It's okay,' she said. 'This will give us a chance to save up for some land.' She had a point. By going out so often we seemed to be going through an awful lot of cash. But on the island I would be forced to put it aside, as there wasn't much to spend it on over there.

Telling Craig and Ada was harder. They took it very badly, begging me to stay, or at least to think it over for a while. Craig said

The island

he didn't want to lose me, that he needed a foreman and the job was mine. He told me how reliable he found me and that I had a good future with him.

My stubborn pride got in the way. More than anything in the world, I would have loved to stay and become the foreman. But I also knew that, somewhere down the line, all the problems I had with reading and writing would get in the way. Somewhere down the line someone – another cabinet-maker, or a customer, or worst of all, Craig himself – would decide that having a dummy in charge was just not good enough for a successful, growing business. And I didn't want to be there when it happened.

Monday morning the clock showed two-thirty. Still no sleep in sight. I had left Jan around midnight and was still wide awake, lying on my bed and watching the minutes and the hours ticking away.

I had only just drifted off when Mum rapped on my door. Within minutes I was ready. I had packed my suitcase before going to bed and, though Mum offered to make me breakfast, I only drank a quick cup of tea.

The morning was very still, with trees outlined against the sky and not a breath of wind. Dawn was just breaking to the east and it looked like the start of a beautiful day. Ian drove me to Cleveland. By the time we pulled up at the wharf a very strong wind had risen out of nowhere, whistling through the rubbers on the car door. People on the pier were clutching their hats and leaning into the wind.

'I think we'll just say our goodbyes here,' said Ian, 'no way am I getting out!'

A gale-force wind hit me when I stepped out of the car and nearly took Ian's passenger door with it. I had to struggle to get it shut again. The sea was pounding the sides of the jetty and my suitcase was doing its best to turn into a kite. 'Forget it!' I told myself. I knew that if I stepped onto the boat I would be seasick. I turned back to the car but was just in time to see it vanish around the corner. With the wind howling in my ears I hadn't heard it drive off.

On my way to the ferry I was joined by an older man clutching an armful of parcels.

'Bit rough today,' he said.

There was a girl walking beside him and she asked me if I was 'the new man'. I told her my name and then she said we had better hurry, because Neil wouldn't wait for us.

What Next You Bastard

The ferry was crowded and it rolled as my feet touched the deck. All the passengers headed straight for the shelter of the single cabin, where the air was foul with the fumes of the diesel. From the porthole it looked as if the whole wharf was moving – up and down, up and down, up ... Locking my jaws together, I headed for the cabin door. But every time I pulled it open, the boat rocked and slammed the damn thing shut again. On my third try I made it through, and only just in time.

With my hands grasping the rail, I heaved over the side of the ferry. Spray from the sea drenched me from head to toe.

And then, as if by magic, the wind was suddenly gone again. The sea became smooth and flat. I returned to the cabin and sat down, glad to rest my shaky knees.

'Ken, isn't it?' said the man I had met on the jetty. 'Come and sit here with us. By the way, I'm George Cavanough and this is my daughter Mandy.'

We were there at last. My legs dragged me off the ferry and onto the pier and after the motion of the water I had trouble keeping my balance on dry land. At the far end stood a bus.

'When you get on the boat,' said Mr Cavanough, 'ask for Harry White. Tell him you're his new man, and that I'll see him later.' Only then did I realise that I had been sitting next to one of the bosses. But what did he mean about 'the boat'? I was supposed to be taking the bus to camp.

The bus journey was nearly as bad as crossing the bay had been. Rough, very rough. We bounced our way over miles and miles of pure white sand with flowering shrubs lining the sides of the track. At the end of it we came to a campsite that had been built between two sand hills. On the left were the men's quarters, to the right was the canteen. None of the men stood around wasting time; they all headed straight towards the quarters. I was left wondering what to do.

'Hey you!' somebody yelled. A head was sticking out of the canteen window. 'Get your gear into a room and be quick about it!'

Men were already leaving the buildings as I arrived, slamming doors as they went. I knocked on a few but there was no reply. My only option was to look into each room and see if it was already taken. So far, all of them were. Running now, I tried each door and only when I opened the thirtieth, did I find a vacant one. I was about to open my suitcase and get changed into my work clothes when the voice boomed again.

The island

'You! Get down to the boat right now! They can't wait!' It made me think of Sergeant Gilbert, so I slammed my door and ran.

Another ferry, but this time a smaller one, was moored to a jetty in a lagoon. So this was the boat Mr Cavanough had meant! It was built of plywood and bobbed up and down in a freshwater swamp. Just what I needed – another boat ride! I was the last to arrive and felt a bit overdressed in my good clothes. At least they were well and truly dry by now.

As I boarded, I felt about thirty pairs of eyes on me. There was dead silence until one man stepped up to me.

'I'm the captain of this boat. May I help you, sir?'

'Yes. I'm looking for a Mr Harry White.'

'See that man over there? Well, that's him. May I say, sir, if it's to do with work, sir, could you please wait till we get to the beach. These men don't clock on till they get off the boat, sir.'

No one spoke a word as the ferry wound its way through the swamp. Small water-hens with their big feet were walking on the lily leaves. There was movement everywhere in the water, but for ten minutes there was no movement on the boat. When we got off at a small pier on the far side of the island, a round little man in his sixties, with a leather satchel under his arm, approached me.

'I believe you wanted to talk with me, sir,' he said. I was amazed at the formal manner of these people, who called their fellow workers 'sir' all the time.

'Yes,' I said. 'George Cavanough told me to report to you.'

'Mr Cavanough sent you?' he frowned. 'Sorry, I'm lost. This matter you need to talk to me about – can you put me in the picture, sir?'

'Well, yes. I'm your new man.'

'New man?' he repeated, looking even more confused.

'That's right. I'll be working with you.'

'I take it that – are you telling me you're going to work *with* me? But – then please tell me, why are you dressed like that?'

'I didn't have time to change my clothes.'

Harry White's face took on all sorts of different expressions, one right after the other. Finally he took an enormous breath and slowly let it out again, with his eyes closed. 'You have made a bad start, my boy,' he said, opening his eyes and looking at me sadly. 'Everyone on that boat thought you were a part of the administration. They'll be watching us all day. Oh well, follow me, boy.'

What Next You Bastard

A hundred yards into the sand dunes stood a small shed. Stacked around it were huge drums holding all sorts of odd materials. Lying beside these were piles of electric cables and power poles which Harry said were for high-tension power lines. Two big brass locks guarded the door and when Harry had unlocked them he led me inside. There was barely room for the two of us to turn around. From floor to ceiling all around us were shelves with hundreds, maybe thousands, of special switches made from solid brass. Everything was brass: nuts, bolts, screws, wire, everything!

'Welcome to my gold mine,' Harry said. 'As you can see, everything in this room could make us very rich, but let me tell you now: I know *every single* nut and bolt in this shed. *Any* of it goes walkabout, I will know! Today, thanks to you, we will have to work outside. All these years I've been working here, this is the first Monday I'm leaving the shed. I see you have no lunch with you, so today will be long for you.' He reached into a tin and produced some keys. 'These two are for the locks. You'll need them. Every single time we leave this shed it must be locked. Leave it open just *once* and you're fired. Come on, we'll get us a vehicle from the garage.'

Three hundred yards further north we reached a building. As we got closer we could hear laughter coming from inside it. Harry put his hand on my arm as an idea came to him.

'Hang on a minute – what I want you to do is walk up to the front door and tell them you need their *best* vehicle.'

There were five men standing around the counter, talking, when I stepped inside. As soon as they spotted me, four of them just vanished. 'Can I help you, sir?' the last one asked.

'I believe you can,' I said, playing along with Harry's little game. 'I would like the best vehicle you have.'

'Certainly, sir. Just one moment, please.' Like a flash of lightning, the man took off to make the arrangements. While he was gone, Harry joined me. In a low voice he said that I would be driving, and that when they brought the vehicle around I should make it look as if *he* was coming with *me*, not the other way round.

The man returned to the counter. 'Did you want a driver, sir?'

'No thanks,' I said, 'I'll be driving. Harry here will be coming with me.'

Slipping into the seat I found the key. The motor cranked over, but just wouldn't fire. 'The stop button, sir,' said the man, 'just push it in.' My hands were searching all over the dash but I didn't find it. 'No, sir, that button next to the gear box. This is a diesel, sir.'

The motor roared into life. As my hand touched the gear lever I noticed that it felt very loose. Looking at it, I saw a diagram for the gears: ten forward and ten reverse gears, as well as a lever for putting it into single-wheel-drive. The clutch was in. I slipped her into gear and, with my foot on the accelerator, let the clutch out. I was concentrating on going forward – so I was taken by surprise when we flew backwards instead, landing in the open garage and crashing into a workbench.

'Sorry, sir,' the man said. 'I must have left it in reverse. Don't worry about the damage, sir, we will fix it.'

During all of this Harry hadn't said a word. He was sitting beside me with his head between his knees. 'You've been set up,' he groaned. 'They *always* leave them in reverse!' But it wasn't until we had put some distance between us and the garage that he burst out laughing.

Coming over the top of that first sandhill I was met with a view that took my breath away. It was high tide. The brilliant blue of the South Pacific Ocean, the two-foot waves breaking onto the beach, the clear waters so transparent that you could see the white sand on the bottom – all these things added up to one: this was paradise! A lone sea eagle sliced through the air; it dived into the sea and returned to the horizon carrying a fish in its talons. Looking south, I found it hard to take it all in. The light blue sky blending into the sea gave the impression that the sea went on and on forever. It was so peaceful here. Miles and miles of dunes blanketed with powdery white sand, running down to meet the blue ocean. Looking north was different, however. There was activity on the beach just a few miles away. I stopped the vehicle and stared towards the south again.

'Sorry, my boy,' Harry said, bringing me back to reality. 'We are here to work, not to admire the scenery. You'll get plenty of time to spend on the beach later. First, let's talk about your job. I am the only linesman on this island and my job is to look after the power lines and the Black Snake. You will be my offsider. All you have to do is what *I* tell you to do. If anyone else gives you an order, just tell them to get stuffed. See that power pole? We'll start there. And, as I said earlier, everyone will be watching us today because they believe you are someone "big" from Brisbane. So, please play along with me.'

As we approached the power pole I noticed a thick black cable on the ground. It was about four inches in diameter and looked to be a good mile long.

'Stop the car. Let me familiarise you with the Black Snake. It carries 50,000 volts and it's the life-line for the dredge.' We both looked at it for a moment. 'Warning! I will only tell you this once: Do *not* drive over it! Do not *touch* it at any time. If you see this cable lying in water, *don't* touch the water! The Black Snake makes no noise and will kill without notice. Now, let's take a look at the poles before smoko.'

We had been driving through the sand dunes for a while, checking for faults in the line, when Harry suddenly said, 'Drive to the beach.' On the damp sand he held his door open and while I kept driving he seemed to be searching for something on the ground. 'This is it, my boy. Hop out and tell me what you see.'

'Footprints,' I told him. 'Just footprints.'

'Aha!' Harry said, 'anything unusual about them?'

'They point outwards – like a duck's.'

'Right, my boy. Those prints belong to Mr Noyce, the meanest boss on the island. He loves to sack people just for the fun of it. I've seen him dismiss a man for just turning up to work! He's been after me for years. Only trouble is, I always know where he is. He leaves a calling-card – his footprints. If you notice his tracks anywhere, be on your guard.' Harry straightened up and hitched his trousers. 'Time to show you the old girl.'

The 'old girl' was enormous. She was sitting on the sand with men and machinery working all around her. In front of her were three D8 bulldozers and welders were busy working on one of her sides. The men crawling all over her looked like tiny ants. The 'old girl' was the dredge. To me she looked rather like a mass of steel tossed together by some art nut, or some crazy giant's toy. She also looked top-heavy, ready to roll over at any second.

'Let's have our smoko over there,' said Harry. As we got closer the men stood up and moved around to the other side, leaving us alone. Harry was sniggering to himself. 'The word about you – it got here before us!'

I didn't think it was all that funny, really. This was only my first day and after this it was probably going to be my last as well. When the men found out I was a fraud I'd be getting the sack for sure. But I didn't say this to Harry. Instead I asked him what was wrong with the dredge.

'They're moving her back down the beach to where they started, then they'll turn her towards Point Lookout, refloat her, and then dredge the same sand again. See, they always overshoot a lot of mineral on the first run.' Harry explained that the dredge couldn't travel through water without operating and it would be quicker to move her one way along the beach than force her to dredge both ways. This move would be a history-making event. Never before, in the Southern Hemisphere, had such a massive piece of machinery been shifted over dry land.

Harry and I spent the rest of the day driving over the dunes, often crossing our own tracks. We were looking for a stockpile of drums and electrical goods that had gone missing after the last big storm. They had been left beside a power pole one afternoon and by morning they were gone. That was the trouble out here, Harry explained, the winds shifted the sand dunes and buried everything.

We finally found the pole, or at least the tip of it, which was just breaking through the sand. Twenty feet below was the base and, hopefully, the goods Harry needed.

Racing along the beach at sixty miles an hour was my kind of fun! I drove and Harry whistled. The wind was blowing through my hair, my good clothes were filthy and my shoes were full of sand. I was famished, my growling belly telling me that I could eat a horse and saddle and still have room for the rider.

With a sudden jerk I was flung forward, then pushed back into my seat. What was wrong? I hadn't touched the brakes! The speedo was reading only ten miles an hour.

'Keep her going! Hit the pedal, boy!' yelled Harry. I stepped on it, but something was holding us back. I looked at Harry and asked him what the hell it was. 'Ugaris, boy, bloody pipi beds! They're like quicksand – don't stop!' Could something as small as shells really be slowing us down that much? We were down to five miles an hour now and the engine was straining. But just when it seemed as if we were going to be brought to a stop, we were up and running again.

'There! Look up on the hill – too late, he's gone,' Harry said.

'Who was it?'

'A spy from the garage! They've been waiting for your return,' he laughed.

We took the vehicle back to the machine shop where every man and his dog was working flat out, doing his best to impress the 'big man from Brisbane'.

The one who had brought me the car hurried over and asked, 'Did you have a good day, sir?'

I just gave a small nod.

'Please, let me show you around, sir,' he said, holding my door open for me. 'Over here we are working on the D8 Crawley gearbox. The truck has a cracked diff. May I ask what you thought of the German Unimong, sir?'

I knew he meant the four-wheel-drive we had been using, because Harry had called it that. So I replied, 'Rough, very rough.'

'I believe your office is looking at a different style, sir.'

'Could be,' I said. 'Look, I can't say any more. Thank you for the tour.'

Back at Harry's gold mine there was an application form addressed to me, which Mr Cavanough had sent over. Knowing that I didn't have a hope in hell of reading the damn thing, let alone writing the answers, I had to think of something fast. Very casually I suggested that, as he was the boss, Harry might like to fill it in for me. He was glad to. It was obvious that he was curious about me and this gave him the perfect excuse to get all my personal details without prying.

'You know, Ken,' he said when the form was done, 'we work twelve days straight before we get three days off. And you must stay in the camp after work. Dunwich is out of bounds for you, as you'll be on call twenty-four hours a day.' He also made it very clear that by three-thirty each afternoon he wanted us to be back here at the shed.

Four-thirty rolled around and we walked down to the boat. Harry took the last seat, so I was left standing.

'Please sir, take my seat,' offered one of the men.

But before he could move, Harry jumped up and said, 'No, no way. Here, Mr Hall, take *my* seat.'

I just shrugged and sat down, wondering what his game was going to be this time. I knew I was being set up for something. And I didn't have long to wait. Harry stood beside me for a moment and then, in a loud voice, pretended that he had changed his mind.

'*Hang* on! No bloody way am *I* standing! Get out of my seat, you stuck-up little prick!'

There was a horrified silence. You could have heard a pin drop on the boat. The captain moved to Harry's side and spoke quietly. 'Harry, what's *wrong* with you?'

The island

'Not a damn thing!' he said, starting to laugh. 'For the first time *ever* I have caught you all out, you bastards!' People were still looking at Harry as if he had gone raving mad, until they heard his next words: 'I would like to acquaint you all with my new off-sider, Ken Hall!'

At this, the men fell about laughing. They slapped Harry on the back and congratulated him for being so clever. They swapped other con-stories and told jokes and Harry's face was split from ear to ear in a huge grin.

I got a few dirty looks, but not a word was said to me all the way back.

I was last off the boat. There was a bit of a climb up to the quarters and I dragged myself to my room. It was like an oven. I opened the window and sat out on the verandah, waiting for it to cool down.

'G'day! Haven't seen you before.' Standing in front of me was a skinny old man with a towel wrapped around his waist. He reminded me of two matchsticks glued together. His smile revealed a mouthful of black teeth. 'Name's Carl. Shower's down there,' he pointed with a thumb. 'Tea's at seven.'

Clean and refreshed, I lay on my narrow bed and rested. I was having trouble keeping my eyes open, but afraid that if I shut them I would miss out on tea. Just as I started drifting off, I heard the bell.

The area between the quarters and the mess was crawling with men. It reminded me of a huge ant's nest, with all the workers heading towards the food. I stopped at the door of the canteen and peeked inside. It seemed to be a friendly place, with everyone talking and joking. The room held about twenty tables and at the far end was a serving bench. Standing beside this was a whale of a man dressed in white, with a very tall chef's hat on his head. When he moved, his fat rolled and quivered like jelly on a saucer. Most of the tables were occupied.

I took a deep breath and entered the room.

The friendly atmosphere I had felt from the doorway burst like a balloon. All eyes were on me. The noise had died.

The fat chef came out from behind his counter to meet me. 'Good evening, sir. Eric's my name. This is your table over here, sir.' The bastards were up to something! 'I will get your meal for you, sir. Tea or coffee? Tea? Please, take a seat,' he said, drawing out my chair.

My table was fit for a prince. There was a white cloth and the cutlery shone in the lights. I looked around and saw that the other tables were pretty bare, because the workers were expected to get their own meals from the counter. And then I read something in the faces of the men – they were sending me a message without talking: 'Play along – don't say a word!'

So I kept quiet and ate my meal, feeling very uncomfortable.

When I was finished I had made it halfway to the door before someone called out, 'Hey Eric! How come he got special treatment?'

Not now, I thought, wanting to run from the room. But then another voice joined in.

'Yeah! Come on! We want to know why! We all work here, what's so special about him?'

'Look,' Eric said angrily, 'I was told by Harry …'

'Told what?'

'Harry said he was to have special treatment – you know, 'cos he's from the office in the city.'

'No way, mate! This man is Harry's offsider, not some boss from the city! Go on, tell him, Ken.'

But how could I? Eric the chef was looking like thunder. His mouth was hanging open and his eyebrows had disappeared under the white hat. The rolls of fat rippled dangerously and two doughy fists were clenched on the bench in front of him. The whole canteen was in an uproar – after being conned by Harry, the men had now got even. Harry was going to be mincemeat after Eric finished with him.

I made a quick getaway.

Back in my quarters I sat and stared at my suitcase. Should I unpack it or just leave it? I knew the bus would be there in the morning and I could be on it. You bloody fool, I cursed myself, you had the best job in your life with Craig and you threw it away! I looked around my room. There was a wooden chair in one corner and a wardrobe by the window. It wasn't Buckingham Palace, but it was better than some places I had stayed in. This made me think back to my time at Tudor Downs. At least this place had a light switch and a power point, but it still felt like a prison. And what was I going to do in my spare time? No way was I going to scribble letters and have people laugh at me! Jan had no idea about my reading and writing problems, unless someone (Mum!) had told her. Maybe she knew already? If not, what would she do when she found out? Would she still want to marry me? If I decided to stay, I would have to be very careful. After the way these men had acted at tea time, I was sure they'd give me hell if they knew about me. A radio – that was it! A radio would break the boredom at night. I might also try to read again. Oh well, I would just have to see what lay ahead of me.

Morning came and, boy, was I hungry. Then I remembered the cook's face from the night before and decided to give breakfast a miss. But someone started yelling for me. They said the cook wanted to see me. So now I would have to go down to the canteen and face him after all.

Things didn't look too good. Every man I passed on the way made some comment about Eric being in a foul mood. A big white shape like a giant mushroom was standing behind the counter when I walked in. Any moment now he was going to turn around and eat me alive.

'Hi! You forgot to leave me your lunch order last night,' Eric smiled. I was so surprised that I mumbled something about no one telling me I had to. 'That's all right,' he said and held out a big white hand. 'Forget about last night – it wasn't your fault. And welcome to Straddie.'

Work? There wasn't any. For more than a week, all Harry and I seemed to do was hide from the boss who walked like a duck. I had managed to get a phone call through to Jan, letting her know that it would be ten days before we'd be seeing each other. She wasn't too happy about it.

On the day before my three-day break the weather turned bad. Rain was pouring down by the bucket-load and it was blowing a gale – 40 to 47 knots, which Harry called a Force 9. We were sitting in his shed with nothing to do. Harry was reading – he loved his Westerns, always carried some around with him in his lunch bag, going through one every two days. Harry looked at his watch. 'One-thirty, that's another ... two and a half hours to go,' he said happily, his eyes already back on the page. How I envied him being able to lose himself in stories about cowboys and Indians whenever he had a free minute. I picked one up now and then and tried to make out the words, but there were no pictures to give me clues and in the end I just gave up. Harry just assumed that I wasn't interested in Westerns.

What Next You Bastard

All of a sudden he said, 'Quick! Get rid of those books. We've got company.' I hadn't heard a thing but, sure enough, seconds later the door flew open.

We were busily cleaning pole conductors with our wire brushes, which Harry had ready for an emergency like this.

'What's going on here?' A short man with blue bird-like eyes and a beaky nose appeared in the doorway. He wore a long trenchcoat and held a dripping potato bag over his head. When I looked down at his feet, I saw that the toes were pointing outwards. So this was Mr 'Duck-Feet' Noyce!

'We're in the middle of cleaning up,' said Harry.

'Who's this?' the man asked, looking at me.

'My new offsider,' Harry told him. 'His name is ...'

'No time for that – I'll get to him later. Right now we have a pole about to go down right next to the dredge. Get to it!'

The rain had eased now but the wind was growing stronger.

Driving along the beach we could see the sand dunes changing shape. Just two days ago, this pole had been bedded in eight feet of sand. Now it was standing in only two, its top swaying in the wind.

'Take that auger and dig three holes six feet from the pole for stays,' Harry shouted over the noise of the wind. 'I'm going to turn the power off.'

The auger was a long boring-tool, about two feet in diameter, with a screw point on one end and a handle that extended way over my head. Turning it on its own was hard enough, but when the damn thing was full of sand and the lift was five feet, it was a real backbreaker. My eyes and ears and mouth were soon full of sand. When Harry got back we placed wooden stays in the holes I had managed to bore into the sand. Then he leaned the ladder up against the pole and went to climb it.

'I don't like it,' he said. 'The wind's getting worse. Give me those brackets.'

Harry got halfway up while I struggled to hold the ladder steady below. He called out something but I couldn't hear what it was. Every time I looked up, the wind blew sand straight into my face. When the ladder was suddenly wrenched from my hands there was nothing much I could do about it. My whole body was thrown backwards with the weight of it and then Harry hit the sand, in exactly the spot I had been standing only seconds before.

The island

'*That's it!* Down tools – get me back to the shed.' Harry was shaking.

Management was not happy. The 'big move' was already behind time. We were told that we were to have no breaks until the job was finished. That pole had to be repaired right away.

Early next morning we were back at the pole again and, though it was still windy, the worst of the gale seemed to be over. Not wanting to take any chances, this time Harry wore his big safety harness. With his leather toolbag and a rope in one hand, he climbed the ladder once more. At the top he passed the rope over the rail until the two ends were on the ground. Then he fastened the ladder to the pole with his safety chain and fixed his harness to the pole.

'Send me up the hand brace,' he ordered.

I tied the brace to one end of the rope, then pulled the other end, just like a lift. A spanner, or any item that couldn't be tied, had to be thrown up. This was a skill in itself. You'd think it would be easy enough to stand on the ground and throw an item up to someone holding his hand out, ready to pluck it from the air. But it wasn't. Many times it would have been quicker for me to run up the ladder and hand it to Harry, or even to tie a bag to the rope.

Old Harry had different ideas, though. He sat up there on that pole, yelling at me to throw it towards his fingertips. 'I won't go anywhere,' he chuckled, 'I'll wait till you get it right.' After a lot of practice I finally got the hang of it. It was in my own interests to learn quickly. Flying tools are dangerous. And what goes up slowly can come down very fast!

It was only two weeks but it seemed like a lifetime before Jan and I were together again. I was so glad to see her and hold her that she had to push me away so she could take a breath. 'I've always said you have four hands, Ken,' she teased, 'but now you've got eight!'

My pay wasn't that great, just £8 a week, but by living at the camp I was spending less and saving more. Buying some land for a house was becoming our dream. We talked about little else. When I returned to North Stradbroke for my next shift I took my surf rod and radio with me.

23. On the beach

Eventually the dredge reached its new destination. An enormous hole was dug around her and a wall of sand built around the edge. She huddled there like a beached whale. Next the hole was filled with water and turned into a lake, making the whole thing look like a sandcastle with a moat. Slowly the sand under the dredge caved in and she floated. She was now ready to dredge again, twenty-four hours a day.

Her crews were made up of four men, each working eight hours a day for seventeen days straight, then for four days at twelve hours. After this they received a well-earned four-day break. There were two crews so that no time would be wasted while the dredge sat idle. The shifts alternated; when the twelve-hour shifts were on, the men finished at midnight and returned eight hours later for another twelve hours. The pay for this was tops: after working eighteen days, the next four were worth triple. I wouldn't have minded being on the crew for that sort of money, but the waiting-list was a mile long.

Whenever I drove along the beach I could see fish in the waves, and there was plenty of bait around – pipis by the thousand. Eric the cook had been complaining about having no fresh fish, so I told him about an idea I'd had. After work, instead of returning to the camp by boat, I would stay on at the beach and fish till the boys from the dredge changed shifts, then return with them. But Eric told me that management would never allow it.

Then something even better came along.

One afternoon I came across two glass balls from a fishing net on the beach. No one seemed to be around, so I bent down to pick them up. They would make a pretty souvenir for Jan, I thought. I was just putting them into the cabin when another vehicle came bouncing over the dunes towards me. Straight away I knew who it was: Duck-Feet!

'You! Come here,' he called. I walked over and waited to be roasted for taking the glass balls. 'I believe you like to fish? Well –

On the beach

any time you like, after work, you can use the boat. You can drive a boat, can't you? Then you can catch us some nice fresh fish. Just make sure the boat is back at camp before 10 pm. See you.'

The boat? Did Duck-Feet mean the ferry? The one we used each day for the trip between the camp and the beach? He must have, I realised, because that was the only boat around. I couldn't believe it.

Next afternoon I returned to the jetty with my fishing gear. For a few minutes I did nothing but stand and stare. I had never driven anything this size before. My only experience with boats had been with Grandad's little rowboat, and this thing was about ten times bigger. It was a ship!

Starting the motor was easy enough. I cast off the ropes and found myself adrift. There was a two-speed gearbox – forward and reverse. I tried the first gear and the boat backed away from the jetty. So far, so good. I was on my way. Steering through the swamp was also straightforward; twice a day I made this trip as a passenger, so I knew which way to go. Pulling in at the small pier on the far side was like riding a bullet – the boat shot right up onto the bank and I hoped like hell that I would be able to launch her again when I was finished.

Parked nearby was the Unimong, ready for the next shift. I threw my fishing gear into the back and drove along the beach till I found a gutter in the surf.

Carrying my surf-rod over my shoulder, I slipped off my rubber boots and I waded into the water till it was just over my ankles. I wriggled my toes around and felt for pipis, ending up with far more bait than I needed.

Fish! My hook only had to hit the water and they jumped on. Two hours later I had a bag full of bream, flathead, dart, tailor and whiting. It had gradually become dark while I was fishing and by the time I drove the Unimong back to the boat, I could barely see my hand in front of my face.

Why did I always have so much trouble finding light switches? I fumbled all over the cabin with no luck. Then I came up with the solution: I would feel for the spotlight on the roof and trace the wiring all the way down to where it entered the cabin, which would lead me to the switch. It wasn't a bad theory, but in practice it was a disaster. Having scrambled onto the roof I lost my grip and ended up in the drink, wellington boots and all. Water-filled wellies are like concrete boots – they keep you under the water longer than you would like. In my mind I was back at the turkey's-nest, with heavy flippers pulling me down ...

My hands thrashed above my head and touched the roughness of a rope tied to the side of the boat. I was saved! Hand over hand, I hauled myself up over the side and collapsed onto the floor of the boat. Bugger the light – I would have to do without it.

Somehow or other I managed to get the boat back to camp.

The canteen was in darkness when I finally got there. Not only had I missed out on tea, but I still had all these fish to clean. With the canteen closed, I had no choice but to go back down to the jetty to do the job. Time didn't matter, so I was taking it slowly, whistling as I scaled and gutted my catch, and was amazed to see the night shift for the dredge already coming my way.

These men were from Dunwich – the tiny little town itself, not the mining camp. They believed themselves to be the cream of the workforce. They pretended not to see me. As they stepped aboard the boat, the first man put his hand just inside the door and the spotlight came on. Silly me, I told myself, why didn't I try that? A light switch is *always* just inside the door!

'Bloody hell – look! The floor's all wet in here. That bugger's been using the boat!' When they had safely boarded, I gave them the Australian two-fingered salute.

Eric had left the kitchen door unlocked. Too bad about missing my tea, but at least I could look forward to a decent breakfast. Lovely fresh fish!

'Gee, Ken,' the big man told me in the morning, 'thanks for the fish! I hope you don't mind, but I sent it all over to the houses.' What a blow – all that work for nothing! Those snooty Dunwich people had copped the lot.

Later in the morning I was doing some work near Harry's shed when Duck-Feet paid me a visit.

'I believe I owe you for my breakfast,' he said. 'My wife really enjoyed the fish. It's the first time we got them already cleaned.' With this he held out his hand. 'The name is Mr Noyce – any time you have spare fish, please think of us.'

Harry and I watched him walk away, leaving his calling-card in the sand.

'You've done it, my boy,' Harry laughed, 'you've actually done it!'

'Done what?' I asked.

On the beach

'Anything you want from now on, Noycie will look after you. You'll be his golden boy. And best of all, he won't worry *me* anymore.'

Harry was right. From that day on, I could be working anywhere, doing anything at all, and if Duck-Feet showed up, he always gave me a friendly nod.

And more often than not, after an evening's fishing, when I delivered my catch to the kitchen, I would find that Eric had saved a meal for me.

I shouldn't have worried about being bored. North Stradbroke Island had plenty of things to occupy me in my spare time. I roamed the beaches and explored the swamps, hiked over sand hills and fished in the surf.

About twice a month I would see men from Point Lookout, on the north-eastern tip of the island, driving along the beach to fish. You couldn't blame them – the beach here was alive with fish most of the year round. Pipis were gathered before the weekends and sold on the mainland to a bait shop, four for a penny. It was easy to fill a sugar-bag with them.

You had to be careful about the pipi-beds, though. As Harry had said, they were like quicksand. In the days before the endless cable, tip-trucks used to carry the mineral along the beach to Point Lookout and then to Dunwich. This could only be done at low tide. One day one of the trucks returning with a heavy load had driven straight onto a very big pipi-bed. It had dropped immediately to the floorboards. By the time the driver was rescued, waves were breaking over the cabin. Two days later there was no sign that the truck had ever been there. Not long afterwards a D8 crawler was taken in the same manner. No wonder old Harry was nervous about driving over them.

Wildlife on the island was the same as on the mainland. Over the years it had migrated by crossing the bay, or by island-hopping at the southern end.

Domestic animals brought over there also found a way to live on the island, even when they were no longer wanted or needed. There was a proper little food-chain going, with one lot of animals always providing for another. Small wildlife was eaten by the feral cats, which bred in large numbers. Their kittens became the main source of food for the local snakes, which were hunted by birds and cats.

The cats themselves were taken by the wild dogs. Domestic dogs learnt to run with the dingoes which also ate the cats, as well as feeding on kangaroos and wallabies and whatever else came along.

Even cows and horses ran the full length of this wilderness.

One day I saw a chestnut mare with a week-old foal standing on the beach. She looked lame and half-starved. As Harry and I drove closer, she moved into the water until she was belly deep, calling for her foal to follow. At first I thought she had been frightened by our car, and wondered why she hadn't run off into the dunes – there was plenty of time for her to get away before we reached her. But she only looked our way once. No, her attention seemed to be taken by something up in the dunes.

Then I saw her problem: waiting in a row at the edge of the sand dunes were seven dogs. Their coats were mangy and their ribs were poking through their skins – three dingoes, a Great Dane, two greyhounds and a cattle dog. As we drew nearer they backed off slightly, giving the mare and her foal the chance to make a break for it. She took it, only to run headfirst into another dog that seemed to have come from nowhere. There was nothing we could do.

Two days later we found the mare dead on the beach. Her throat had been torn out and one eye was missing, but the rest of her had been left intact. She couldn't have been more than seven years old, yet her teeth were worn down to the gums. Harry said this was caused by the sand, which covered everything she ate. Her feet had suffered the same treatment – walking on sand all her life had worn away her hooves. The foal, or what was left of it, we found a few yards away.

Not all the animals roamed wild. A few were kept as pets in the camp.

Most of the men kept cats, but some of them had snakes. The cat-lovers hated the snake-keepers, with good reason. When kittens were born, it wasn't unusual to find a carpet snake lying in the sun with bumps along its length. I saw one of the cat-lovers return from work one evening just in time to see his newest kitten disappearing down the neck of a twelve-foot carpet snake. The man leapt into action. He jammed a wooden plank between the snake's jaws, stepped on its back to pin it down, sliced the snake open with his pocket-knife and cut the frightened kitten out. For added punishment he skinned the snake alive. The snake's owner threatened to do the same to the cat-lover and the two had to be forced apart.

On the beach

The University of Queensland had a team of scientists at the camp. Their job was to trace the water-flow that ends up in Eighteen Mile Swamp, which runs the eastern length of the island. The water-level in this swamp never rises or falls, even though millions of gallons always find their way into the sea. The fresh water starts its journey high up in the Toowoomba Ranges, flows through Gatton and Ipswich to Redland Bay, then disappears under the bay and turns up on the far side of North Stradbroke Island.

One of these scientists was an expert on reptiles. He gave a long lecture one night on how to care for them and then asked if any of the men kept snakes in their rooms. Proudly, three of the snake-lovers put up their hands. One boasted that he had three green snakes, a second man said he had a black, the third kept two death adders. Identifying themselves was a big mistake. Even before the lecture was over, the cat-owners crept from the room and hunted the enemy down. All six pet snakes came to grief that very same night.

Stray snakes on the island were something you always had to look out for. Death adders, especially, had a habit of curling up under rubbish or equipment, so we always checked before we moved anything. Quite often we came across dead snakes which had crawled under a drum to rest, only to suffocate when the sand built up around them and blocked their escape.

Violent storms hit the island regularly. There was nothing between us and the Pacific Ocean to break the winds, leaving us exposed to the foulest weather.

During one of these storms – a Force 11, with 63-knot winds – we sat in the shed for four days, with not a damn thing to do. Harry had his books, but I was going crazy. When I told him I was going for a walk to the beach he tapped his head and gave me a look that said: 'Madness!', but turned the page and kept right on reading.

I had to bend almost double to keep myself from being swept away. Walking headlong into the wind was like trying to break through a wall of sandpaper. I wondered if I would have any skin left by the time I got back.

Climbing the last dune, I took a peek through my sleeve. Straight in front of me was a sizeable fishing fleet, just past the breakers – five small boats and a very large mother ship. They were so close that I could see the Japanese crew. And some of them were waving!

What Next You Bastard

I had been told that our fishing boundary was twelve miles out and no Jap boats were allowed in the area. So what were they doing here, in the middle of a storm?

Harry didn't seem surprised when I told him about this later. He said that it happened all the time when bad weather was forecast. They knew that none of our boats would come out to catch them, so they made the most of it. Sometimes they came at night, he told me, sneaking in under cover of darkness to spread their nets just off our beach. He also said that whenever reports of these sightings were made on the radio, the government would always answer, 'There are no Japanese boats in our waters; if there were, it would be illegal.' Who were they fooling?

After a storm the beach was always littered with rubbish and odd gear. Wooden planks and pallets from the decks of the big carriers lay half-buried among the seaweed. For most of the journey this wood was used to secure cargo on the decks, but before entering port the crew would throw it over the side, as our customs officers would not allow the timber into the country. The stupid part about it was that it always ended up on our shores anyway, and people collected it for building projects at home.

Probably the strangest thing we ever found on the beach after a storm was a metal ball. It was about two feet in diameter, round and spiky, and looked a bit like a mine. Harry froze on the spot and said, 'It *is* a mine!' The army was called in to dispose of it. They treated it with kid gloves at first, then stood back and fired a few shots at it. Nothing happened. Finally they placed a charge beside it and blew it to kingdom come, leaving one bloody big hole on the beach.

Friendships between workers at the camp were not common. Most of the men closed their doors and spent their evenings alone in their rooms. Like Harry, many read books to pass the time. Of course, I didn't, so for me the nights were very long. Even listening to the radio got to be boring after a while.

The company didn't provide much in the way of entertainment, other than a room with two table-tennis sets and a couple of dartboards. One night I decided to have a game of ping-pong. When I arrived at the rec room, I saw that one of the tables was being used by two men, a few more were playing darts, and two more were just sitting talking.

On the beach

'Anyone for a game?' I asked.

The two who were seated looked at me.

The younger one was about five-foot four and wouldn't have been older than eighteen: 'Not me, that's a sissy's game!'

'I'll play,' said the other bloke, standing up. 'My name's Trevor – just arrived here a week ago.'

'Go on then, play the silly game,' jeered his friend. 'I don't care.'

'Don't listen to the young fool, he's only been here three days and don't like it,' Trevor told me. It didn't worry me anyway. I only needed one partner.

We had played two sets and were getting ready to play again.

'No, you don't,' said the boy. 'I wanna have a go.'

'Sorry, Mick, we're going to play one more set,' Trevor said. 'Maybe after that.'

'I wanna play now!' yelled Mick, jumping up and grabbing the little white ball. He crushed it in his fist. Trevor had a spare ball, so we ignored him and started playing. The youth threw himself onto the table and with his outstretched hand snatched the ball. 'I play, or I bust this one too!'

I'd had enough of this. 'You break that ball and I'll break your face!'

Looking me square in the eye, young Mick held the ball up to my face and squeezed it flat. My fist hit him dead centre on the jaw. He flew backwards into the wall and I followed, nailing him with every punch. Blood was pouring from his nose and lips. I stepped away from him and waited.

'Let me take my shirt off,' he said, but didn't bother to fight back. So I punched him again. Once more I stood back and waited for him to hit me. Nothing. Instead he begged me again, 'Please, let me take my shirt off.'

Why not? 'Go on then, take it off,' I said. Looking anxious, Mick quickly peeled off his shirt and flexed his muscles. And what muscles they were!

'I'm a top amateur fighter,' the boy said proudly. 'And now it's my turn.' With that he pinned back my ears, flattened my nose and then dropped me with one iron fist to the chin. As I rose slowly to my feet, young Mick the fighter held out his hand.

'Let's be mates,' he said, and smiled through his bloodied teeth.

I couldn't figure it out then, and I still don't know the answer. What difference did the shirt make?

'Ken, over here,' Duck-Feet waved. 'You may have heard that the captain is retiring. Well, I have a new job for you. As from tomorrow, you will be driving the ferry.'

Was he joking? There had been rumours that the captain was leaving, and lots of guesswork about who would be taking over from him – but what about my work with Harry?

'By the way, Harry is also leaving us.'

I stood there in shock and watched Duck-Feet waddle away. There must be some mistake, I decided, because Harry would have told me if he had plans to go. We had become good mates.

He was reading in his shed when I caught up with him. I asked him if Duck-Feet was right.

Harry put the book down and started packing his bag. Not even looking at me, he said, 'That's right. I'm retiring as of today, and tomorrow you start a new job.'

'That's it?' I asked, feeling hurt. 'Our friendship means nothing?'

No handshake, not a friendly word of goodbye. Harry White just picked up his bag and walked out the door.

Being the ferry driver wasn't as good as I had imagined. After taking the men to the worksite in the mornings, I would wait for the night shift to board, return them to the camp, then wait for the afternoon shift, take them across, and bring the morning shift home again. I was on call twenty-four hours a day, so fishing – or going anywhere at all – was out of the question. I missed my walks and drives through the dunes.

And there was one other thing that bothered me: for some reason no one ever spoke to me.

One quiet afternoon I was halfway back to the camp with the day shift aboard and a boat full of men. Most of them were just ordinary workers, but in one corner sat the crew from the dredge.

One of these men produced a small bomb from his bag.

It wasn't the first time I had seen one on board. The dredge sometimes sucked up practice-bombs from the sand. During the Second World War, Stradbroke had been used as a target for the new fly-boys out of Eagle Farm. This particular bomb hadn't gone off and the men huddled together, trying to see what made it work. They started fiddling with it.

'Look! It's smoking!' someone shouted.

Everyone on board ran across to the opposite side so fast that the ferry leaned over dangerously. The steering wheel was ripped from my hands, the rudder was completely out of the water, and men were falling on top of each other. The one with the bomb was laughing his head off.

'Get rid of it, you stupid fool!' yelled one of his mates.

'It's only smoking,' the bomber said, holding it above his head with one hand and hanging onto his seat with the other. He was the only one left on the high side of the boat and I was still fighting for control.

It was too much for one bloke. 'Get rid of it right now, or you'll go in with it!' he threatened.

The smoking bomb flew right across the boat. It sailed over the heads of the crouching men and splashed into the water behind them. 'There. It's gone! Happy now?'

I had the wheel back in my hands, but she wouldn't respond. We were all starting to panic now. Water was sloshing in over the side and we were going over ...

'Get back!' I screamed, 'get back to your seats!'

The crowd moved as one, making the rudder answer so quickly that it drove us straight into the bank. The fool who had caused all the trouble was still laughing. He couldn't see what all the fuss was about. I felt like killing him – so did many of the others on board – but he was one of the 'sacred' dredge-operators and no one dared touch him.

A fews days later Eric had a message for me. The management wanted the ferry back at nine in the morning. A special trip was being arranged.

By nine I was ready. Ten o'clock came and went, but nobody turned up. At eleven I walked into the kitchen to see whether Eric knew what was happening. The noise was deafening! Eric was in a rage, throwing around pots and pans and whatever else he could put his hands on. He had been ordered to prepare a meal for eight guests and at the last minute they had cancelled. I couldn't help smiling, though – Eric was so hot and bothered that he looked like a melting snowman.

Down at the ferry I had to wait two more hours before they arrived: Mr Cavanough, two stiff-collar workers from administration and five Japanese businessmen. The Japanese seemed to enjoy the ferry trip through the swamp, pointing at any wildlife we passed and smiling shyly behind their hands. Only one of them spoke English, in a very broken fashion. He was trying to tell Mr Cavanough about a new kind of four-wheel-drive vehicle and the strange word *toyota* was being thrown around a fair bit. Whenever it was mentioned, the other four Japanese went into a frenzy of bowing and shaking hands. Mr Cavanough was quick to catch on. By the time we were heading back, he was using *toyota* to keep the smiles on their faces. I wondered what it meant. Probably some kind of Japanese greeting.

Just before he left, Mr Cavanough asked me something very odd. 'Can you play tennis, Ken?'

'Yes, I play a bit.'

'Good. Be at my house around seven this evening. My daughter Mandy wants a game.'

That night I dressed myself in the best clothes I could find. It wasn't easy. Most of my things were already in my dirty-clothes bag, waiting to go home and be washed on my next weekend off. I had to settle for slightly crumpled trousers and shirt, which I splashed with after-shave to hide the stale smell. There was no choice of shoes – I wore the only leather shoes I had to my name.

Trevor, the ping-pong player, was already running around the court with Mandy. Mr Cavanough was sitting at a table, beer in hand. I greeted him and apologised for not having tennis shoes or a racquet.

'Don't worry, we have some racquets,' he said. 'Sit down and have a beer with me. After hours we all belong to one big family around here.' Three beers later we were all on the court together.

When I arrived at the jetty the next morning, I could hear the motor of the ferry running. Someone I had never seen before was at the controls.

'Hey, what's going on?' I asked.

'Would you be Ken Hall?' When I nodded, the man said, 'Well, I've got a message for you from Mr Cavanough. He said you've got a new job, and that you're to stay here till Mr Noyce sees you.'

I knew I shouldn't have beaten that man at tennis!

What on earth was Duck-Feet Noyce up to? I waited for hours. It was nearly ten o'clock by the time he arrived. As usual, he didn't waste words.

On the beach

'You start on the dredge at four. Don't fail me.' And then he walked away.

This time I was really stunned. Something was wrong here; jobs on the dredge didn't come up just like that. Men put their names on a waiting list that was three years long! Even then, to begin with they were only allowed to fill in part time for someone who was sick or on annual leave. I knew all about it because the subject often came up among the men, who were all envious of the top wages the dredge-crew got. And here I was, landing the job for no reason I could think of.

The men would really hate me after this. Around here, queue-jumping was the worst sin a man could commit.

By three-thirty my stomach was in knots. I walked into the kitchen and found Eric. He gave me my tucker-bag of sandwiches, but wouldn't talk to me. News travels fast on an island.

At five to four I stood by the ferry, ready to board. A vehicle pulled up and out jumped the dredge-workers from Dunwich.

'Mongrel!' yelled the Frenchman. (It sounded like 'mern-grill'.)

'Who said that?' The leading hand was furious. 'I'll have none of that on my shift!'

It was strange being a passenger on the ferry that, until just yesterday, I had driven. The leading hand was a man in his early fifties. He didn't introduce himself, but I heard the others call him Max. The rest ranged from eighteen to thirty. I didn't have to be a mind-reader to know that I wasn't welcome.

On the other side another vehicle stood waiting for us. I was last to climb in. The men spread themselves and their gear out, making things as uncomfortable for me as they could. The only place was on the floor. Only once during the drive did anyone speak to me. It was the Frenchman again.

'We don' like what 'appened, and you *stink*!' With that he put his foot into my ribs. The others laughed.

When we pulled up at the dredge I heard that it had been closed down for a while because the tail-pipe was covered in sand. Max told me to follow him. We walked over to a floating bridge that ran from the beach to the dredge. I remembered Harry telling me that the tailings, or waste, from the dredge was pumped through eight-inch pipes back onto the beach, and these pipes were fastened to metal floats to keep them from dragging on the ocean floor. Across the top of these floats ran a walkway. It was nearly a hundred feet long, eighteen inches wide, and had no side rails. The water below was covered with a very thick brown foam. As I watched Max walk across, my mind flashed back to the fallen tree-trunk at the Wacol army camp. Sitting down and sliding across wasn't going to be an option this time.

I took a deep breath, gritted my teeth, and followed him. The wind and the waves rocked the platform. I could feel it rise and fall beneath me. Getting to the other end was quite a balancing act, but somehow I made it.

Everything aboard the dredge was wet. Under my feet the floor was slippery, above my head water either poured or dripped down, depending on where I stood. We climbed some steps to the next level and entered a dry cabin.

'Got a raincoat? No? Well you need one on this job. And those rubber boots look too old,' said Max, frowning as he looked me up and down. 'What *did* your uncle tell you about this job?'

'Uncle? What uncle?'

'Mr Noyce.'

'He's not my uncle!'

'Come off it! He must be related to you somehow.'

'No way!' I told him. (Duck-Feet's nephew? What a laugh!)

'Okay then! You tell me how you got this job ahead of all the others who have been waiting for years,' the leading dredge-operator said, hands on hips.

There was no explanation. I wished I had one. All I could do was describe what had happened since I came to the island. Then I shrugged.

Max had one of those faces that were hard to read. Did my story make things better or worse for me? They didn't think much of Mr Noyce, so it was good that I wasn't a relative. On the other hand, the men resented me for jumping the queue without a proper excuse. And that was bad.

After a while he nodded and said, 'For your own sake, I hope you're not lying. Frenchy and the others have plans for you after work. Nothing I can do about it. Bring your bag and follow me.'

Back down to the lower deck again. We entered the hull and I was told to leave my bag here. Then we climbed to the very top of the dredge.

'This is where you'll be working. Listen very carefully. The sand is pumped from the bow of the dredge and makes its way up here.

On the beach

Then it runs down these spirals. The heavy mineral sand falls to the inside, and this is the sand we want. Your job is to get that sand away from the ordinary sand. To do this, we have built-in rubber splitters. They trap the mineral sand and run it down to the deck and into a bin. There are fifteen rows of spirals, each row has ten spirals, each spiral has six splitters in it. What you have to do is open the splitters when the mineral sand is heavy, and close them when the mineral is light. You do this by hand. Remember, we don't want the plain sand, we only need black sand. Got it?' Max didn't wait for an answer. 'I have to go now,' he said. 'Someone will check on you later.'

I was standing twenty feet above the deck on a steel grate. There were rails on both sides and on the stern. The only windbreak was the wall that faced the bow, where some sheets of iron had been bolted into place.

Heights still made me uncomfortable, but the view from up here was terrific. It reminded me of my perch on the windmill at Tudor Downs Station, but the scenery couldn't have been more different. From where I stood I could look back over the beach from the stern; from the port side into the dunes; the other side faced over the ocean.

Far below me, men were working on the tail-pipe, which had two jobs: one was to get rid of the waste sand, and the other was to fill the holes that we left. Someone shouted that it was fixed, and the men started making their way back to the dredge.

There was a vibration through the floor. Not knowing what to expect, I stood next to the spirals. Then came a noise like gushing water and before I could move, I was drenched by water pouring down the spirals. Now the dredge was starting to shake and water was flowing from everywhere.

Without warning, sand started to pour down the spirals. It was white. My hands worked overtime, trying to close the splitters. I had only done half of them when black sand was running down the spirals and going straight out the tail-pipe. I ran back and opened them up again. Just as I did, the stream of black narrowed! This meant that I had to get them closed again ... open, close, open ... It was hopeless. I couldn't keep up. How could anyone keep up? There were too many splitters for one person to handle.

I was wet from head to tail and my cigarettes were a soggy mess in my pocket. I had no way of telling the time. The sun had set long ago and the lights above me cut my vision down to a few feet. I was doing my best, but getting nowhere. Cold, back aching, hungry, dying for a smoke – I found the only corner out of the wind and stood there shivering.

What was that? Above the roar of the dredge I heard something. Turning, my eyes caught a glimpse of a figure in the shadows.

'Hey you! It's time to go home,' somebody called out. 'Hurry up, we haven't got all night!'

My first long day on the dredge was over. We had finished the shift at midnight and were due back at work by eight, which meant I had to meet the boat at seven-thirty in the morning. Back at my quarters I threw off my wet clothes, dragged myself into the shower and fell into bed. My stomach rumbled, reminding me that I hadn't eaten all day, so I opened the tucker-bag that Eric had given me.

These were grown men, not schoolboys, but you wouldn't know it! The rotten buggers had poured sand all over my sandwiches; they had even punched holes in the fruit and filled it up with the damned stuff.

Burying my head under my pillow, I decided two things. Firstly, from tomorrow on, I wasn't going to let my bag out of my sight. And secondly, it would take a hell of a lot more than gritty sandwiches and a sulky Frenchman to get rid of this boy!

Max had been watching me for a while. Just before noon on my second shift he stepped up to me and shook his head.

'No, no, that's not the way, watch me.' He spent the next couple of hours showing me all sorts of short-cuts and I finally learnt how to control the spirals without knocking myself out.

When it was almost dark, Max sent a young lad around to show me 'the ropes'. His name was Adam. He showed me where the mineral sand from the spirals ended up. It was his job, he said, to pump it up to the beach where it was loaded into buckets. Adam explained it all very thoroughly, saying that I would have to do this job sometime and I might as well learn about it now.

He showed me how to measure levels, turn valves, pump water and sand, and how to tell if the pump was in danger of blowing up. I learnt how to check the tail-pipe every hour or so, what to do if it became blocked, and when to shut 'her' down. There were ballast tanks and holding tanks, steel casings and steel clamps, rubber inserts and bilge pumps. Adam described how everything was built, how it worked, and what caused it to break down. 'Steel and sand don't get on very well,' he said grimly.

I was about to return to my work with the spirals when Adam put his hand on my arm. 'Look, mate – I've got nothing against you,' he said, 'but I'll give you a warning: Frenchy's got you set up. There's money on it, so be careful.'

It turned out that Frenchy had a friend in town who was waiting for a job on the dredge. His name had been next in line before I came along and stole it out from under him. Adam hinted that Duck-Feet Noyce had something against Frenchy and his mate, which was why he gave the job to me. At least it explained my sudden promotion.

We were dredging in very heavy mineral sand one day when we got more than we bargained for. Bullets were entering the spirals. They weren't just ordinary bullets, either; they were the heavy-calibre type and they were everywhere.

All at once the dredge gave a grunt, pieces of shredded metal were filling the spirals and the main pump started screaming. It had sucked up something big.

Slowly, the dredge was shut down. When the nose was lifted to see what the trouble was, we found something strange on the end of it – the wing from a plane! As more of it was exposed, we could see that it belonged to an old warplane. The lettering on the metal was in fair condition and the serial number was perfect. The phone line between the dredge and the office was running hot as Max kept them informed of the latest details.

Meanwhile the main pump was being stripped. The men knew that the rubber inserts must have been chewed into little pieces as the smell of burning rubber was overpowering. As the pump came apart, bullets spilled onto the deck. Then, without warning, a five-pound bomb struck the floor.

'Out! Everyone out on the beach!' screamed one of the men.

We were out of there so fast that only when we'd hit the beach and looked back did we realise that no one had told the leading hand. We started jumping up and down on the beach, waving our arms and shouting to Max in the cabin. It took ages before he finally turned and looked our way. At first he just stood and stared at us, probably wondering what the hell we were up to, judging from the way he scratched his head. When he finally got the message he lost no time joining us.

'Okay. We're all out here,' said Max. 'Now, what's the story?'

All the men agreed there was a fifty-fifty chance that the bomb was a live one.

'Did any of you get a good look at it?' Max asked.

'No, we all just ran for it!'

'Did anyone see it hit the floor?'

'Yes, we all did.'

'Yeah, we were splitting the pump. Bullets were pouring out left, right and centre, then this bloody bomb sticks her nose out and falls on the floor!'

'You did say "nose first", yes?'

'Sure did.'

Max thought for a moment. 'Okay,' he decided, 'we'll give it twenty minutes, then I'll check it out.' When the time was up we watched him board the dredge and enter the hull. The minutes felt like hours before he reappeared, carrying the bomb and placing it carefully on the sand. 'It should be safe,' he told us. 'It's not been primed.'

During all this, the office had been in contact with the Australian Air Force. The serial number from the wing finally closed a very long search for a plane that had gone missing after a mission with a full crew. Orders from the War Department reached us, that we were to bypass the entire area. All items that we had dredged aboard were to be returned to the site. They sent over a clergyman from Brisbane to say prayers for the dead crew.

From time to time, other war relics were uncovered – bullets and practice-bombs, even some old lifejackets and lifebuoys – but most were untraceable because the names of the craft were missing. It was always exciting, though.

Mineral sand was worth its weight in gold but, funnily enough, gold itself was considered worthless.

On board the dredge we had an oldtimer, a man by the name of Carl. He was the one who had told me where the showers were on my first day. No one knew how old he really was, but the biggest mystery of all had to do with his even being there. Nobody could figure out how he held down his job. Old Carl could never be found when needed, and when he was around he always got in the way. The other workers had no patience with him, telling him, 'Go and hide, Carl,' every time he showed up.

For the past two days we had been working in an area that contained a lot of gold. The spirals were full of it. Word from management was straight to the point regarding this particular metal: 'Send it through the tailings. It's not worth the trouble.'

Old Carl had a 'thing' about gold – he could smell it from miles away. This day he had taken over the spirals, placing jars below the splitters and filling them with gold particles. After work I helped him carry a couple of jars back to his room and in the morning he was at it again.

After another trip to Carl's room the next night, he talked me into staying for a whiskey. He told me about the mines he had worked in from the age of twelve.

'But this one's going to make me rich,' he said.

'Why is that, Carl?' I asked, not really interested.

'You young fellows don't get it, do you? *Gold*, boy – bloody gold! The owners of the mine don't want it. You and I can have it all, it's worth a fortune! They don't realise that if they mined the gold, it would pay the wages of every worker here.' He shook his head at the idea of such waste. 'Look, I'm offering you a partnership, son. You get the gold from the spirals, I treat it and sell it, and we share the profits. What do you say?'

'Gold,' I said. 'Gee, sorry mate, it's got no value to me. No thanks, Carl, I'm doing all right.' If the management didn't think it was worth anything, and even people like Frenchy and Max thought it was a waste of time, then I had no use for it either.

'You stupid young lad,' Carl said and showed me the door. 'I can tell you, one day you will remember this and regret it. Gold can give you riches! You can have anything you want!'

Maybe he was right. And maybe not. Right now, though, the only thing I wanted was to hold down my well-paid job. Teaming up with Old Carl would have made me a laughingstock, just when I was finally being accepted as one of the boys. Or men.

24. Spell Australia for me

Jan wasn't happy. Being apart for twenty-one days at a time was not her idea of the perfect engagement. If we couldn't see each other every week, she said, then at least we should write.

Reading her letters was good practice for me. Whenever I had a spare moment I would take the latest one out of my pocket and puzzle out any words I didn't know. Showing them to my workmates just wasn't on, so I struggled through alone. If I was stumped by a word, I tried to memorise the rest of the sentence and, while I worked the splitters on the dredge, or walked along the beach, I tested what word best fitted in with what she was telling me. Sometimes it would take me days to figure out a single sentence.

Usually her letters were full of news about her family and her work. In one of them Jan told me that her girlfriend, Pat, the senior office girl, had been caught stealing from the till. No wonder she always had so much money to throw around! Some of her letters made me laugh and others made me cry. But she always ended up telling me she wished we could spend more time together.

And asking me why I hadn't written back.

After some time I was feeling so guilty about not replying that I worked up the guts to give it a go. I was afraid that if I didn't send something soon, she might stop writing to me. It was one of the hardest things I had ever done. My only experience with letter-writing so far had been when I was a young jackaroo out west, when I was still in my teens, and I was a grown man now. Mum was the only person I had ever written to, but there were things I wanted to tell Jan that I had never said in letters to my mother. I wanted to tell her how much I missed her, how I loved her with all my heart, and that I could think of nothing else but being with her again. Somehow the words that were so easy to say were torture to write. Close to thirty sheets of writing paper ended up in the fire before I had a page that looked okay.

It would have to do.

By the next morning I was already having second thoughts. This letter might change everything between us. For a long while I just stood there, holding the envelope with Jan's name and address into the hungry red mouth of the postbox, afraid to let go. There is something so final about posting a letter: once it's done you can never change your mind and get it back again. Then someone walked past and gave me a suspicious look, so I dropped it in. Clunk.

On my next visit to Jan's house I was terrified. I stood on the front porch and couldn't bring myself to ring the doorbell. What had she thought of my childish scribbles? Was she wondering what she was letting herself in for, as the wife of a dummy? Did her brothers and sisters think I was a walking, talking joke? Had they passed my letter around the room, taking turns to read it out loud, killing themselves laughing? Or, worse still, maybe they hadn't been able to read it at all. And, more to the point, what about Jan's parents? They might have told her not to marry me …

The door opened. It was Jan's mother, Mrs Greer. She said she had seen me from the window. She smiled at me and said not to be shy, I should come inside, and then she called Jan.

Fresh and glowing from her bath, Jan looked happy to see me and kissed me hello.

'Thanks for your letter. It was nice – you should write more often,' said the most wonderful girl in the world. Not a single word about my shocking printing and my hit-or-miss spelling!

She did have some startling news for me, though.

While I had been busy on the island, Jan had been busy planning our wedding.

Word was out that we wanted to get married, but that Jan's parents weren't able to afford another wedding so soon after her brother's. So all the family members had put their heads together and come up with an idea. Some of Jan's relatives, who had just started a catering business, offered to supply the food and crockery and glassware; an aunty would make and ice a three-tiered wedding cake, and one of the uncles would print the invitations. As for the music, why not let the other uncles play in their newly formed band? All that Jan's parents would have to do was organise the church and the hall. The lucky young couple only needed to set the date. Problem solved.

Jan described this all to me as we sat in the car that night.

The drive-in tickets had been a bit of a waste, as we hardly even looked at the screen. In the flickering light she looked so excited and proud of herself and her family for working it all out. Now there was nothing stopping us, she told me happily, and I didn't have the heart to burst her bubble.

Not that I had anything against our getting married sooner than planned – I was all for it! – but two things stood in our way.

The first was money.

Only a short time earlier Jan and I had pooled our savings and put a deposit on a small block of land in Greenbank, but at the time we thought we would have years to pay off the balance and build a house on it. Now that we'd be getting married much earlier, we would have to make different plans. All Jan's wages and savings would be needed for her wedding dress and the bridesmaids' outfits, and mine would have to be spent on a suit, two wedding rings, the marriage licence and beer for the reception.

The second problem was – where were we going to live?

There were no quarters for married men at the mining camp. Maybe we could get a house at Dunwich? But one thing was for sure, the land at Greenbank would have to go, even if it meant losing our deposit.

We talked it over and decided that getting married sooner was worth giving up the block, and that somewhere down the line we would find another one. We also set a date.

Back on the island, the nights were very long. My mind was on the wedding. Not the ceremony and the reception, but the part that comes afterwards!

On November 22, 1963, I had just come off a twelve-hour shift, tired and hungry and looking forward to breakfast. But when I entered the kitchen I saw something disturbing. Instead of scrambling eggs and frying bacon, Eric was sitting on a stool, wringing the hell out of his apron. His face was a pasty white; his eyes seemed to be fixed on the ceiling, and he was muttering something about 'Kennedy'. As I came closer, he groaned and shook his head.

'Bloody war, take it from me, that's what's coming.'

'War? What the heck are you talking about, Eric? Is Kennedy going to take on the Russians or something?' I asked.

Eric gave me a strange look. 'Haven't you heard? They *shot* Kennedy this morning.'

I closed my eyes. No wonder Eric was looking like a ghost. Kennedy shot by the Russians! War! I could be called up within a

Spell Australia for me

minute if Australia got involved. Our Prime Minister would ... yes, knowing him ... he would go with the Yanks!

My appetite was gone. Instead of eating, I sat in the kitchen all morning with Eric, eyes and ears glued to the radio. News reports about the shooting were coming in non-stop. The announcers and all the people they interviewed gave the impression that we'd be fighting the Red Army any day now. They were all convinced that President Kennedy had been shot by the Russians because of the Navy blockade of Cuba.

All I wanted to do that night was to get off the island, take Jan and disappear. After what had just happened, our wedding plans weren't looking too good. All over the camp the workers had their radios on, passing on the latest details from man to man. Early next morning things looked even worse. The whole of Stradbroke was buzzing with the news that war was coming.

I was tempted to quit my job and get to Jan – it would be easy enough to get myself fired if that was the only way – yet something stopped me.

Something inside, that I had never felt before. Resentment.

Deep, strong, blood-boiling anger and resentment at people I had never met – people I never would meet, who lived half a world away, human beings I had no ties to, nothing in common with – who could make decisions that might affect me and my life. Who the bloody hell did they think they were?

Look at all these powerful men around the world, I told myself, not one of them was my age. They were probably all married, had children, and had already lived full lives. All I wanted was to live quietly, have a little love and a bit of happiness and a family to care for. The last thing I wanted was to hurt anyone. If they wanted a war, well, let them fight and kill themselves. But this boy wasn't going to be in it.

As it turned out, I needn't have worried. Kennedy had been killed by an American bloke, not by the Russians (though the bloke did have a Russian wife!), so there wasn't going to be a war after all. And the Prime Minister didn't call on me to lay down my life for my country, whether I had wedding plans or not. Just as well.

Now that the immediate threat of dying on foreign soil had passed, I was faced with something else: I only had a few weeks left to find accommodation for the two of us. The wedding was planned for

March and we were in January already. All the houses in Dunwich were taken by the married shift-workers. Renting was not going to be easy, because every house had a waiting list of at least six names before ours.

Just when I was starting to lose hope, something came along to save my bacon.

Some of the single men on my shift shared a very old house that had been divided into six rooms. Through the grapevine I heard that one of these rooms would be coming up for grabs soon, so I asked one of the tenants about it. He said he might be able to help me, but it would cost me a tenner. Stuffing the money into his pocket, he said he would get a message to me when the room was vacant, and then he hurried away. I stood there wondering if I had just blown £10 for nothing.

That same night, as I waited for the boat to take me to work, a slip of paper was pushed into my hand. Most of it looked simple enough, but there were three important-looking words that had me stumped:

ROOM AVAILABLE IF YOU CAN GET YOUR BAG
IN THE ROOM FIRST TOMORROW

I knew the word 'room' and I was fairly sure about the other short words, but the longer ones might make a big difference to the message. I tried spelling them out. I tried sounding them out slowly, but only got myself more and more confused. Now I was in a bit of a jam, because if I showed the note to anyone, they might beat me to the punch. There had to be some way ...

The notice-board, the one in the hull that the fitters used! I hurried down there and, when no one was looking, copied out part of the message onto a scrap of paper – just those words I didn't know. I decided to try out Adam, the young dredge-hand, first.

'Hey Adam,' I said casually, 'I found this message in the hull. Looks a bit strange. Can you make head or tail of it?'

Adam said, 'Let's see it: "Available first tomorrow". Doesn't make sense, mate. Feed it to the gulls.' I shrugged and walked away, but my plan had worked perfectly. Adam had read it out loud.

In the morning, straight after my shift, I ran from the boat but missed the Dunwich bus anyway; all I caught was a glimpse of it as it went over the crest. Some of the Dunwich workers were driving home in their own cars, but asking one of them for a lift would be a stupid idea. If they worked out why I wanted to get to town instead of going up to the camp, they would give me the longest drive ever around the island.

Kicking the sand, I headed for the canteen and forced myself to admit that I had missed the bus in more ways than one. The room would be taken by the time I could walk there. Then I saw one of the office staff from Dunwich coming through the doors, swinging a set of car keys. I asked him if he was heading back to town and if there was any chance of getting a lift. He warned me that it wouldn't be a very fast trip.

Parked behind the canteen was a brand-new four-wheel-drive vehicle. I had never seen one like it before, so I asked the man what kind it was.

'It's a Toyota,' he told me. So! Now I knew what the word *toyota* meant. It was a Japanese car, not a Japanese greeting! 'This vehicle is powered by a straight six. On the flat she flies like a bird, but when it comes to hills, she dies. Hop in, you'll see.'

When we came to the first hill, it crossed my mind that the handbrake must be on. It wasn't, but it felt as if we were dragging an anchor. The driver changed down into first gear.

'The Japs have sent us two for testing on the beach. We already tried one out there. Half a mile, and the four-wheel lock broke.'

As we approached the biggest hill, he stopped, turned the vehicle completely around so that we were facing downhill, then reversed all the way up. 'They back up all right, it's just that they're too heavy at the front to drive forward in the sand.'

At Dunwich I thanked my driver and ran to the rooming house. I barged through the front door, found the spare room and staked my claim.

It was a large room, twelve feet wide by eleven feet long. A single frame bed, with a heavily stained mattress that sagged in the middle, stood along one wall. This would have to go; Jan and I would be needing a double bed anyway. The floor was partly covered with lino that was so old the pattern had almost disappeared; in places it was worn right down to its tar base. A large wardrobe frowned angrily at me from a corner of the room; it was leaning to one side with the door hanging open. When I went to shut it, the door, and the mirror on the front, fell to the floor with a loud crash. It wasn't a hopeful beginning.

Seven weeks before the big day, Jan took me to meet the minister of her local Presbyterian church. He had made it very clear that he expected her husband-to-be to attend services each Sunday until the wedding. When she had explained how impossible this would be, he reluctantly agreed to accept me, but only if I would meet with him at least once.

The minister, a skinny man in his late thirties with a wife and three children, took us aside after the service. In his small office, he closed the door and advised us on marriage and all it involved. He explained that it was his duty to prepare us for 'not only the spiritual side, but also the physical side' of our lives together.

'Now, Kenneth and Janice, as this will be the first time the pair of you will sleep together ...' he said, and then coughed discreetly, 'sorry, I should say, after the wedding it will be your first time ... well, I would like to tell you what to expect.'

He folded his hands in his lap and looked out the window. 'First, it's nice if you get ready in separate rooms, then turn out the lights before going to bed. Kenneth, as you are the man, you ...'

'Hang on,' I said, not liking where this was headed. 'I think this is between Jan and myself, sir. It's for us – and only us – on the said night.'

'But marriage is – it can't be taken ...'

I stood up and told Jan we were leaving. No way was this man, a stranger to me, going to tell me what I could or couldn't do on my own wedding night!

'Well, just a minute,' he said, holding his arm out like a traffic cop. You could see he was someone who wasn't used to having his lectures interrupted. 'I have a special book for you both. At least take it home and read it.' Seeing the look on my face, he turned to Jan. 'Please, Janice, read it. It's a must! The book is by a very well-known doctor. It'll tell you everything you need to know about marriage. And Kenneth,' he said sternly, 'I would like to see you and Janice here one week before the wedding, so we can get the paperwork done on the licence.'

Everyone seemed to have advice for the engaged couple. Some of it was useful, some of it was offensive and all of it was unasked-for. Mrs Greer even took Jan aside one night and gave her some motherly advice on what she called The Special Needs of Men.

My own mother was more concerned with something else. And

she threatened to call the wedding off if I ignored the advice she had for me.

'But ... what are you saying, Mum?' I asked.

'I'm saying: If you can't get a house before you're married, there's no way I'm letting this wedding go ahead. You can't take a newly-married girl to a room.' And the way she spat out the word 'room', I knew she was deadly serious. 'Janice is to be given respect. She's going to be your wife, not some ... No house, no wedding.' At this Mum folded her arms and refused to listen to any excuses about the shortage of accommodation on Stradbroke Island. If I couldn't get a house on the island, she told me, I would just have to move back to the mainland and find a new job. 'No house, no wedding,' she repeated.

With only one week to go, I was lost. Houses for rent in Dunwich were harder to find than hen's teeth. Then old Joe Meadows, the local store owner, came to the rescue. He had heard I was about to get married and said that he and his wife had a house coming up in three weeks' time. Would we like to move in?

When Jan and I returned for our second appointment with the minister, he led us straight to his desk, where he had set out two chairs. He seemed a little stiff this time. I could tell he didn't like me.

'Janice and Kenneth, come on in. I have the forms here on my desk. Please sit down and each fill out one of these. There are two pens on the desk.'

I watched Jan write down her details and this helped me with mine. It was mainly a matter of filling in our names, addresses and birth dates. Nothing too difficult, even for me. But I needed help with all the o's and r's in my home suburb of Coorparoo (who wouldn't?).

And then I said, 'Jan, how do you spell Australia?'

'A-u-s-t ... ' Jan started, but never got the chance to finish.

'Excuse me, Janice!' the minister interrupted. 'I have known your family for eight years or more ... Don't tell me you're going to marry an imbecile; you can do better than ... that!' He flicked his hand in my direction as if I were a thing, not a person.

At the time I didn't know the true meaning of the word imbecile (mentally weak, a stupid person, an idiot, moron, or fool), or I would have crowned the man with the heavy glass paperweight on his desk. It was very tempting, all the same. His tone of voice was enough to tell me that he didn't think much of his young parishioner marrying someone too dumb to spell the name of his own country.

The minister shook his head slowly from side to side. He looked at Jan as if her entire future had just flown out the window. 'Oh, my dear girl.'

Holding myself in control, I gave him a dirty look and asked Jan to start again. He could rot in hell for all I cared. All that mattered to me was how Jan felt. She was the one I was marrying, after all, not some stuck-up preacher who was supposed to help people, not insult them.

If Jan was embarrassed, she didn't show it. She spelled Australia for me.

On Saturday 14 March, 1964, I watched my bride gliding down the aisle on her father's arm and got a lump in my throat.

Her long white gown caught the rays of light falling through the stained glass windows, making rainbow patterns dance on the skirt with every step she took. Her eyes shining, and her smile trembling, Jan looked every inch the fairytale princess.

I was so happy, I had to remind myself that grooms are supposed to be nervous. But the only thing I could find to be nervous about was the thought that this beautiful girl trusted me to look after her, and I only hoped that I would never let her down.

The reception at a large hall in Paddington passed by in a blur. From what I remember, everything went off according to plan and all the guests seemed to enjoy themselves. Mum soaked a few hankies with her tears, saying over and over again that she had never expected me to live long enough to get married. Jan's parents seemed happy to welcome me into their tribe of eight children (including the newest baby); the uncles' brand-new band was a smash hit, and my brothers disappeared for a while before coming back into the hall with guilty faces.

By ten-thirty that night we were on our way to Palm Beach on the Gold Coast, with 'Just Married' soaped onto the back window of the car, and white ribbons streaming from the antenna. The boys sure had been busy! It was dark when we left, and would still be dark when we arrived, so we decided not to worry about removing the decorations till later.

Spell Australia for me

It was after midnight when we slowed down and pulled in to the caravan park, where we had booked a van for nearly three weeks.

'What's that rattle?' Jan asked. I was just wondering about it myself. Out on the highway I hadn't noticed it, but now it was loud enough to wake the dead. And the sleeping! From out of their caravans and tents came wide-eyed people, all trying to see what the racket was about. The more slowly I drove, the louder the noise seemed to get. Along with their other work, the boys must have put stones or bottle-tops into the hubcaps.

With lights coming on all over the park, and people standing around with torches, the newly married couple crept into their honeymoon quarters.

So much for privacy.

We were still awake at five in the morning, testing the springs on the creaky old van, when a loud voice frightened the daylights out of us.

'Knock, knock! Ice man!'

'Not now, thank you,' I called. Jan giggled softly.

'Ice, sir,' he called, 'you'll be needin' your ice today. Bein' Sundy, the shops are closed.'

'No thanks,' I yelled, 'we'll be all right.'

'But, sir, it'll only take a minute to get the ice, you can ...'

'Look!' I shouted, really getting ropeable. 'I'm in bed, and I *don't* feel like getting up. We'll get our ice tomorrow!' I thought I heard a snicker or a giggle, but I had no way of being sure.

'But the young lady – have you arksed her?'

'Bugger off! *Now*!'

'Has he gone?' whispered Jan.

'I think so,' I said, and hoped it was true. 'Now – come here, *Mrs* Hall.'

In the first week of April we moved into the house at Dunwich. I was glad now that Mum had insisted, because it was a much nicer place to start our married life than the rooming house would have been. Only trouble was, my bride was bored.

For the first time ever, she had nothing to do all day. While I was at work, Jan was alone in the house. And with my long hours, most of the time I spent at home was used for catching up on sleep.

Hearing that Jan was looking for some sort of work to keep her busy, Mrs Meadows gave her a job working behind the counter in

What Next You Bastard

the shop. It solved one problem, but caused another one, because now we saw even less of each other. As I was coming home from the night shift, Jan was leaving for work, and in the afternoons it was the other way around.

Jan had been hoping to start a family right away. When she had still not fallen pregnant after four months, she took a day off and made the long trip to the doctor's. It was late when she arrived home. I was watching TV, almost due to leave for work.

She couldn't keep it to herself. Tears ran down her cheeks as she told me, 'I've got bad news. I can't have any children.'

I was out of my chair in a flash, comforting my wife. This was a shock. Never in our wildest dreams had we ever considered that our lives might be empty of children. Since before our wedding we had been talking about the big family we would have one day soon, but now ... maybe everything was going to be different.

'What did the doctor say?' I asked, stroking her back and pressing her face against my chest.

'I'm not a woman,' Jan sobbed.

I gasped with shock. 'Did he say that! Just wait till I see him! How dare ...'

'No, no, I mean I feel like I'm not a woman. I can't have babies. I've got a twisted womb. They said it was the worst they'd ever seen.' She cried quietly for a while and I used the time to let it all sink into my brain. 'It's impossible for me to have children, Ken. You'd better go and find someone else to have your babies.' Jan took a deep breath and wiped her eyes. 'So – just leave me alone from now on.'

'Look, I'll take you to a specialist, we'll go and ...'

'Forget it, will you?' Jan said, pushing me away angrily. 'I'm not a woman! And look at the time, you'd better get off to work.'

Our little house was a sad place for the next few weeks. Children were not mentioned.

Now and again we had visitors from the mainland. They loved it here. Everything was so peaceful that they never wanted to go home. One of our visitors was Grandad George, who came down from Hervey Bay to see how the fishing measured up. Having him around took my mind off all the unhappiness for a while, but it also made me realise for the first time that when I died, my branch of the family would come to an end. No children to carry on from here.

During one of our talks, I said something about being the first of our bloodline to live here on North Stradbroke Island.

But Grandad shook his shaggy head. 'No, you are wrong, boy. My father and his sister were quarantined here when they arrived from Germany in 1865. Their ship, *La Rochelle*, spent 35 days right here at Dunwich. Yes. Many of them were sick when they arrived, from the water. Not seasick, you understand, but poisoned! The water barrels on the ship had not been washed out properly before they were filled, and the dirty wood contaminated the drinking water. A graveyard is around here somewhere – about six died. My father's sister lost her husband, Heinrich Hofmann, and also their little son, Bernhard. So, you see, you have come back to the very beginning.'

I had relatives – ancestors – buried nearby! No wonder people kept saying that life is a circle.

When Jan became pregnant after all, we couldn't believe it.

She had been feeling sick for a few weeks and had gone to the doctor on the mainland, a different one this time. There was no mistake, they assured her, when she argued that it couldn't be true. A baby was definitely on its way. We were both over the moon with excitement.

On one of our rare nights home together, Jan and I sat down to discuss what the future might hold. I had never been one to plan far ahead, partly because no one had ever expected me to live long enough to make the exercise worthwhile, and partly because I had always been too busy just getting through one day at a time.

But now that I was a husband and a father-to-be, for the first time I allowed myself to dream that there truly might be a tomorrow, a next week, even a next year. My own health problems seemed to have settled down, despite the daily aches and pains I had learnt to live with. The doctors had seemed happy enough with my last check-up, though somewhat puzzled that I had managed to survive these past twelve years after they had sent me home to die.

Jan loved hearing all about the properties I had worked on out west and, though we didn't want to move too far from Brisbane, we both liked the idea of raising our children in the country. Stradbroke Island was no place for settling down. Apart from food and electricity being far more expensive here than on the mainland, the long-term opportunities just weren't enough. We also wanted to be closer to Jan's doctor and to both our families when the baby came. It was time to leave the island and make a fresh start.

There was just one last piece of unfinished business to take care of.

On a hot and steamy night in late January, I had my long-awaited showdown with Frenchy. In a way I was glad it was finally going to happen, because he had been getting harder and harder to work with. He had also heard on the grapevine that I might soon be leaving Straddie, and he sent word to me that it was time to pay up – with interest.

We had been on afternoon shift, so it was just past midnight when we stepped off the boat and into the 'boxing ring'. A group of cars with their headlights on had been parked in a circle near the jetty, and the men led us into the centre of it. One of them acted as referee. 'We want a fair match,' he called. 'On the count of three, come out fighting.'

Frenchy and I faced each other warily.

Neither of us knew how good the other one was.

Up till now it had all been talk, and if talking counted for anything, then Frenchy would win by a mile. On the other hand, I was quite a bit bigger, so he wasn't going to be trying anything too stupid.

For a few minutes, all we did was give each other light jabs.

As we danced around, I noticed that my legs felt like lead – the boots, my heavy wellington boots, were slowing me down. If I could only … (I laid a couple of punches into Frenchy's midriff) … if I could just stop and slip my boots off … maybe kick them off one after the other without stopping the fight …

Frenchy wasn't big on boxing; wrestling was more his cup of tea. Over and over, he tried to wrestle me to the ground, but each time he tripped over his own rubber boots and I managed to pull clear of him. Every time I put an arm out, he tried to grab hold of it.

After some more dancing and shuffling and dodging and circling we were both starting to slow down.

The men had seen enough. They were as tired as we were.

'Come on, you two! We want to go home.'

'Yeah, shake hands and forget it.'

'Fine by me,' I said. Besides, I wanted to get home to Jan in one piece.

A little nervously, I stepped forward and offered my hand to the Frenchman. Would he shake it, or would he dive in under it and knock the wind out of me? For a moment everyone was quiet, while Frenchy opened his fist and closed it again, opened it and closed it, and then he shuffled his feet in the dust, sniffed twice, and shook my hand once.

The other men patted us on the back, happy that the matter was finally settled and there were no bodies to bury in the dunes.

In late February 1965 I said goodbye to my workmates and even joked with Frenchy that he could finally give his mate my place on the dredge. Duck-feet was furious when I told him I was leaving, asking me why I had to go when he had done so much for me, and demanding to know who would provide the fish from now on. Mr Cavanough and Mandy wished me well, and I bowed and said 'Toyota!' to his back when he walked away.

So long, Straddie, I told the sand dunes as the ferry took us away for the last time. My ancestors had landed here a hundred years ago and had only stayed thirty-five days, but I had stuck it out for nearly three years.

Jan looked up from the magazine she was reading and smiled at me.

We had never really discussed my reading and writing difficulties, but in many small ways she had already shown me that she knew what a struggle it was for me, and that she was prepared to help me when needed. From her I learnt the most important lesson: I was illiterate, not stupid. And there was a world of difference between the two. With her at my side, I knew I would be able to face anything.

I had come a long way, I reminded myself as I watched the sandhills grow smaller and smaller behind us. And I still had a long way to go. But with some money in my pocket, the first of our four children on the way, and a wife who loved me despite everything, it was sure to be a wonderful journey.

Epilogue

Some of my early health problems have caught up with me again, others never left me. It became obvious over the years that not all of the medical conditions were diagnosed correctly, and much of the treatment was unnecessary. These days my back gives me more and more trouble and the hospital tests are starting again. But I'm not complaining. I've had a good run. I've even outlived a lot of the doctors who predicted my early death.

I still have trouble with reading and writing, but all the tests show that I am not dyslexic, in case you were wondering. My literacy problems are due to medical reasons and a lack of schooling. My handwriting hasn't improved much over the years and without a computer I would be lost. Officially, I am still illiterate. My own children and grandchildren are only now starting to realise this, because I have managed to hide it for so long. Admitting my handicap to my family and friends has been very hard, but it is a relief to finally bring it out into the open.

Soon after my fiftieth birthday in 1990, I attended the Maryborough Rehabilitation Centre, where literacy tutors did their best to teach me reading and writing. I was not one of their best pupils. Try as I might, I was simply not able to start at the beginning and learn all the necessary basics. My short-term memory problems just wouldn't make the connections I needed for these new skills. Besides, all I really wanted was to learn enough to get my story written.

Finally Belle Coyte, a retired school teacher, took pity on me and offered to take my illegible scribbles and piles of messy computer printouts home. She corrected my countless spelling mistakes and even added something called 'grammar'. I now had something to work with, and was determined to carry on. I owe her a lot.

But I am a story teller, not a writer. I had never even read a book, so I had no idea how to present my story to others. My notes were still not in a form suitable for publication, so for years I hunted around for someone to do this job for me. Through one

Epilogue

of the publishing houses I eventually found Monika McFerran. She sorted through my boxes of notes, interviewed me, asked a thousand questions, and spent two years writing my story. Monika now knows almost as much about my past as I do. Now that it is all down on paper at long last I can relax and give my memory a rest. I am very grateful.

These days all my time is taken up with a project I have called 'Radio For All Australians'. My idea is that illiterate adults and sight-impaired people would benefit from having the old radio plays brought back. Even though cassettes are available (Talking Books, etc.) it is not the same thing as a play – where you have all the sound effects, different character voices and 'action'.

I also spend a lot of my time trying to make the politicans understand what it is like to live in a world where reading and writing is a daily struggle. I get no finanical help, but each Sunday I send out twelve faxes to make sure every politican and organisation knows about people like me.

There are many ways to help illiterate people, but the biggest problem is that the rest of the community just cannot understand how we feel about our handicap and how ashamed we are of it. Admitting it is one of the hardest things of all, especially when we know that others will look down on us.

I hope that through this book – which I will never be able to read properly myself – people will become aware of the problems that illiterate people face. I also hope that our education system and hospitals start paying more attention to children with learning difficulties and make sure they do not slip through the net as I did. For many people, the standard you have when you leave school is what you carry with you all through life.

And, sometimes, that just isn't enough.

It is too late for some of us, no matter how hard we try to catch up. Most people take reading and writing for granted. You might be one of them. If you are, I would like to ask one small favour.

Please remember, we are illiterate, not stupid.

Ken Hall

ACKNOWLEDGMENTS

Ken Hall wishes to thank:
Mrs Belle Coyte, retired school teacher, for making my earliest notes and scribbles legible and for giving me hope. My wife Janice for her understanding, tolerance and help over the years. My children, Toni, Kim, Michael and Janine and their families, especially Kim Twidale for her beautiful illustrations. John Casey of Hervey Bay for keeping my computer programs up to date, when they went down, from 1986 to 2000. Two Tone Electronic of Hervey Bay for helping me to stay up with the latest computers since 1984. Many thanks also to the Hon. Warren Truss, MP for his assistance, and to the community of Hervey Bay for their ongoing encouragement and support, particularly the RSL and Lions Clubs, and to the Hervey Bay City Council for a travel grant.

Monika McFerran wishes to thank:
My husband John McFerran for his endless patience and cups of coffee while I was glued to the computer. My children and friends for their faith in my ability. My parents Dr Elisabeth Wieden and Maximilian Wieden for their constructive criticism and for giving me the confidence to persevere. The Bourke, Gaffney & Sim families for proofreading the manuscript and making helpful suggestions. Colin Turner in Sydney for his boundless energy and positive approach. Mrs Dina Browne AO, for her guidance and expertise.

We both wish to thank:
Margaret Johnson in Perth, for her assistance with editing the manuscript and her determination that the story be told. Thank you for helping to make it happen. Bert Hingley and Sylvia Hale, our publishers, for their enthusiasm and faith in the book. And to all others who offered support and encouragement along the way. This book is for you.

Sketches by Ken Hall's daugher, Kim Twidale, appear as follows: the windmill at Tudor Downs p.1, the house at Tudor Downs p.77, Gannon's Hotel at Julia Creek p.93, the Railway Hotel at Julia Creek p.154, the butcher's shed at Kilterry Station p.165, the house in Coorparoo where Ken Hall was born p.176.

PHOTO BY: ANNETTE DUNN

PHOTO BY: YME TULLENERS, KIRKLAND PHOTOGRAPHY

KENNETH WILLIAM HALL was born in Brisbane in 1940. Owing to ill health as a child, he has never been able to read or write properly, but his remarkable memory allows him almost perfect recall.

After years of hiding his shame, Ken finally went public in an attempt to bring awareness to the problem of illiteracy in this country. He now spends all his time on a project he has called 'Radio For All Australians', a national radio service devoted towards helping anyone who is unable to read, whatever the reason.

Ken is married with four children and ten grandchildren and lives in Hervey Bay, Queensland, where the fishing is terrific.

MONIKA MCFERRAN (née Wieden), the second of four daughters, was born in 1955 in Cape Town, South Africa, to Austrian parents. The family emigrated to Melbourne in 1964. Married with two children and three step-children, she lives on Queensland's Gold Coast.

After various careers, including business management, sales and design, her lifelong interest in human nature finally prompted her to study personal relationships and behaviour. She now has her own professional counselling practice and writes in her spare time.

A single meeting with Ken Hall inspired her to take on the enormous challenge of writing his life story. This is her first book.